COMPUTER BOOK SERIES FROM IDG

References for the Rest of Us!®

Are you intimidated and confused by computers? Do you find that traditional manuals are overloaded with technical details you'll never use? Do your friends and family always call you to fix simple problems on their PCs? Then the *. . . For Dummies®* computer book series from IDG Books Worldwide is for you.

. . . For Dummies books are written for those frustrated computer users who know they aren't really dumb but find that PC hardware, software, and indeed the unique vocabulary of computing make them feel helpless. *. . . For Dummies* books use a lighthearted approach, a down-to-earth style, and even cartoons and humorous icons to diffuse computer novices' fears and build their confidence. Lighthearted but not lightweight, these books are a perfect survival guide for anyone forced to use a computer.

> *"I like my copy so much I told friends; now they bought copies."*
>
> **Irene C., Orwell, Ohio**

> *"Quick, concise, nontechnical, and humorous."*
>
> **Jay A., Elburn, Illinois**

> *"Thanks, I needed this book. Now I can sleep at night."*
>
> **Robin F., British Columbia, Canada**

Already, hundreds of thousands of satisfied readers agree. They have made *. . . For Dummies* books the #1 introductory level computer book series and have written asking for more. So, if you're looking for the most fun and easy way to learn about computers, look to *. . . For Dummies* books to give you a helping hand.

IDG BOOKS WORLDWIDE

WORDPERFECT® 3.5 FOR MACS®
FOR DUMMIES®

WORDPERFECT® 3.5 FOR MACS® FOR DUMMIES®

by Mark A. Kellner

Foreword by Teri Robinson
Contributing Editor, *Communications Week*

IDG Books Worldwide, Inc.
An International Data Group Company

Foster City, CA ♦ Chicago, IL ♦ Indianapolis, IN ♦ Braintree, MA ♦ Dallas, TX

WordPerfect® 3.5 For Macs® For Dummies®

Published by
IDG Books Worldwide, Inc.
An International Data Group Company
919 E. Hillsdale Blvd.
Suite 400
Foster City, CA 94404

Library of Congress Catalog Card No.: 95-78776

ISBN: 1-56884-913-3

Printed in the United States of America

10 9 8 7 6 5 4 3 2 1

1I/RU/RS/ZV

Distributed in the United States by IDG Books Worldwide, Inc.

Distributed by Macmillan Canada for Canada; by Computer and Technical Books for the Caribbean Basin; by Contemporanea de Ediciones for Venezuela; by Distribuidora Cuspide for Argentina; by CITEC for Brazil; by Ediciones ZETA S.C.R. Ltda. for Peru; by Editorial Limusa SA for Mexico; by Transworld Publishers Limited in the United Kingdom and Europe; by Al-Maiman Publishers & Distributors for Saudi Arabia; by Simron Pty. Ltd. for South Africa; by IDG Communications (HK) Ltd. for Hong Kong; by Toppan Company Ltd. for Japan; by Addison Wesley Publishing Company for Korea; by Longman Singapore Publishers Ltd. for Singapore, Malaysia, Thailand, and Indonesia; by Unalis Corporation for Taiwan; by WS Computer Publishing Company, Inc. for the Philippines; by WoodsLane Pty. Ltd. for Australia; by WoodsLane Enterprises Ltd. for New Zealand.

For general information on IDG Books Worldwide's books in the U.S., please call our Consumer Customer Service department at 800-762-2974. For reseller information, including discounts and premium sales, please call our Reseller Customer Service department at 800-434-3422.

For information on where to purchase IDG Books Worldwide's books outside the U.S., contact IDG Books Worldwide at 415-655-3021 or fax 415-655-3295.

For information on translations, contact Marc Jeffrey Mikulich, Director, Foreign & Subsidiary Rights, at IDG Books Worldwide, 415-655-3018 or fax 415-655-3295.

For sales inquiries and special prices for bulk quantities, write to the address above or call IDG Books Worldwide at 415-655-3200.

For information on using IDG Books Worldwide's books in the classroom, or ordering examination copies, contact Jim Kelly at 800-434-2086.

For authorization to photocopy items for corporate, personal, or educational use, please contact Copyright Clearance Center, 222 Rosewood Drive, Danvers, MA 01923, or fax 508-750-4470.

is a trademark under exclusive license to IDG Books Worldwide, Inc., from International Data Group, Inc.

About the Author

Mark Kellner has been published as a journalist since 1972, when as a high school student he wrote a weekly column for the *Queens Tribune* in New York City. He's written the "On Computers" column for *The Washington Times* since March 1991. During this time, Mark's published more than 200 weekly articles evaluating Windows and Macintosh hardware and software, as well as the Internet and other leading technologies.

Along with the "On Computers" column, Mark writes about technology for many national publications. He is currently contributing to *Communications Week, InfoWorld,* and *Nation's Business* magazines and has written for *PC World, InformationWeek, MacWeek,* and *Computer Buyer's Guide and Handbook* magazines.

From 1993 to 1994, Mark was Editorial Director of and then Editorial Consultant to *Mobile Office* and *Portable Computing* magazines. For *Mobile Office*, Mark also created, compiled, and edited a special software section. Prior to that, Mark was editor of "The Report on AT&T," an independent newsletter based in Alexandria, Virginia. He was also Washington Correspondent for *MISWeek* and a Senior Reporter for *Federal Computer Week,* as well as a Senior Editor of *UNIX Today!*. He was a general assignment reporter for the *Wilkes-Barre Times Leader* in Pennsylvania, and has been published in newspapers and magazines in Canada, Britain, and Australia.

Outside of technology, Mark has written on a variety of subjects for *Delta Sky* magazine, *Travel Weekly*, Religious News Service, *Christianity Today*, and *The Detroit News*. An avid stamp collector, Mark is editor of *The Philatelic Communicator,* the quarterly journal of the American Philatelic Society's Writer's Unit.

Mark currently resides in Reston, Virginia, with his wife, Jean, and their cats, Tony and George. His next book, *God on the Internet,* will be published by IDG Books Worldwide in early 1996.

Welcome to the world of IDG Books Worldwide.

IDG Books Worldwide, Inc., is a subsidiary of International Data Group, the world's largest publisher of computer-related information and the leading global provider of information services on information technology. IDG was founded more than 25 years ago and now employs more than 7,700 people worldwide. IDG publishes more than 250 computer publications in 67 countries (see listing below). More than 70 million people read one or more IDG publications each month.

Launched in 1990, IDG Books Worldwide is today the #1 publisher of best-selling computer books in the United States. We are proud to have received 8 awards from the Computer Press Association in recognition of editorial excellence and three from Computer Currents' First Annual Readers' Choice Awards, and our best-selling *...For Dummies*® series has more than 19 million copies in print with translations in 28 languages. IDG Books Worldwide, through a joint venture with IDG's Hi-Tech Beijing, became the first U.S. publisher to publish a computer book in the People's Republic of China. In record time, IDG Books Worldwide has become the first choice for millions of readers around the world who want to learn how to better manage their businesses.

Our mission is simple: Every IDG and Compaq press book is designed to bring extra value and skill-building instructions to the reader. Our books are written by experts who understand and care about our readers. The knowledge base of our editorial staff comes from years of experience in publishing, education, and journalism — experience which we use to produce books for the '90s. In short, we care about books, so we attract the best people. We devote special attention to details such as audience, interior design, use of icons, and illustrations. And because we use an efficient process of authoring, editing, and desktop publishing our books electronically, we can spend more time ensuring superior content and spend less time on the technicalities of making books.

You can count on our commitment to deliver high-quality books at competitive prices on topics you want to read about. At IDG Books Worldwide, we continue in the IDG tradition of delivering quality for more than 25 years. You'll find no better book on a subject than one from IDG Books Worldwide.

John J. Kilcullen

John Kilcullen
President and CEO
IDG Books Worldwide, Inc.

Dedication

With appreciation, love, and joy, this book is dedicated to

My wife Jean, who put up with much during the weeks of writing, revising, and editing, and who for many years urged me into book writing. Thanks, sweetheart.

My parents, Jacques and Arlene Kellner, who instilled a love of reading and writing and books that has never left, resulting in a too-large personal library.

My best friend, Nathan Bergerbest, whose encouragement and support goes back more than two decades to the McGovern press bus in 1972.

An outside inspiration and acquaintance, author Peggy Noonan. Her sparkling, precise, and prescient writing has at once entertained, inspired, and challenged me to write better, and then better again.

To you all, my most sincere thanks.

Acknowledgments

No book, at least none produced in the last five years of the 20th century, is ever the product of one individual. Even when something is written by one person, the efforts and help of many people contribute to taking that product from idea to manuscript to finished product.

My thanks, then, to:

Greg Croy, Acquisitions Editor par excellence at IDG Books. He took me seriously when I walked up to him at Macworld Expo and said, "Acquire me!"

Megg Bonar and Suki Gear, who hammered out the details of the contract, held my hand, sent me money, and never failed to be nice even in tough situations.

Tim Gallan, one of the most patient and persuasive editors on the planet, a generous soul who softened the rough edges of this volume, and did so very well.

Dennis Cohen, whose technical edits validated what you read here. However, any errors are to be charged to me, and not him.

Keri Walker, one of the most valuable people Apple Computer has ever employed. In charge of the editorial product loan program, Keri's phenomenal attitude and terrific spirit exemplify all that is admirable about Apple. This business needs more people like her.

Matt Gerber and the team at Power Computing in Austin, Texas. They make a dynamite Mac clone that costs less than equivalent Macs and runs like a champ. Thanks for a product that saved me midway through this project!

Dave Harding, Liz Tanner, Nancy Pomeroy, Roger Bell, Blake Stowell, and the whole Mac team at WordPerfect. You aren't going to find a better bunch of people in the applications game without a pile of searching! Particular thanks to Marsha Terry of WordPerfect, who answered a multitude of questions with speed and grace and who helped me document features you won't read about in the WordPerfect manual.

Brooke Cohan, of Stirling and Cohan, who knows her way around the PR biz and who hooked me up with Power Computing and Visioneer. Ditto for Cathy Cloud of McLean PR, who helped with Apple and a bunch of other folks.

Margaret Ryan and Karen Johnson of America Online, thanks for some great assistance, and thanks to AOL, which became my direct link from home to IDG Books!

My friends Joe Frye of Memphis and Ken Sanford of Geneva, who offered useful bits of inspiration for this book.

Derek McGinty, Joe Barber, and the WAMU-FM staff in Washington, D.C., for having me on to talk about software, including WordPerfect for Macintosh.

Anne Veigle, Harvey Kabaker, Dean Honeycutt, and Anne Marriott of *The Washington Times*, for more than four years of great teamwork; and to *Times* editor-in-chief Wesley Pruden, a super-sharp writer, for his encouragement.

Chuck Ashman, Sandi Roth, Liz Montgomery, and Debra Miyasato of Cowles Business Media, for support and friendship and opportunities to work together.

Tony Snow and Kim Komando for saying nice things about me!

Finally, a great big thank you to Teri Robinson, the best editor I've ever worked for and with, a master of rock trivia and knowledge, a dear friend, and the writer of the foreword to this book.

To any whom I've inadvertantly omitted, my sincere apologies. And again, to all who've helped, my most sincere thanks.

(The Publisher would like to give special thanks to Patrick J. McGovern, without whom this book would not have been possible.)

Credits

**Senior Vice President
and Publisher**
Milissa L. Koloski

Associate Publisher
Diane Graves Steele

Brand Manager
Judith A. Taylor

Editorial Managers
Kristin A. Cocks
Mary C. Corder

Product Development Manager
Mary Bednarek

Editorial Executive Assistant
Richard Graves

Acquisitions Assistant
Suki Gear

Production Director
Beth Jenkins

Production Assistant
Jacalyn L. Pennywell

**Supervisor of
Project Coordination**
Cindy L. Phipps

**Supervisor of
Page Layout**
Kathie S. Schnorr

Production Systems Specialist
Steve Peake

Pre-Press Coordination
Tony Augsburger
Patricia R. Reynolds
Theresa Sánchez-Baker

Media/Archive Coordination
Leslie Popplewell
Michael Wilkey

Project Editor
Tim Gallan

Editorial Assistants
Constance Carlisle
Chris Collins
Stacey Holden Prince
Kevin Spencer

Technical Reviewer
Dennis Cohen

Associate Project Coordinator
J. Tyler Connor

Graphics Coordination
Shelley Lea
Gina Scott
Carla Radzikinas

Production Page Layout
Brett Black
Linda M. Boyer
Todd Klemme
Jill Lyttle
Anna Rohrer
Michael Sullivan

Proofreaders
Kathleen Prata
Christine Meloy Beck
Gwenette Gaddis
Dwight Ramsey
Carl Saff
Robert Springer

Indexer
Sherry Massey

Cover Design
Kavish + Kavish

Contents at a Glance

Cartoons at a Glance

By Rich Tennant

Page 271

Page 157

Page 57

Page 7

Page 141

Page 71

Page 102

Page 287

Page 186

Page 204

Table of Contents

Foreword

· ·

*W*ordPerfect has long taken a bad rap. Consider, for instance, a recent high-profile slander. When criticizing fellow Dream Team attorney Robert Shapiro on his low tech office set-up, F. Lee Bailey sneered derisively that Shapiro only had WordPerfect — and the original version at that.

I can't speak for Shapiro, but Bailey's comment sure was a backhanded slap at WordPerfect, and not the first delivered either publicly or privately. The truth be known, though, despite the criticism, WordPerfect is just about the best word processor around for the Macintosh. This is a well-kept secret, however, because in the public mind, WordPerfect often takes a backseat to other word processors such as Microsoft Word. But does Word let users create a hyperlink to a Web page as does WordPerfect? I don't think so. That's just one of the many hidden pleasures in WordPerfect.

So there's no better time than the present for *WordPerfect 3.5 For Macs For Dummies* to right that wrong perception and take users through the rich feature set and the new enhancements that make the current version of WordPerfect a potential powerhouse.

Now, don't let the title fool you: this book is not just for dummies after all, but for anyone who's ever struggled with the nuances of WordPerfect. (Although if being a WordPerfect dummy were a prerequisite for reading this book, I'd gladly count myself among their number.)

Unfortunately, it's not just the dummies who have remained mystified by some of WordPerfect's twists and turns, earning the program the moniker "Word Imperfect." Even the most computer-literate among us needs guidance to get the most out of this delicious, but complex, program.

And what better place to find a helping hand than from this witty, hip, informative, and often irreverent book by Mark Kellner. Kellner parlays over two decades worth of journalistic expertise into an informative tome that's easy to follow and doesn't make the reader feel like, well, a dummy. He is a master detective who investigates and reports all the angles while plumbing the depths of WordPerfect's potential.

Plus, *WordPerfect 3.5 For Macs For Dummies* is infinitely more interesting reading — downright entertaining, in fact — than any user manual. And, by the way, that's the only other place that you might find such comprehensive information on WordPerfect. I expected no less from the talented writer and insightful teacher Kellner — and I wasn't disappointed. You won't be either.

WordPerfect 3.5 For Macs For Dummies is set up like the typical user thinks. The chapters are self-contained and broken down into individual pertinent topics. You don't have to read the complete tome just to find the answers you seek as you slog through WordPerfect on your desktop. You can jump around or quickly flip to much-needed information without interrupting your workflow. Or you can read this guide cover to cover and become an instant expert — you'll also discover a few clever rock 'n' roll references that you can co-opt when chit-chatting with other WordPerfect users.

WordPerfect keeps its many secrets well hidden. We can all use the help uncovering them. And *WordPerfect 3.5 For Macs For Dummies* is just perfect for dummies — and the rest of us.

Teri Robinson
Contributing Editor, *Communications Week*

Introduction

● ●

This Is the Mac . . . It's Supposed to Work!

One of the first major books about the Macintosh was called *The Macintosh Bible*. In it, creator Arthur Naiman postulated several rules for Mac usage, the first being: "This is the Mac. It's supposed to be FUN."

Users of word processing on the Mac today might have a different request. All they want is for their word processor to *work*. The fun can come later.

That's because many users of Microsoft Word 6 for Macintosh (hereafter referred to as "Brand X") don't own the computer firepower needed to really run that mega-program to its best advantage. They may not own a Power Macintosh or double-digit quantities of RAM — and even a nice program such as RAM Doubler (discussed in Chapter 21) is of limited use.

One friend of mine begins her work day by switching on her Mac Quadra, starting up "Brand X," and then going for a cup of coffee. By the time she returns to her desk, some 10 minutes later, that program is still loading.

But enough about word processors that *don't* work. I'm here to help you along with one that *does* work — and very well, I might add. It's called WordPerfect for Macintosh, and whether you process words for pay or for fun, you will find this program helps you, in ways big and small, to make the job a painless one.

WordPerfect for Macintosh has taken about four years to evolve into its present form. Once a gangly attempt at making the popular WordPerfect compatible with the Mac, the program today is a powerful tool for creating and managing documents that just happens to run on the Mac platform.

The fact that WordPerfect is a great system for document creation and management, by the way, is comforting news as far as computer users go. Industry experts predict that it is the *document* and not the *operating system* that will be the basic building block of computing in the years to come. So starting with WordPerfect as a way to manage your documents might well be a good beginning.

What You'll Find Here

Inside the pages of this book, you'll find all the basics of running WordPerfect for Macintosh, explained in clear English. You'll also learn some tricks and techniques for making WordPerfect behave the way you want, as well as some rather advanced features of this remarkable program.

Want to write a letter, begin the Great American Novel, or just polish off the quarterly report to headquarters? *WordPerfect 3.5 For Macs For Dummies* will show you how to best use the software to achieve these goals.

Need to prepare a thesis for college? A research paper for a medical journal? Maybe a grant application for your local nonprofit? Here, too, *WordPerfect 3.5 For Macs For Dummies* will show you great ideas on format and presentation, from setting up cover pages to adding footnotes, from automatically creating a table of contents, to generating an index you'll be proud of.

Along with these important tasks, you'll learn some of the neat advantages WordPerfect for Macintosh offers a user. Take every time I've mentioned WordPerfect for Macintosh so far. I only typed the actual name of the program once, long ago in fact. Thanks to a feature called QuickCorrect, discussed in Chapter 10, I now only have to type the initials "wpm" to get the full program name. (You might want to use this feature to insert the name of a business, say the law firm of Dewey, Cheatem & Howe, if you happen to work there.)

That's spiffy, yes, but it's not all. There are literally tons of great features in WordPerfect that will save you time and trouble. And embarrassment, too. If your grammar isn't becoming to you, you should be coming to WordPerfect, because it includes a great grammar checker. Got the itch to create a newsletter for your block association? There are graphics and layout tools aplenty here to help.

In business, WordPerfect contains enough math power to total up an expense report, enough smarts to handle mailing labels and form letters, and even enough style to transmit your work via e-mail (from within the program) or publish it on the Internet's World Wide Web using the Hypertext Markup Language (HTML) standard. You'll learn about all of these right here. You can even skip the rest of this intro (please don't) and learn about them right now.

How to Use This Book

The short answer is to use *WordPerfect 3.5 For Macs For Dummies* any way you want to use it. Want to read it straight through to grasp the scope and sweep of this program? Fine. Need to dip in and answer a tough question? No offense taken. I've arranged this book to satisfy both kinds of readers — the ones who like to linger and those who don't have a lot of time at the moment. (If you've ever picked up a reference book in a hurry before, you'll know there are some moments where you need answers, pronto!) This book is here for you.

If you are using *WordPerfect 3.5 For Macs For Dummies* as a guide to learning the WordPerfect for Macintosh program, I'd suggest going through this book from front to back. Taken in sequence, you'll learn about the basics of using the program and progress from simple tasks to more complex ones.

Are you a current WordPerfect user upgrading to a new version? Or do you have different needs? Then *WordPerfect 3.5 For Macs For Dummies* will offer you a buffet of capabilities, ready for you to load up on your computing "plate" as desired.

But along with these two methods of using this book, let me suggest one other. When you've mastered the basics of using this amazing program, consider the advanced features described here as a kind of graduate school for your continuing education. There are many, many layers to WordPerfect for Macintosh that offer tremendous benefits. Even if you only want to write letters or reports — and I'll show you how to best do those things — I would encourage you to let your curiosity run wild. Try your hand at a newsletter or presentation. Experiment with the graphics tools. Heck, even stick a table in your note to grandma.

The nicest thing about "taking a chance" with WordPerfect is that it's pretty impossible to screw up. You can always undo something you've done and try it again. (And if that doesn't sound like much, look up the Undo instructions in *Stonecutting For Dummies*!)

The skills you add with such experiments could well be invaluable to you. When your boss or your friend or your significant other asks, "Can you help me with _____?" and you answer "Yes," it's a great boost to your self-esteem, and it could add to your paycheck, too.

How This Book Is Organized

Part I covers the basics. If you need to get started right away with opening, saving, and printing documents, here's where you look.

In Part II, I deal with some of WordPerfect's editing, layout, and graphics features. None of this stuff is hard to master, but you'll look like a pro in front of your friends and coworkers when putting into practice the information you gained from just a few minutes of reading.

Part III contains a mix of WordPerfect's more advanced, power-user features. From style sheets to HTML, if you want to use WordPerfect to its fullest potential, you'll find what you need to know right here.

Part IV, The Part of Tens, is a standard in every *Dummies* book. I use this part to offer some optional advice that you can take or leave, and I even throw in an appendix on installation (a $2.95 value thrown in at no extra charge).

Icons Used in This Book

Not only is *WordPerfect 3.5 For Macs For Dummies* an easy book to grow with, it's easy to follow. That's thanks in part to the six little icons that follow. Any time they appear, there's something you should take note of:

This icon indicates that I'm about to present a set of steps. You may want to be sitting in front of your computer.

When I want to offer my own, personal opinion about some topic, product, or procedure, I use this icon to give you fair warning. The opinions expressed by this author may not be those of IDG Books Worldwide, Inc., its janitorial — oops, editorial — staff, its parent corporation, International Data Group, or its founder, Pat McGovern.

When I don't want you to forget some juicy bit of information, I use this icon.

This icon points out the finer details that you can ignore if you just want to find out how to use WordPerfect, do your job, and leave the office at 5 o'clock every day.

I use this icon to indicate shortcuts, secrets, good advice, and other cool info.

Any text flagged by this icon ought to be read carefully. Trust me: a little extra time spent reading will save you from heartache, headaches, lower back pain, and bad karma in general.

What Your Computer Needs to Run WordPerfect for Macintosh

Besides the obvious — you need a Macintosh computer or one of the new clones just starting to appear on the market — your computer should have the following as basic equipment:

For a regular Macintosh:

- System 6.0.7 or later
- 2MB of RAM (if you're running System 6.0.x) or 4MB if you're running System 7.0 or later)
- A hard disk with 9MB free for a complete installation of WordPerfect for Macintosh

For a Power Macintosh:

- Hard disk with 11MB free for a complete installation
- At least 4.5MB of RAM, but I'd recommend a minimum of 8MB
- System 7.1.2 or later

You'll also want to have a Mac-compatible printer — inkjet or laser is your best bet — and a good display screen.

There are several other items you can get that will make word processing with WordPerfect more enjoyable and productive. One of the joys of working with WordPerfect — and the Mac itself — is that you can enhance both the program and your computer for maximum effectiveness. See Chapters 21 and 22 for more suggestions on what extra equipment and other useful tools you should consider.

What's New in WordPerfect for Macintosh 3.5

Plenty. For one, this new release fixes a couple of "bugs" (or, undocumented features, as the cognoscenti call 'em) and adds some significant features.

Perhaps one of the most important — as everyone contemplates merging onto the Information Superhighway — is *HTML* support. HTML stands for *Hypertext Markup Language*, and it's the way people prepare documents for electronic publication on the World Wide Web. If *you* want to reach the world with your thoughts, HTML will be very important to your use of WordPerfect for Macintosh. If, on the other hand, you don't have a clue about the Web, pick up a copy of *The Internet For Macs For Dummies* — after you finish this book, of course.

Now Get Started

By now, I hope you're excited enough about WordPerfect to want to dive into the program itself. So get over to your Mac, turn a page, and get ready to begin!

Happy computing!

Part I
Beginner's Luck

The 5th Wave   By Rich Tennant

In this part . . .

"*O*nce upon a midnight dreary, as I pondered weak and weary . . ." — whoops, wrong story. It could be bright and early one morning, the middle of the afternoon, or, yes, 3 a.m.

Whatever the time, you want to fire up WordPerfect and get going. You've got a Macintosh, you've got the desire (or necessity), and you've got a deadline, maybe. What you may not have is the knowledge of the software. At least not yet.

In this part, I show you how to create and save a document, how to print that document out (the basics, at least), and other fun, albeit somewhat basic, stuff. Then I'll talk about the menus, the button and ribbon bars, and even the "Zen" of WordPerfect.

Chapter 1

Firing Up WordPerfect, or It Was a Dark and Stormy Night

. . . .

. . . .

*I*t was a dark and stormy night, and the writer sat facing a blank screen, knowing his editor wanted 5,000 words by morning, wondering what to say, and remembering that one successful author of his acquaintance started by typing one word — "The" — on top of the screen and waiting for inspiration to take over.

Six long, agonizing hours later, the writer was still staring at his screen. His eyes ached. His soul was parched. That one word, "The," stared back like a cyclops, daring him to continue.

He did. He typed, ". . . heck with it." and printed out the page. Not caring that Margaret Mitchell had assigned the same words decades before, he said to himself, "Tomorrow is another day."

Your Boss (Teacher, Partner, Client) Wants It When?

You may not face the exact challenge our imaginary writer confronted, but I'll bet you face some other demands in your life, and they're demands that WordPerfect for Macintosh can help you solve. You have to write a report, prepare a pitch for a new client, apply for a job, finish a term paper, or begin the Great American Novel. (Free hint: Keep some coffee handy for that one.)

It may seem strange to some readers, or even surreal, but way back in the dark ages before the Macintosh, say about 12 or 15 years ago, many of us depended on something called a typewriter to handle these tasks. Sometimes these machines were manual — they depended on human power to move the keys and advance the carriage. Toward the end of their widespread popularity, most were electric or electronic, but they were still noisy and few had the native intelligence that sits before you with your Mac and WordPerfect.

In those days — trust me — typing a few thousand words was a chore. You had to have enough paper at hand, make sure the paper was aligned properly in the typewriter and hope you had either enough correcting tape or Liquid Paper (the latter invented by Monkee Mickey Dolenz's mother, by the way) to correct your mistakes. If your work was, say, for a college thesis or legal brief, not only did you have to use special paper, but you had to be even more careful — some professors didn't allow excessive errors, and neither did some courts.

Fast forward to today and just think of how much easier it is. You can type what you want and see what it will look like on paper before you print it out. Want to change the typeface? You couldn't do that with a manual typewriter — unless you changed machines. On the Mac, it's just a couple of mouse clicks to a whole new look.

Go beyond simple customization to more complex demands. Did you just write that term paper and find out the instructor wants the footnotes at the end of the document instead of on each page? No sweat: a few minutes at the keyboard and you're set. Want to do a newsletter with justified text (even on both sides) and columns that balance on a page? My friend, Joe Frye, in Memphis, Tennessee, will tell you it's tough going. For the better part of a decade, he put out a 20-page newsletter, circulated internationally, every quarter with an electric typewriter and a lot of patience. (He later became a WordPerfect enthusiast, even if it was the Windows version!)

One neat way of thinking about word processing with WordPerfect for Macintosh — particularly if you're making the transition from a typewriter (or something equally ancient, such as MS-DOS) — is that many of the basic operations of this program are very much like using a typewriter, only much better and much more powerful.

Just about any task you can associate with putting words on paper can be done more easily on a Macintosh. And, frankly, WordPerfect offers a host of neat and nifty tools to help you accomplish just about any task you can associate with putting words on paper. In this book, you'll learn how to accomplish many of these tasks — as well as learn how to use the tools for going even further.

So if your boss (or teacher, or partner, or client) says that he or she needs something in a hurry, you'll have the wherewithal to accomplish the job. For now, let's begin at the appropriate beginning with the answer to one of the key questions any first-time user of word processing might ask:

Why Is My "Page" Blank?

Start up WordPerfect, and you'll find a screen that looks very much like Figure 1-1.

It's pretty blank up there. You are basically on your own when starting off — or are you?

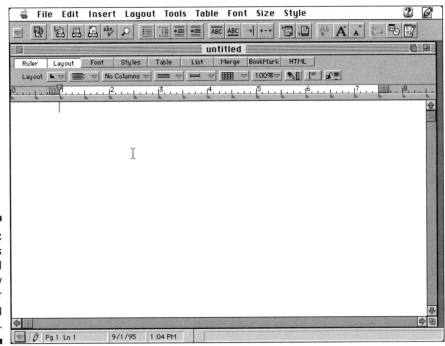

Figure 1-1:
This is what you'll probably see after launching WordPerfect.

What Are All Those Buttons on My Screen?

Let's take a look at this screen. Your typing area *is* clear, yes, but there are some tools available to help you. Starting just above the blank screen, you see the *ruler,* as shown in Figure 1-2. Just like the old margin setting devices on some typewriters (remember those?), this ruler shows you what your left and right margins are (the default is an inch around each side of the page) as well as the *tab stops* that are set in the document. These are just like tabs on a typewriter: they help you line up items in a tabular form but are easier to change than with a typewriter. In WordPerfect, you can move these tab stops and have the text move with them.

I'll discuss the ruler in greater detail soon. For now, just know that it's a good guide to the boundaries of your document, and know that it can later be modified to meet your specific needs.

Figure 1-2:
The ruler.

Just above the ruler is the first of several *ribbon bars* (see Figure 1-3), which allow you to select and easily use various special functions of WordPerfect for Macintosh without having to dash through a bunch of menus. The ribbon bars are great if you don't want to have to hunt for a given command, and they're also helpful if you want to see various settings as you are working (which helps answer the ever popular question: "Gee, did I select **bold** or *italics* — oh, and what is this font I'm using called?").

Figure 1-3:
WordPerfect's
ribbon bars.

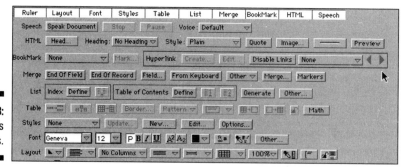

Above the Layout bar are control buttons for a variety of other functions: font selection and attributes; styles (for text and other elements); creating and editing tables, as well as two for creating various lists (such as a table of contents or an index) and one that puts various merge functions at your fingertips.

Rounding out the screen that's before you are three more important items — aside from the Macintosh menu bar, which is common to all Mac programs and with which you should be familiar. (In WordPerfect, you can access almost every command from the Mac menu bar, but you probably figured that one out.)

Some other items you'll see on-screen include a *title bar,* which shows you the name of your document (and contains a button to switch between open windows — more on that later); and a *status bar* at the bottom of the screen, which shows the page and line you are working on, the date, time, and other functions (see Figures 1-4 and 1-5).

Figure 1-4:
The title bar of a document.

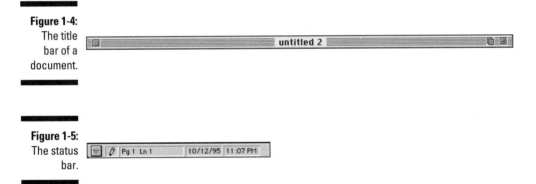

Figure 1-5:
The status bar.

Last up on the display, just above the title bar and below the Mac menu bar in this example, is a *button bar* showing a variety of functions you can access (see Figure 1-6). Want to draw or modify a graphic? Need to spell check or do some special formatting? The default settings on the button bar will help you. For more detail, turn to Chapter 3. Meantime, just be glad you've got this extra resource handy.

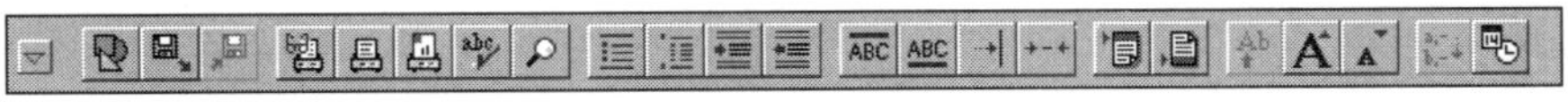

Figure 1-6:
The button bar.

Type Something! Anything!

Now that you have a sense of what's available on your screen, just begin typing. The blinking cursor tells you where you can start typing.

For those who are making the transition from a typewriter, a gentle reminder: Unlike typewriters, the computer will move the cursor from the end of one line to the beginning of the next automatically. You *do not* need to press the Return key in order to advance. It'll take some practice, perhaps, but you'll get the hang of it, I promise.

But wait . . . there's more! Not only can you zip the cursor around the screen, but you can easily move about within your document with other features of the keyboard and WordPerfect. For one, there are the arrow keys, which can be found near the bottom row of both the regular and extended Apple keyboards. Using these keys, you can move within a paragraph or line, up or down, left or right. Hold these keys down and you can keep moving until you reach a desired destination. Use them in combination with the Option key, and you can move left or right one word at a time, or one screen at a time.

Next, look at the shaded bars at the right and bottom edges of your document. These are called scroll bars and you can drag the buttons on each bar either left or right or up or down. The right scroll bar is a particularly good way to move through a long document with some speed.

Making All Things New

If you ever need to create a new document — even while you're working on another one — check out the New command on the File menu (or you can use the ⌘-N key combination to create a new, untitled file). This new file can be a handy "parking place" for spare notes or scraps of information from a big document, or a place to rough out ideas. And if you ever find yourself in the middle of one job and needing to start another, the New command is your best friend (see Figure 1-7).

If It Was Worth Your Time to Type It, You Ought to Save It

Once you've typed something, you'll probably want to save the file and give it a name. Naming files, of course, helps you identify them and find them later. Saving a file on disk (either a floppy or hard disk) stores your work for retrieval

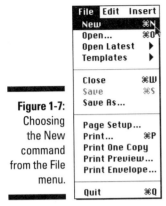

Figure 1-7:
Choosing
the New
command
from the File
menu.

another time. You access the Save command by choosing the Save command from the File menu. You can also press the key combination ⌘-S. Figure 1-8 shows the Save dialog box, which pops up when you try to save a new document for the first time. It also appears when you choose the Save As command, but that's another story; see Chapter 5 for the details. For now, let's look at the basics.

Straight off, this screen tells us several interesting things. For one, it shows you where on the hard disk or floppy disk the file will be saved. It also has a place for you to specify the name you want to give the file. And it also lets you tell WordPerfect what format you desire this file to be saved in, which is handy when you're sharing work with others who aren't as enlightened as you are about choosing a word processor!

Figure 1-8:
The Save
dialog box
allows you
to name
your
document
and choose
the location
in which you
would like to
save it.

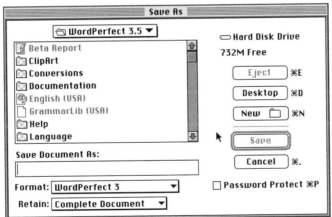

Once the Save dialog box appears, you need to give your document a name. You type it in the Save Document As section.

One of the nice aspects of the Macintosh is that you are able to use a *real name* for a file, up to 31 characters and spaces, such as My Letter to Chloe re Contract. This is better than DOS or Windows, where you are limited to 11 characters, 8 before a required period and three after. For now, just name your newly created document whatever you choose. (Yes, I know that Windows 95 lets you use even longer names for files than the Mac does, but it's still Windows, and you may have heard the saying: "Windows 95. Macintosh 84." There's no doubt that we who are Mac fans have had it easier for many years now.)

You now need to decide where you want the file to be saved. "On my hard drive, you idiot!" is probably what you're thinking, but *where* on your hard drive? If you've been using your Mac for a while, I'm sure you have folders set up for your documents, perhaps by project or kind of document or whatever you desire. Just maneuver over to one of those in the Save As dialog box and click the Save button. Piece of cake.

For new Mac users, the process is a little more complex, but it's still very easy, so don't panic. If you don't have a separate folder created to store your documents, here's what you do:

1. **Click the Desktop button in the Save As dialog box.**

2. **Now click the New Folder button.**

   The button actually has the word "New" with a picture of a folder on it, in case you weren't sure. It's just below the Desktop button.

   A little dialog box appears asking you to name the new folder.

3. **Type** WP Documents **and click the OK button.**

   You now have a folder named WP Documents sitting on the desktop of your Mac's Finder.

   On the left side of the Save As dialog box, your new WP Documents folder is selected, meaning that when you click the Save button, your new document will be saved in that folder.

4. **Click the Save button.**

Congratulations! You now have a document stored in the WP Documents folder on the desktop of your Mac. Later on, you may want to move this folder to another place on your hard drive.

By the way, if terms like Finder, desktop, and even folder are meaningless to you, you need to familiarize yourself with the workings of your Mac's operating system, a subject which is beyond the scope of this book. I suggest that you pick up David Pogue's *Macs For Dummies* or Bob LeVitus's *Macintosh System 7.5 For Dummies,* both excellent and both published by IDG Books.

For now, let me add that organizing your hard disk and doing the right job of filing not only make sense, it could also make your computer run better. I'm not kidding: my wife, one of the most organized people on Earth, says her Macs run faster when organized properly. And considering that both a friend of mine and I each complain of slow computers — and we each could have better organized hard drives — maybe she has a point. In any case, anybody who uses a Mac will benefit from learning the basics of file management.

How to Print One Copy without Really Trying

This next bit is easy — assuming, of course, that you have a printer attached to your Mac, and that it is turned on and has paper in it. I shall also assume you know about the Chooser and how it works in selecting which printer you wish to use. (If you're unclear on either of these concepts, see the two basic Mac texts referred to in the preceding section.)

You can do one of two things to print a copy of your work. One is to simply click the Print icon in the button bar at the top of your screen. This action brings up the Print dialog box, which lets you specify the number of copies you want to print and many other options. Figure 1-9 shows a picture. For now, just click the Print button in this dialog box, which should result in the printing of one copy of your document. More discussion of print options appears in Chapter 17.

Figure 1-9:
A Print
dialog box
for a
LaserWriter
SC.

Personal LaserWriter SC 7.0.1	**Print**
Copies: `1` Pages: ◉ All ◯ From: ___ To: ___	Cancel
Paper Source: ◉ Paper Cassette ◯ Manual Feed	
☐ Every Other Page ⌘E ☐ Print Backwards ⌘B	
☐ Print Selection ☒ Print Overlay Layer ⌘L	

If you only want one copy of what you're working on, here's a little trick: pull down the File menu and choose the Print One Copy command (see Figure 1-10). That's all you do: WordPerfect for Macintosh does the rest and prints out a copy of your work in a jiffy.

Figure 1-10: Choosing the Print One Copy command from the File menu.

File	Edit	Insert
New		⌘N
Open...		⌘O
Open Latest		▶
Templates		▶
Close		⌘W
Save		⌘S
Save As...		
Page Setup...		
Print...		⌘P
Print One Copy		
Print Preview...		
Print Envelope...		
Quit		⌘Q

I'm Outta Here

Well, not really, since there's more — much more — to cover in WordPerfect for Macintosh than what I've explored here. However, for now let's assume you want to take a break. After all, if you're totally new to WordPerfect, or even the Mac, you've just assimilated a lot. Let it soak in for a spell. Go have some coffee, or take a walk.

I'm not joking about the take a walk idea. Even though it's tough, getting up out of your chair and away from your keyboard is one of the best things you can do while operating a computer. During periods where you have to be in front of the machine for a good amount of time, try to get up and stretch every 15 or 20 minutes. The health you will save will be your own!

Anyway, to exit WordPerfect, press the ⌘-Q key combination on your keyboard or choose the Quit command from the File menu. This command takes you out of the program until your next time. By the way, if you have open documents that you haven't saved recently, WordPerfect will ask you whether you want to save them before quitting. How nice.

You will want to make sure your files are saved before quitting the program — and especially before shutting off your Macintosh. WordPerfect is a very forgiving program, but it is also a forgetful one: once you quit, it forgets anything you've created or edited but haven't saved.

Chapter 2

Mastering WordPerfect's Menus

· ·

· ·

*N*ow that we've gone through the basics of firing up WordPerfect for Macintosh and creating a short document, let's move on to a more involved level. I'd like to suggest you consider a new, more personal relationship . . . with the menu system built into this program. It's a fast, easy way to get around WordPerfect, and a good working knowledge of the menu system will save you time and heartache as you go about your business.

But as straightforward as the menu system might appear, there are some surprises and little-known features you need to learn about. That's what I'll help you with in these pages, so hop on board the menu express and get on the fast track to WordPerfect proficiency.

Meet the Pull-Down Menus

From the beginning, way back in 1984 (long before Microsoft Windows came up with the idea) Apple Computer scored one in the marketplace with — ta da! — *pull-down menus*. At the top of the Mac screen, there's a *menu bar* that contains several words. Click on a word and a menu drops down, full of exciting choices you can make. Figure 2-1 shows a pull-down menu.

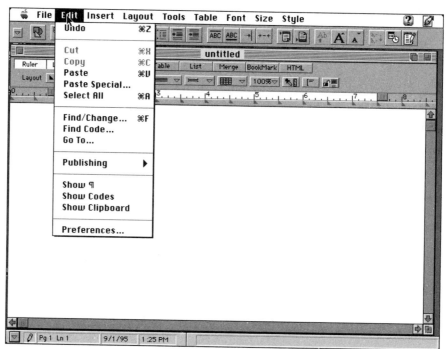

Figure 2-1:
WordPerfect's
Edit menu.

By now, this may not seem so revolutionary. Way back then, however, our best hope, in MS-DOS or even for those brave souls still using CP/M (remember that?), was a combination of keystrokes that were difficult to understand and remember. Using a pointing device known as a *mouse* allows you to point and click on various options, something you can't do with a key combination.

For many people, taking a hand off the keyboard and using the mouse quickly becomes second nature. Indeed, some users bridge the gap between keyboard and mouse by having a stationary device called a *trackball* alongside the keyboard (or even built into it), reducing the distance a hand has to travel in order to point and click.

Whichever access method you choose, the pull-down menus of WordPerfect are there to make life easier. And they're easy to use, too. For one, many of the basic commands — open a file, save a file, print a document, or quit the program — are standard throughout Macintosh applications. That's a rule, or convention, Apple insists upon in its operating system. What it means for you is that if you know the basic Mac commands, you're more than halfway there when it comes to using WordPerfect. (But keep reading this book — there's a great deal to learn when it comes to WordPerfect!)

If you're at once new to Macintosh computers in general as well as WordPerfect, take heart. The pull-down menus really are your friends. Read on, use the menus, and reap the rewards!

There are nine pull-down menus in WordPerfect you'll work with, and they are rather straightforward. Figure 2-2 shows a close-up.

Figure 2-2:
The menu
bar.

The File menu

This File menu, shown in Figure 2-3, deals with key file actions: creating, opening, closing, saving, and printing a file. From here, you can create a new file, open an existing one, open the latest version of a file, and perform other tasks including the printing of a file. Some of these are Mac standards: ⌘-P is a universal print-file command; ⌘-Q is the equally standard command you can use to quit, or exit from, a program.

Neat trick

Also found here are a couple of really neat, time-and-effort-saving features. One of these is the Open Latest menu, which displays as many of your recently opened files as you like, up to — no joke! — 255 of them. That's a boon to those of us who keep files in different spots on a hard disk or a network: if you lose your way, the Open Latest submenu (see Figure 2-4) can help you get back to where you once belonged!

Figure 2-3:
The File
menu.

File	Edit	Insert
New		⌘N
Open...		⌘O
Open Latest		▶
Templates		▶
Close		⌘W
Save		⌘S
Save As...		
Page Setup...		
Print...		⌘P
Print One Copy		
Print Preview...		
Print Envelope...		
Quit		⌘Q

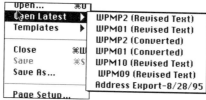

Figure 2-4:
The Open
Latest
submenu.

Neat trick part deux

The other great asset of the File menu is the Print One Copy command. Choose this one and pow!, you're printing. No print dialogues; no advanced setup. Just click and go. When you're in a hurry and your paper trays are loaded, Print One Copy gets things moving in a jiffy.

Two other commands are worth special attention here. Print Preview takes the what-you-see-is-what-you-get aspect of the Mac and WordPerfect one step further: you get to see what the finished document will look like on-screen. Print Envelope, which will be discussed in greater detail in Chapter 13, is even more brilliant. Use it to grab a recipient's address from a letter and see how your envelope will look before it's printed. Very cool, if you ask me.

The Edit menu

The Edit menu (see Figure 2-5) is command central for the key functions of WordPerfect, at least when it comes to editing text. Here, you can cut, copy, and paste blocks of text, as well as *publish* and *subscribe* your documents with or

```
 Edit  Insert  Layout
 Undo              ⌘Z

 Cut               ⌘X
 Copy              ⌘C
 Paste             ⌘V
 Paste Special...
 Select All        ⌘A

 Find/Change...    ⌘F
 Find Code...
 Go To...

 Publishing      ▶

 Show ¶
 Show Codes
 Show Clipboard

 Preferences...
```

Figure 2-5:
The Edit
menu.

from other Macintosh files, either locally or on a network. (A complete discussion of publish and subscribe is found in Chapter 15, so relax, Caddie.)

At the bottom of the Edit menu is one of the most wonderful areas of WordPerfect, the Preferences command. Choose this item and a world of choices opens up to you. This is a program that you can make truly your own by adding all sorts of shortcuts and enhancements — right here. More on preferences in Chapter 19, but for now, just know that it's there.

The Insert menu

The Insert menu, pictured in Figure 2-6, adds to the power you have in controlling WordPerfect's editing functions. Here, you can add a page break or column break or have the program automatically place the date and time. You'll also find the Symbols command, a point-and-click way to add special characters such as the pound symbol — £ — used to denote British currency, or the Σ, that handy Greek alphabet letter used in many scientific equations and some fraternity mailings (not to mention a raft of others).

The Layout menu

The Layout menu (see Figure 2-7) is where you'll find even more document publishing power. It's a menu that lets you set margins, tab stops, even the spacing of letters (called *kerning*). Come to Layout menu country when you want to want to rope a border around a paragraph or make sure a bunch of lines stay together.

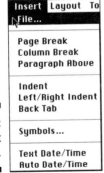

Figure 2-6:
The Insert
menu.

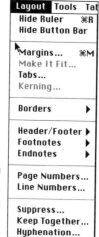

Figure 2-7:
The Layout
menu.

The Tools menu

But wait, there's more! You say you want to check your spelling? You say you need a synonym for grandiose (how 'bout haughty or pretentious, Biff?)? You say you want to check your grammar (that's language, not a female relative)? You say you get paid by the word and need to count 'em all up?

Well, wait no more, friends. WordPerfect for Macintosh is open 24 hours a day for your spelling and lexicographical pleasure. No, you don't get Webster's New World Dictionary online, but you do get a spell checker with several thousand words, a thesaurus containing many thousands more, and tools to count words, check grammar, and do lots of other nifty things. And it's all found on the Tools menu, which is shown in Figure 2-8.

The Table menu

Setting a table used to involve fine china, linen table cloths and napkins, crystal glasses — you get the idea. In WordPerfect, as you will see in Chapter 6, setting a table is much less complicated, and no one will know if you forget to use your salad fork! In the Table menu (see Figure 2-9), the two commands visible when no table is present are New and Calculate. The first, naturally, lets you create a table. The second permits you to ask WordPerfect to calculate all mathematical formulas in a table or an entire document — rather handy when preparing a budget report, wouldn't you say.

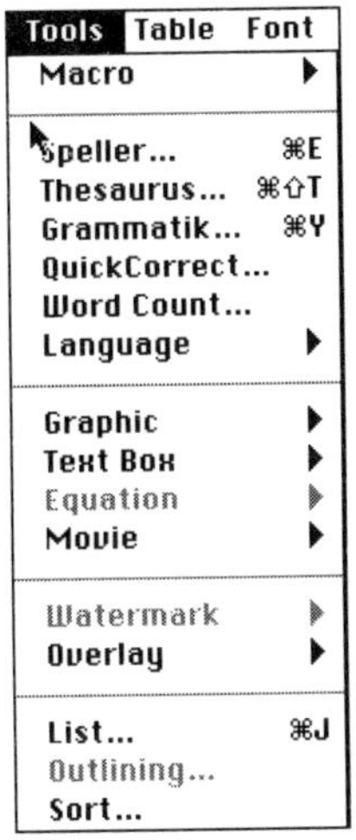

Tools Table Font
Macro   ▶

Speller...   ⌘E
Thesaurus...   ⌘⇧T
Grammatik...   ⌘Y
QuickCorrect...
Word Count...
Language   ▶

Graphic   ▶
Text Box   ▶
Equation   ▶
Movie   ▶

Watermark   ▶
Overlay   ▶

List...   ⌘J
Outlining...
Sort...

Figure 2-8:
The Tools
menu.

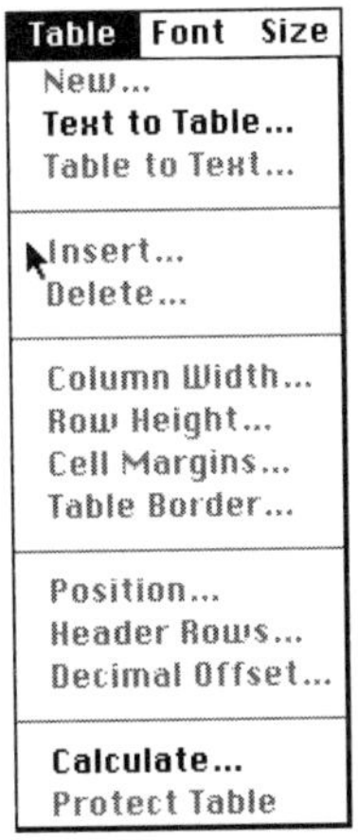

Table Font Size
New...
Text to Table...
Table to Text...

Insert...
Delete...

Column Width...
Row Height...
Cell Margins...
Table Border...

Position...
Header Rows...
Decimal Offset...

Calculate...
Protect Table

Figure 2-9:
The Table
menu.

Twin menus: Font and Size

Birds of a feather flock together, the saying goes, and so it's somewhat natural to find the Font and Size menus next door to each other (see Figures 2-10 and 2-11). From the first, you can select a desired font with WYSIWYG ease. From the second, pick your style, from tiny 9-point (a contract-writer's favorite) to end-of-the-world-headline-size 72 points, which is large enough to get just about anyone's attention.

Figure 2-10:
The Font
menu.

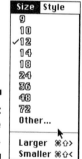

Figure 2-11:
The Size
menu.

The Style menu

And then there's Style. Indeed, where would we be without Style? Pretty bland, I'll tell you. As you can see in Figure 2-12, this is the menu to pick when you want to get **bold**, or <u>underline</u> your points, or even *put a different slant on things*. Whether you are writing in business or for school or college, you'll need these different attributes to either make a point or fit the proper form for a footnote, bibliography, or table of authorities.

Style
Plain Text   ⌘T
✓**Bold**   ⌘B
✓ *Italics*   ⌘I
<u>Underline</u>   ⌘U
Small Caps
Superscript
Subscript
Other...   ⌘H
Redline
~~Strikeout~~
Remove...
Uppercase
Lowercase
Initial Caps

Figure 2-12:
The Style
menu.

And, yes, it's just a point and click to get the text style you desire. Spend a little time with these three, and your writing will never look the same.

As I discuss later, you *can* get too much of a good thing. Be judicious in applying styles and using various typefaces in a document. Otherwise, your job application letter to join the White House staff could look like a ransom note made up of clipped magazine letters. Remember E.F. Schumacher: Less *is* more.

Quick and Easy Menuing with Key Combinations

At the start of this chapter, much was said about the virtues of the pull-down menu and how much better it is than the arcane keyboard combinations of the bad old days of DOS and CP/M.

Well, I fibbed. Sort of. There's no doubt that a mouse makes a lot of things easier, not the least being the selection of a portion of type that needs to be changed, cut, copied, or dragged to a new location. And as I've tried to show, the point and click of the mouse is an ideal way to move through these menus and select the features you need.

But along the way to a mouse-filled nirvana (something my cats, George and Tony, might welcome), the people who study how the rest of us use computers made an interesting discovery: sometimes, often even, it was better to just stick to the keyboard and issue program commands from there, as well as type in words.

Needless to say, WordPerfect takes note of this need. Along with the standard Mac commands discussed earlier, you can use numerous keystroke combinations to achieve your ends. Heck, you can even make up your own for functions which do not have a keystroke combo assigned.

Finding the keystroke combinations is easy. Simply look at the pull-down menus. All these menus — except for the Font menu — include pre-set key combinations that you can use if you desire.

For me, the most common combos are as follows:

- ✔ ⌘-O: Open file
- ✔ ⌘-P: Print file
- ✔ ⌘-S: Save file
- ✔ ⌘-W: Close window

I also use key combinations to change text attributes:

- ✔ ⌘-B: Boldface
- ✔ ⌘-I: Italic
- ✔ ⌘-U: Underline

You'll bump into many other keyboard shortcuts along the way in your journey through WordPerfect, so keep your eyes open!

Customizing Menus

Unlike other areas of WordPerfect, there's not too much to customize in the setup of menus. In fact, it boils down to two areas: You can add more key combinations, and you can change the number of files you can list in the Open Latest menu.

To add more key combinations, select the Preferences command in the Edit menu. When the Preferences dialog box appears (it's shown in Figure 2-13), click the Keyboard button. The Keyboard dialog box appears, where you'll get a list of commands showing existing key combinations where applicable (as shown in Figure 2-14).

Figure 2-13:
The
Preferences
dialog box.

Figure 2-14:
The
Keyboard
dialog box.

Select the task you want to customize, and if it has a key combination defined, you'll see it and can copy it down. If there is no combination present, click the Assign button. The Assign Keystroke dialog box opens (see Figure 2-15), and as you press potential combinations, WordPerfect will tell you if that combination has already been assigned.

Once you find a combination that's (a) easy to remember and (b) not taken elsewhere, make a note of the new combo and then click the Accept button. You're done.

You can really go crazy with this feature of WordPerfect. I haven't tried every keyboard combination known to humankind, but you'll want to exercise some care. For example, you can replace the normal Save command, ⌘-S, with any combination you like, or you can assign the ⌘-S key combination to another function. The bad news is that if you make your copy of WordPerfect too personal, others in your office or home might have difficulty using it when and if they have to.

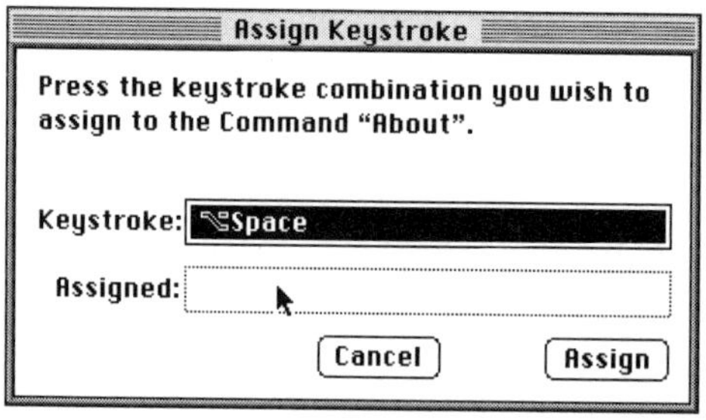

Figure 2-15:
The Assign
Keystroke
dialog box.

```
╔═══════════ Assign Keystroke ═══════════╗
║ Press the keystroke combination you wish to    ║
║ assign to the Command "About".                 ║
║                                                ║
║ Keystroke: ▓Space                              ║
║                                                ║
║ Assigned:  [              ▶               ]    ║
║                                                ║
║             ( Cancel )      ( Assign )         ║
╚════════════════════════════════════════╝
```

That caution aside, the assigning keystrokes feature of WordPerfect is a delight. If you perform a task frequently that few others do, WordPerfect might not have thought of you. Customizing the keyboard is one way to keep this program running the way you want it to.

What are some popular combinations? One of my favorites (set up by the program but not visible on the pull-down menu) is Word Count, which is Option-F3. A press of these two keys tells me I have about 2,645 words in this chapter, so far. Your mileage may vary.

Other combinations can be used to apply styles to a document or to run macros, something that I discuss in Chapter 18. The most important thing to remember here, however, is that you can make this program work the way you do, with just a little effort and imagination.

Hidden Secrets of the Menu Bar

There are a couple of great features on the menu bar which WordPerfect for Macintosh users, new and old, will appreciate. One of these is the Open Latest feature in the File menu, which is discussed in some detail in previous sections of this chapter.

Another very good one is easy access to the extensive amount of help available just under the Balloon Help icon found on Macs running System 7 and above. In this little menu, which I call the Help menu and you can see in Figure 2-16, you can access just about every aspect of WordPerfect for Macintosh's help facilities, which are discussed in greater detail in Chapter 23. Right now, know that if you're stuck and want to see the online help that this program provides, a click on the help balloon (it looks like a comic strip dialog balloon with a question mark inside) will get you there.

Figure 2-16:
The Help
menu.

Just before we leave behind the menu bar, one final thing to notice is the Application menu at the upper-right side of the screen (see Figure 2-17). This menu shows all the applications that are open at any given moment. On my Macintosh, it's usually WordPerfect, Claris Emailer (an electronic mail program) and the Finder; sometimes QuarkXPress (a high-end desktop publishing program) and GraphicConverter (which handles photos and the like) join the list. On your system, your open applications might be just WordPerfect and the Finder.

The point of the Application menu is something that escapes the Windows designers at Microsoft: With one click of a mouse, Apple users can see, and switch to, all of their applications. The Windows user, even under the much-hyped Windows 95, has to press more than one keyboard button to do the same thing. Personally, I like the Mac's way of application switching better, and you might prefer it as well.

That's about it for the menu bar. No cocktails and no hors d'oeurves, but no tipping and no hangover either.

Figure 2-17:
The
Application
menu in all
its glory.

Chapter 3

Pressing Your Buttons (and Manipulating Your Ribbons)

· ·

· ·

*A*fter reading all about the menu commands in Chapter 2, you may be anxious to learn about other aspects of WordPerfect's interface, namely the buttons.

But first, a word from our sponsor. Well, actually, a couple of pages from me about the wonderful world of buttons in WordPerfect and how they will change your life.

Really.

In your look 'round the screen in Chapter 2, you saw how to operate the major features of WordPerfect from the pull-down menus, as well as by using command combinations on the keyboard. But the menus aren't the only way to get this program to hup to. No sir, no ma'am! Uh-unh. The button bar — and those handy-dandy ribbon bars just below — are a boss way to boss WordPerfect around.

But change your life? Well . . . perhaps. I mean, if you use the buttons correctly and get your work done faster, you can go to that softball game or museum opening you'd hope to attend. While there, you could just bump into the person who becomes (a) your spouse, (b) your company's biggest new customer, or (c) your new best friend. Any one of these could easily have an effect on the quality of your life, and all because you used buttons.

Returning to Earth and reality, let's contemplate WordPerfect for Macintosh's button bar from a practical standpoint. Simply put, it's a great and easy way to keep your most-used features within easy reach. Remember the Print One Copy command and how easily it started the printing process? Well, the button bar can put that command — or virtually any other — within arm's reach. No menus to slink through, no command key combinations to memorize or keep handy. Nope, just point and click! Spiffy, no?

Spiffy, yes! Now let's get down to brass tacks.

Our Friend the Button Bar

Nestled just under the menu bar or along the left side of the screen (the choice, as you'll see, is yours), the button bar offers neat storage space for icons representing frequently used tasks (see Figure 3-1).

Figure 3-1:
The button
bar.

On my screen, one icon — the second from the left — is a picture of a floppy disk, which represents the Save command. I can't save a file often enough, you know, and placing an icon here makes it even easier to do the saving.

Other icons sitting atop my screen make short work of other tasks:

The little printer with a pair of eyeglasses tells WordPerfect to give me a quick preview of a document before it prints. This function is officially called Print Preview.

Next, the plain vanilla printer icon issues a "print this file" command. There's a button for the envelope function (don't cha just love it!). And there's even a button for the ever-popular find-and-replace.

Next are four buttons for positioning and formatting text: two each with bullets or indents of various types. I explore the uses of these bullets and indents in Chapter 6; for now, just know that if you highlight a paragraph or two and click on the first bullet button, each of the highlighted paragraphs will be automatically indented and a bullet (like this •) will be added.

Two other buttons add (or delete) a border above or below a given paragraph, while the next two either align text with the right-hand margin or between the left and right margins.

Continuing our rightward march across the button bar (step carefully, please!) are two buttons for creating headers and footers. Select some text and you'll see the next button over change from being grayed out, or inactive, to a state of readiness. Click on it, and you'll change lowercase text to Text With Capital Letters On Each Word. That's known as "Title Case," and an automatic conversion can help a student (or you) with a bibliography.

If you don't need to make a "Title Case" out of some text, perhaps you need to make it larger or smaller. The next two buttons contain a capital "A" with either an up arrow or down arrow. Click on the first and selected type will increase one point in size. Choosing the second means the type you've highlighted will drop down a point in size. This button can be especially useful when trying to fit a lot of copy on a given page.

Our last three buttons are real time-savers for the office. One will take a list of words and sort them in alphabetical order, which is great if you're organizing a company directory and the front office hires "Carter, Julie" when already you're up to "Zigmund, Edouard." The next inserts the date (i.e., May 27, 1995) at your cursor's location. The last, by default, opens the "Memo" stationery template file, which lets you create a memo on the fly. (Using templates is discussed in Chapter 8.) All these buttons are designed to make your editing easier, saving time and steps in performing "routine" tasks.

Except for the Save button, which I added to the button bar back in Figure 3-1, all the buttons described previously form part of the *default* bar of buttons for use with a document file, and each is displayed across the top of my Mac's monitor. Separate, predefined button bars come with WordPerfect for Macintosh for day-to-day editing, equation editing (see Chapter 14), and graphics (discussed in Chapter 7).

Customizing Button Bars

Customizing the button bars is easy — and it's worth it. Creating the bar you want gives you the program you want. It's very much like setting up your work area or home office the way you want it to be. Assign your most-used tasks to buttons and work can move more quickly.

Editing the button bar begins with the small button at the left or top of the bar. This one has an arrow pointing down. Click on it and a pull-down menu appears (see Figure 3-2). You have the choice of creating a new button bar or choosing to edit an existing one. (Other options involve selecting the position of the button bar and opening up the other bars supplied with the program.) For now, let's Edit the Default bar. When you select the Edit command, the Edit Button Bar dialog box appears, as shown in Figure 3-3.

Figure 3-2:
The pull-down menu on the button bar.

Figure 3-3:
The Edit Button Bar dialog box.

Here, you have a wide range of choices for customizing your menu bar. Look down the list in the left-hand panel and you'll initially see names representing the features found in the menu bar. Click on each name and buttons representing the various tasks in the submenu appear on the right. Just click on one of the buttons and drag it to the menu bar. That's all you have to do to add a task to the button bar.

While it's easy to add buttons to the button bar, you *can* add too many of them. Up to a point, the buttons will adjust in size to accommodate the new ones. But after 26 buttons or thereabouts, the buttons furthest to the right (or at the bottom) will scroll off the screen. So pick your buttons carefully, but know that you can put a lot of functionality at your fingertips! (This limitation obviously depends on the size of your monitor. A user with a 21-inch display screen can probably fit a larger number of buttons across the top or left side than someone using a Color Mac Classic with its tiny nine-inch display.)

Ribbons, Ribbons Everywhere

If nothing else, WordPerfect is a program that delivers a little something extra every time you use it. Don't believe me? Just open a new document window and up pop several things at the top of the screen.

There's the ruler (see Figure 3-4) and there are two *ribbon bars* that immediately appear with a new document: Layout and Font. As with the pull-down menus, these ribbon bars put commands within easy reach.

Figure 3-4:
The ruler.

Above these two ribbon bars is — you guessed it — yet another ribbon bar. This one contains a series of buttons, which, when clicked, give you more ribbon bars. (Pay attention: there's a quiz at the end of this chapter.)

With the click of a mouse, you can select ribbon bars for working with styles, creating and editing tables, handling lists such as indexes or table of contents, and using mail merge functions. (If your Mac is hooked up to a network, you'll also have the option of a Mail bar, which is discussed in Chapter 15.)

The good part of the ribbon bar is that it puts a lot of functions within easy reach. The bad part of the ribbon bar is shown below, where you can fill up half the available writing space (on your average Mac screen) with ribbons. Figure 3-5 shows almost all of the ribbon bars.

There's a technical word for a display like this one: *Yeech!* There's nothing inherently wrong with filling up your screen, but you're putting a lot of stuff in your face when trying to write. So why do it?

In a word, convenience. As with everything else, the presence of ribbon bars in WordPerfect is designed to make your life easier. Instead of having to remember a keystroke combination or jump up to the menu bar, find a keyword, click on it, and then select from choices — and perhaps visit a submenu or three — instead of doing all that, you've got the commands you need right at hand.

As you'll see in Chapter 9, for example, having the Merge bar displayed when creating a mail merge letter and a mailing list to merge into that letter makes a lot of sense. You can jump up to that ribbon and specify the end of a field or record when creating the mail list; another one-click action inserts a merge field into a document.

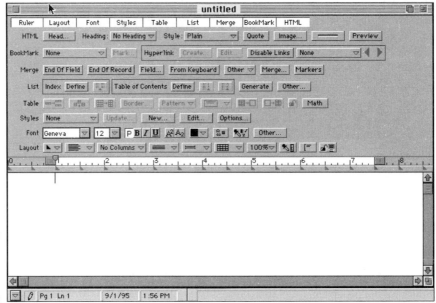

Figure 3-5:
The ribbon
bars.

Or think about working with tables. The Table bar moves the various functions for editing tables within reach. (For reasons best known to the programmers, you still have to go to the Table menu and then choose the New command in order to create a table, but I digress. (If you want to digress to setting tables, Alfonse, flip over to Chapter 6.)

And if writing a thesis or book is your goal, having the List bar means never having to go too far to mark an index or table of contents entry, or to generate an index or TOC, as it's called. Yes, you can go hunt through the menus for these commands, but why bother when they can be right there in front of you.

Using the ribbon bars is sort of like using table salt at a sit-down dinner: be sparing and it will enhance the flavor. Pour on too much and it's just plain gross.

Customizing Screen Layouts

By pressing the right buttons, you can create a custom screen layout in WordPerfect. At the start of the program, you can display as much on your screen — or as little — as you want. You can change the background color, the foreground color, and even the highlight color (highlighting is what you see when you click on the mouse and drag the cursor across a letter or word group).

To begin, choose the Preferences command found at the bottom of the Edit menu. You're greeted with 11 icons that present a variety of choices (see Figure 3-6).

Figure 3-6:
The
Preferences
screen.

Changing the screen display

Of these, you'll be interested in two choices for now. The Environment icon lets you set what is displayed when the program starts up, as well as the screen colors of your choice. Go wild, if you want, and pick a hot pink background, neon green letters and white highlights. (Just get ready for a trip to the eye doctor pretty soon thereafter.) A more likely combination could give you white letters on a blue background — something that many DOS users of WordPerfect will well remember because it was the screen color setup of that pioneer version of the program. Figure 3-7 shows the Environment screen.

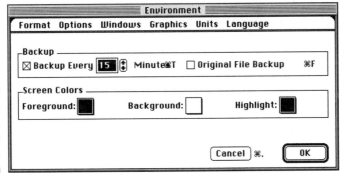

Figure 3-7:
The
Environment
screen.

The other button that'll customize your screen display is Show Bars, which won't get you a list of local night spots, but it will let you decide which rulers, button bars, and ribbon bars are displayed at startup (see Figure 3-8).

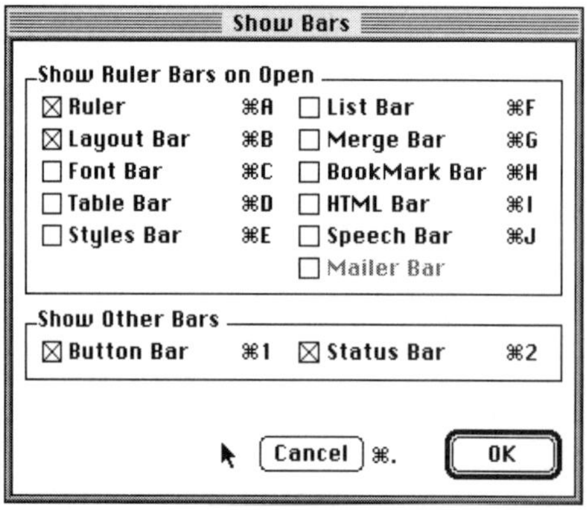

```
┌─────────────────────── Show Bars ───────────────────────┐
│ ┌─Show Ruler Bars on Open ─────────────────────────────┐ │
│ │ ☒ Ruler           ⌘A   ☐ List Bar          ⌘F        │ │
│ │ ☒ Layout Bar      ⌘B   ☐ Merge Bar         ⌘G        │ │
│ │ ☐ Font Bar        ⌘C   ☐ BookMark Bar      ⌘H        │ │
│ │ ☐ Table Bar       ⌘D   ☐ HTML Bar          ⌘I        │ │
│ │ ☐ Styles Bar      ⌘E   ☐ Speech Bar        ⌘J        │ │
│ │                        ☐ Mailer Bar                  │ │
│ └──────────────────────────────────────────────────────┘ │
│ ┌─Show Other Bars ─────────────────────────────────────┐ │
│ │ ☒ Button Bar      ⌘1   ☒ Status Bar        ⌘2        │ │
│ └──────────────────────────────────────────────────────┘ │
│                                                          │
│              ▸     ( Cancel ) ⌘.        ( OK )           │
└──────────────────────────────────────────────────────────┘
```

Figure 3-8:
The Show
Bars dialog
box.

In the Show Bars dialog box, you can select which ribbon bar options you want to be able to view — or have your users view — when using WordPerfect. For me, it's important to see the ruler and Layout ribbon bar, while the button bar and status bar each are nice to have as well. If you select each of the bars, however, you'll end up with a rather crowded opening display, as you saw back in Figure 3-5.

Just click on the ones you want, and that's what you'll get when starting WordPerfect. Remember, you always have the option of adding or removing ribbon bars by clicking on the ribbon bar buttons at the top of the screen.

What's that stuff at the bottom of the screen?

Two of the nicer features of WordPerfect for Macintosh are the status and help displays at the bottom of the screen (see Figure 3-9).

Figure 3-9:
The status
bar.

```
▼  ∂  Pg 6 Ln 24      9/1/95   1:59 PM
```

At a glance, you can see what page and line of the document you're presently at, today's date and time (so you can tell how late you're working), whether the caps lock is on, and even a display of the physical page the cursor is on. At the right of a small bar in the middle of the line is a help display. Put your arrow pointer on any button or ribbon bar element (or any part of the status display), and you'll see a small explanation of what it does. These instant "cue cards," for want of a better phrase, are a nice part of the program for new users. Experienced users can turn off the help display by selecting the Hide Help command via the small button at the left end of the status/help line.

This button is actually a menu, which is shown in Figure 3-10.

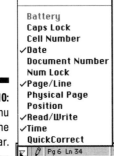

Figure 3-10:
The menu
on the
status bar.

This menu also lets you change what's displayed in the status bar, which appears on your screen by default. You can see whether the Number Lock is on or off, see whether or not QuickCorrect (see Chapter 10 for details) is on, and even keep track of the number of documents you have open.

Can you learn a lot from the status line? Oh, yes. Is it hard to set up and use? Oh, no.

In Conclusion . . .

By now, you may have had more than your fill of setting up and customizing WordPerfect. If you're happy with the program the way it is, then poking under the hood may be boring at best, confusing at worst.

The nice thing about word processors in general and, yes, WordPerfect for Macintosh in particular, is that you don't have to change things if you don't want to — *and* that you can always change them if you want to. For you, and you alone, this program can look just the way you want, or you can keep it in the same pristine condition it has out of the box. Isn't that kind of freedom of choice nice?

You might be itching to get to work right now and do some real word processing. Or you might just be itching, for which I heartily recommend Gold Bond Medicated Powder.

But if you *are* itching to get to work, go take a look at Chapter 4. There, you'll see what you need to do in order to scratch that working itch!

Chapter 4

Basic Editing and Formatting

· ·

In This Chapter

▶ Typing and maneuvering

▶ Editing text

▶ Basic text and document formatting

▶ And more!

· ·

Into Everyone's Life, a Little Typing Must Fall

The previous chapters covered such topics as customizing WordPerfect's display and mastering the menus, buttons, and ribbons that are placed before you. Along the way, I've also presented the basics of typing, saving, and printing a short document.

That's all fine and good, and indeed many people won't want to go beyond these basics in order to get their immediate work done. But you're different from the rest, aren't you? You're not satisfied with a scant knowledge of your software. Oh, no, you want to know how to get things done right the first time, every time.

Can't say I blame you. There's enough power in WordPerfect for Macintosh to satisfy just about every user, and learning it starts now.

Basic Keyboard Skills & Tricks

I talked about using keyboard combinations to issue program commands back in Chapter 2. Think of the keyboard as your command center, the place where you tell WordPerfect what to do and when.

Invaluable to making this program work for you, I believe, is touch typing, the kind where all ten fingers are on the keyboard (OK, OK, in touch typing the thumbs generally rest on the spacebar, and if you're right handed, the left one sees little use, but you get my point).

If you're not a touch typist, don't despair. You can be very effective with WordPerfect using two fingers — or even one. That's because the program can do a lot of the work for you. But there's no doubt that using all your available fingers for the keyboarding task makes life a lot easier.

However you type on the keyboard, you'll be happier knowing some, ahem, "key" features. Get familiar with your keyboard and it will reward your efforts.

Putting It Together

You were promised strategies on editing a short document, and strategies you will get.

Important digression: which keyboard do you use?

Maybe it's a neurosis on my part, but I can't go any further without asking you a personal question: Which Mac keyboard do you use? The answer could have an impact on your success with WordPerfect, as well as your overall happiness with the Mac and even your health.

Many Mac users must content themselves with the basic Mac keyboard, which includes the basic function keys and not much else.

This keyboard will allow you to accomplish most tasks, but frankly, experienced computer users will quickly become frustrated with its odd placement of cursor movement keys, the lack of a numeric keypad and some of the other bells and whistles commonly found on PC system keyboards. Until recently, upgrading meant buying the Apple Extended Keyboard, an expensive item that had all the extras. Nowadays, you can spend under $80 for the Apple Design keyboard, which includes the items found on the extended keyboard, but for less money. If you're struggling with the basic Apple keyboard — and if you plan to spend a fair amount of time word processing — I'd suggest you give some serious thought to splurging and upgrading your keyboard.

(Oh, and you will want to give some thought to the ergonomics of your working setup. A great book called *ZAP! How your computer can hurt you and what you can do about it,* written by Don Sellars and published by Peachpit Press, is must reading for those who want to enhance their computing safety.)

Why devote much thought to your keyboard and how it's set up? Having an extended keyboard gives you more power to use the commands available in WordPerfect, and that makes working easier. The setup issues — which are better discussed elsewhere — can help safeguard your health as you work. It's that simple and, frankly, it's that important.

To begin at the beginning, either Open an existing file or create a New one. You open a file by choosing Open from the File menu or by pressing the ⌘-O key combination. Create a New file by clicking on the New option in the File menu or by pressing ⌘-N. (You can also put a "Create New File" icon on your button bar, as discussed in Chapter 3.)

How you open or create a file usually isn't a big deal unless you have restarted WordPerfect after a crash. In these cases, albeit rare, WordPerfect will likely tell you that backup files exist and ask if you want to open these. If you had to restart abruptly, this option could be your best chance of recovering some or all of your typing. (Another solution for saving work in progress is discussed in Chapter 21.) How can you decide whether or not to open the backup file? It depends on when you last saved your work. If you had just saved your file before a system crash, you're probably OK. If it had been a few minutes since your last manual save, the backup file could be a big help — you'll recover at least part or most of your work.

Basic Editing Made Easy

(Note: If you have never sat down at a computer before, you might want to take a quick look at Chapter 1 to review some of the most basic computer skills necessary to successfully operate your Mac and WordPerfect.)

Moving around within a document is usually accomplished either with the cursor keys or the mouse. The cursor keys, as noted elsewhere, are usually on or near the bottom row of keys on your keyboard. They each show an arrow pointing either up or down, left or right. One press and the insertion point, the solid line which indicates your place on a line, will move as you desire.

The mouse, when moved across text in WordPerfect, changes its arrow cursor to what's known as an I-beam, a long thin line that looks like an overgrown capital "I." When placed in a paragraph and clicked, the program moves the insertion point there.

To go from one part of the document to another, you can use the scroll bars, described in Chapter 2, or the Home and End keys, which with a press will take you to either the beginning or end of a document.

You can zip from one end of a line to another by combining the left or right arrow keys with the ⌘ key. Use that same ⌘ key with the up and down arrow keys, and you zoom up or down one screen-full of typing at a time.

When writing a letter — or anything else with WordPerfect — remember what experienced computer users have learned early on in their computing careers. The Return key is very much like the one found on electronic typewriters, but with a key difference. You can press it after each line of a return address, let's say, but you won't want to press it at the end of a line as you're typing a paragraph. You'll see the cursor wrap from one line to the next without having to hit the return key. It'll easily become second nature with practice, but if you're new to computing, you'll want to keep an eye on when you press Return.

Entering Text

This is the easy part. Just type as you would on a typewriter or with another computer program. Remember, as discussed before, you don't want to hit the Return key at the end of each line, just at the end of a paragraph. Isn't that simple? Repeat the "just-a-return-at-the-end-of-each-paragraph" routine throughout your document, until you get to the end.

While you are typing away, don't worry about advancing to a second or third (or fourteenth) page in your letter. At the bottom of each page, WordPerfect for Macintosh moves you along to the next page, with an on-screen representation of the *page break* to indicate this division, as shown in Figure 4-1. That's one of the other joys of word processing veterans discover early on: you don't need to remove a page and insert another as you go along.

Hitting the highlights

Selecting (or highlighting) text is something you'll probably do many times when working in WordPerfect. You might recall that in Chapter 3 I mentioned a button that indents text. To get the text you want indented, you need to select, or highlight it, *before* you click on the one of the indent button. This same principle applies when you want to do other forms of formatting. If you want to underline or italicize a word, sentence, or paragraph, you highlight that piece of text before initiating the command to perform the formatting.

You highlight text by clicking with the mouse button and dragging. For example, to highlight a word, place the cursor at the beginning of the word, hold down the mouse button, and drag the mouse to the end of the word. Then let go of the mouse. You know that the word is selected (highlighted) because WordPerfect changes the text's background (see Figure 4-2). Whether you're using a monochrome or color screen, you'll be able to tell what you've selected.

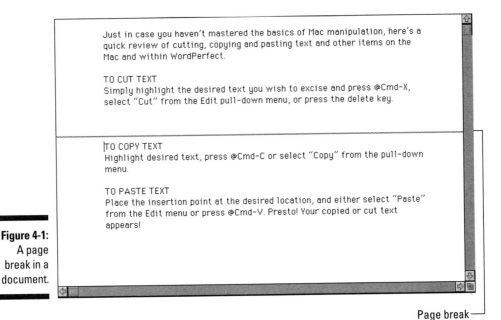

Just in case you haven't mastered the basics of Mac manipulation, here's a quick review of cutting, copying and pasting text and other items on the Mac and within WordPerfect.

TO CUT TEXT
Simply highlight the desired text you wish to excise and press @Cmd-X, select "Cut" from the Edit pull-down menu, or press the delete key.

TO COPY TEXT
Highlight desired text, press @Cmd-C or select "Copy" from the pull-down menu.

TO PASTE TEXT
Place the insertion point at the desired location, and either select "Paste" from the Edit menu or press @Cmd-V. Presto! Your copied or cut text appears!

Figure 4-1:
A page
break in a
document.

Page break

Figure 4-2:
Highlighted
text.

Watermark Software Inc., of Burlington, Mass., last week announced a pact with Biscom Inc., of Chelmsford, Mass., to integrate Watermark's $295 Windows imaging software with Biscom's fax server products.

If you want to select every last bit of your document, the Select All command on the Edit menu or the ever-popular ⌘-A keystroke combination will do the trick.

Making the cut

Deleting text is another necessary step in any writer's life. OK, so you might not feel up to slicing out a stretch from Ernest Hemingway, but you and I aren't Papa, and it's likely both you and I can benefit from some judicious editing. (Like right here, maybe.)

To delete text, you can backspace (using the large Delete key in the main part of the keyboard) over a character or two, or as many characters as you desire. That's fine for small trimming, but what if you need to knock out a paragraph or six? (No, not here, please. This is good stuff, I tell ya!)

That kind of major surgery requires you to highlight the text you want to cut and then either hit the Delete key, press the ⌘-X key combination, or choose the Cut command from the Edit menu to finish the job.There's more about the Cut command in the next section, so read on.

Other slick text tricks

Just in case you haven't mastered the basics of Mac manipulation, here's a quick review of cutting, copying, and pasting text and other items on the Mac and within WordPerfect.

To cut text

Simply highlight the desired text you wish to excise and press ⌘-X. You can also select the Cut command from the Edit menu.

To copy text

Highlight desired text and press ⌘-C. You can also select the Copy command from the Edit menu.

To paste text

Place the insertion point at the desired location, and either select the Paste command from the Edit menu or press ⌘-V. Presto! Your copied or cut text appears!

OK, Mark, you're saying. I get the idea of how to slice and dice my text, but what if I want to rearrange my paragraphs, sort of like how my wife likes to surprise me and rearrange the furniture every so often? Well, I can't solve your home dilemmas, but I can help you switch around your text with some ease.

Moving text is an absolute delight in WordPerfect. Once you've selected a block of text (as little as a character or as much as you like), you can click on the highlighted area, hold the mouse button down, and drag that text anywhere in the document you desire. Have two or more document windows open at the same time and you can drag text from one window to another. It's really neat.

As you drag your text towards its destination, the highlighting disappears and instead you see a rectangle around the dragged text (see Figure 4-3). You'll also see an insertion point that moves as you move the block of text. When you find the desired place for the moved text, release the mouse button and, presto!, the text moves over there. Like I said, it's really neat.

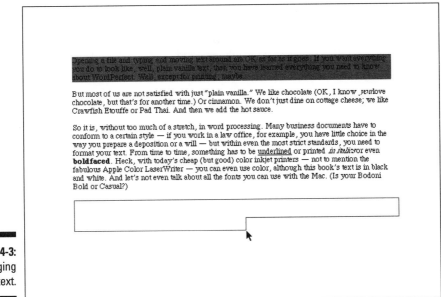

Figure 4-3:
Dragging
text.

You can't go home again, Thomas Wolfe once said, but then he didn't have the Undo feature. In case you've moved — or cut — your copy in a way you didn't like, simply press ⌘-Z or choose the Undo command from the Edit menu. WordPerfect will revert to its last state. It's a handy way to recover from a move you later regretted.

Making It Look Good: Basic Formatting

Opening a file and typing and moving text around are OK as far as it goes. If you want everything you do to look like, well, plain vanilla text, then you have learned everything you need to know about WordPerfect. Well, except for printing, maybe.

But most of us are not satisfied with just "plain vanilla." We like chocolate (OK, I know *you* love chocolate, but that's for another time). Or cinnamon. We don't just dine on cottage cheese; we like Crawfish Etouffe or Pad Thai. And then we add the hot sauce.

So it is, without too much of a stretch, in word processing. Many business documents have to conform to a certain style — if you work in a law office, for example, you have little choice in the way you prepare a deposition or a will — but within even the most strict standards, you need to format your text. From time to time, something has to be <u>underlined</u> or printed *in italics* or even **boldfaced**. Heck, with today's cheap (but good) color inkjet printers — not to mention the fabulous Apple Color LaserWriter — you can even use color, although this book's text is in black and white. And let's not even talk about all the fonts you can use with the Mac. (Is your Bodoni Bold or Casual?)

How do you accomplish all these feats? There's a variety of ways, Jocasta. By judiciously using a combination of fonts and styles — you don't want your work to look like a ransom note, do you? — you can achieve the desired result you need, and even surpass expectations.

Fonts are great things to use, but be sparing in their application. Mixing too many fonts on a page, or mismatching fonts in a document such as a newsletter or proposal, might win a prize for creative art, but it can distract and confuse readers. I know folks who actually get a headache when they confront too many fonts on a page. A good rule of thumb is to use no more than two or three different fonts in a document unless there's a very good reason to exceed this limit. Try to pick fonts that are easy to read — Times Roman is so popular for text such as newsletters and magazines that most daily newspapers use some variant of it for their text. (In order to get a full understanding of this subject, you'll want to read a good basic Mac text like *The Mac Is Not a Typewriter* by Robin Williams (Peachpit), which contains excellent discussions of the ins and outs of fonts.

About (type)face

When you open up WordPerfect, the basic (or default) font is Geneva, the Mac's version of Helvetica, a clear, simple typeface that looks like this:

This is a sample of Geneva in 12 point size.

If you click on the Font button, the Font ribbon appears, as shown in Figure 4-4.

Figure 4-4:
The Font
ribbon.

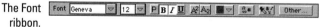

It shows the font name, size, and several styles, plus a color selector. To select a new font straight off, before you do any typing, you can click on the down-pointing arrow next to the font name and a list of all available fonts appears. Figure 4-5 shows all of my available fonts. Your list is probably different (and shorter I hope).

As you saw in Chapter 2, you can also see the fonts available by clicking on the Font menu in the menu bar at the top of the screen. It's a matter of personal choice; I like having the Font ribbon bar available, particularly if I need to change text color.

Next to the font name window is a selector for the size of type, which also duplicates the size menu from the menu bar. Here, the choice of size is a bit more limited than the pull-down menu, but you can type a custom size — say 11 points — in the window, and WordPerfect will obey your command.

Alongside these two windows are buttons for Plain, Bold, Italic and Underlined text; just click on these and either your highlighted text or the text following your present insertion point will take on the appearance you desire. Using bold, italic, and other character styles requires some care — again, you want to avoid the ransom note syndrome — but with the Font ribbon menu, you've got these choices available.

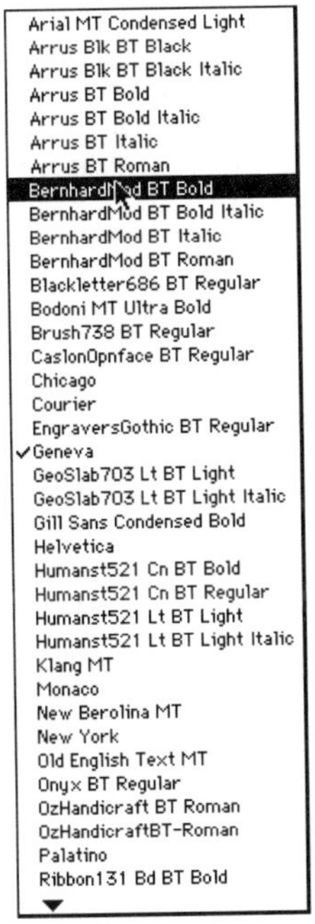

Figure 4-5:
My font list
on the Font
ribbon.

Arial MT Condensed Light
Arrus Blk BT Black
Arrus Blk BT Black Italic
Arrus BT Bold
Arrus BT Bold Italic
Arrus BT Italic
Arrus BT Roman
BernhardMod BT Bold
BernhardMod BT Bold Italic
BernhardMod BT Italic
BernhardMod BT Roman
Blackletter686 BT Regular
Bodoni MT Ultra Bold
Brush738 BT Regular
CaslonOpnface BT Regular
Chicago
Courier
EngraversGothic BT Regular
✓Geneva
GeoSlab703 Lt BT Light
GeoSlab703 Lt BT Light Italic
Gill Sans Condensed Bold
Helvetica
Humanst521 Cn BT Bold
Humanst521 Cn BT Regular
Humanst521 Lt BT Light
Humanst521 Lt BT Light Italic
Klang MT
Monaco
New Berolina MT
New York
Old English Text MT
Onyx BT Regular
OzHandicraft BT Roman
OzHandicraftBT-Roman
Palatino
Ribbon131 Bd BT Bold
▼

There are some other features to note on the Font ribbon menu. After the four type style options are two buttons to create ^{superscript} or $_{subscript}$ text. Most often, this formatting is used in scientific and legal documents, as well as academic settings.

Wonderful world of color

WordPerfect's default setting is to show type in black. And for most of what we type, that's just fine. But there's been a dramatic increase in the use of color printers both at home and the office in recent years, and there's no reason why you can't take advantage of the availability of color. As with typefaces, you will want to be careful in how you use color — and how much you use — in your document.

When you click on the Color button, you see a palette of color ranging from white to red to green to yellow to blue, with a host of combinations in between. Because this book is printed in black and white, Figure 4-6 won't do the color palette full justice. Be sure to click on it to see what you're getting.

Applying color to highlighted text — or specifying which color appears after your current insertion point — is easy. Just select the color you want from the palette and presto!, you're more colorful than your homeroom teacher ever thought you'd be.

One final, colorful thought: Along with being mindful of how much color to use and where to use it, you'll also want to count the cost of your printer's consumables. Using up color can be tough on your consumables and your wallet.

Figure 4-6:
The Color palette (in glorious black and white).

More Font ribbon bar features

Now that I've dispensed with color, three other features of the Font ribbon bar commend themselves to your attention. To the immediate right of the Color button is a little button which does an amazing thing: click on it and you can instantly insert all sorts of special characters in your document, such as Ÿ, ™, ß, •, £, or §. You might not need these or other special characters, but it's awfully handy to have them nearby if you do, and this Symbol button does the trick.

Our last two buttons on the Font ribbon bar are useful when you want to keep your typestyles consistent across a document. The first will copy the character attributes at the insertion point or in highlighted text to the Mac's Clipboard, from which they can be pasted over another bit of selected text. This sounds more complicated than it is; just know that if you want to copy the exact type style of a given block of text and then apply it to other blocks, you can do it, starting with this button.

The last button, deceptively labeled "Other," brings up the Character Format dialog box (see Figure 4-7), which can also be accessed via the Style menu or ⌘-H.

As you see from this box, most of the formatting and type style tricks it will perform for you have been described elsewhere in this section because you can do them in other ways. For me, the most interesting features of this dialog box include the ability to see a sample line of text in a desired typeface, and to impose format options such as <u>double underline</u> or SMALL CAPITALS simply by highlighting the desired text, opening this dialog box, and clicking on the desired feature and then the OK button.

With that, we come to the conclusion of our magical mystery font styling tour. Watch your step as we move to the next platform.

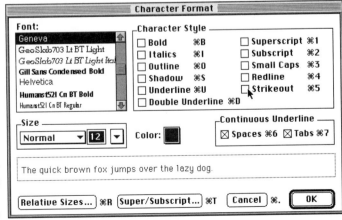

Figure 4-7:
The
Character
Format
dialog box.

Living on the Margin . . . and Running Your Tabs

Now I take you to your ruler . . . the ruler above the document window, that is. On this line, you can accomplish several important things in your document.

I've got to say that I *like* this ruler. It's better than most rulers in most word processing programs because it really lets you do useful things. Take setting margins, for example. In other programs, even in WordPerfect 3.1 for Macintosh, using the ruler to set margins could be a challenge. Here, there are buttons on either side of the default margins (one inch on each side) that you can click to stretch or shrink the margins. (You can do this for a highlighted section of text, if you so desire.)

Figure 4-8:
The new, improved ruler bar.

Another way to change the margins is to pull down the Layout menu. From there, the Margins command (also accessible with the ⌘-M key combination) will bring up a dialog box that looks like this Figure 4-9.

WordPerfect's default margins are one inch on each side. You can adjust this setting to any measure you like that is consistent with the size of page you're working on, which in the United States is a default of 8 ½ by 11 inches.

Notice the smaller button next to the left margin button on the ruler. Click on this one (it resembles a small arrow or shovel blade) and you can set a *first-line indent* for the paragraphs in your document or in a selected area of text.

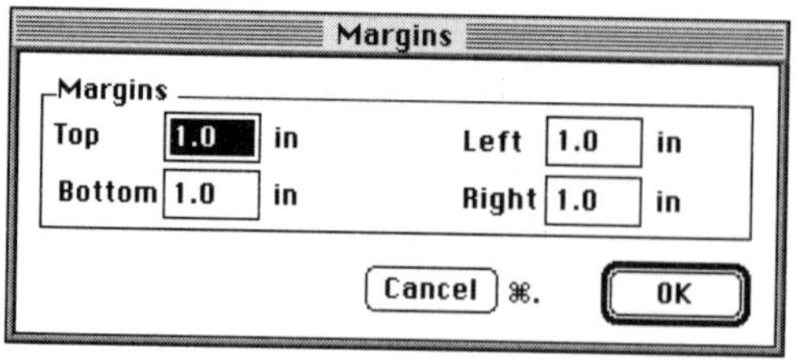

Figure 4-9:
The Margins dialog box.

Margins			
Top	1.0 in	Left	1.0 in
Bottom	1.0 in	Right	1.0 in

Cancel ⌘.   OK

What is a first-line indent? Well, sometimes we keep paragraphs flush left, which means every paragraph starts at the left margin, just like most of the paragraphs in this book. But some of us enjoy having the first line of a paragraph indented from the left edge a few spaces. It's more pleasing, visually, and breaks up the blocks of text a bit more.

How do you indent the first line of a paragraph? There are two ways. The easiest is from the Layout ribbon bar. Click on the fifth button from the left, the Paragraph Spacing button, and go down to the Other option. This will take you to a dialog box that allows you to both set the spacing between paragraphs *and* the first line indent. Both have default measures in inches. Personally, I like a quarter-inch indent at the start of a paragraph, so I enter 0.25 in the dialog box, as shown in Figure 4-10.

Figure 4-10:
Setting a
first-line
indent of
0.25 inches.

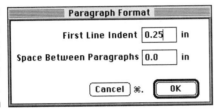

Click on the OK button and every paragraph thereafter will have the quarter-inch indent on the first line. You'll also see one of the indicators on the ruler line scoot over a quarter-inch, which also indicates another way to set a first-line indent: click on the "middle row" triangle in the ruler bar and drag it across the ruler to the desired point. As you drag, you'll see a dotted line drop down across your screen, and most importantly, across the inch marks on the ruler line. This line lets you position that indent exactly where you want it placed.

Between the lines (and paragraphs)

Setting the spacing between paragraphs allows you to avoid another common maneuver from typewriter days: Hitting two or more carriage returns to separate paragraphs. On a typewriter, a return is a return is a return. With a computer and a program such as WordPerfect for Macintosh, however, a return carries with it formatting information and other details that you may or may not wish to duplicate time and time again. Also, using a return as a paragraph separator can cause problems when you try to do desktop publishing tasks with WordPerfect (see Chapter 12). Getting the spacing of lines and paragraphs to your liking means a trip to the Layout ribbon bar.

The fourth button from the left on the Layout ribbon bar is the line spacing button, from which you can select among 1, 1.5, and 2 line spacings for your text; clicking on the Other button will bring up the dialog box shown in Figure 4-11.

From here, you can enter any inch value — from 0.123 inches to 5.697 inches or greater — for your line spacing, or *leading,* as it is sometimes called (and it's pronounced "ledding"). It all depends on your whim, but as with the first-line indent setting, your choice here carries for each new paragraph until you change it again.

Figure 4-11:
The Line
Spacing
dialog box.

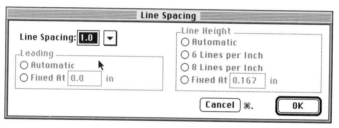

Chapter 5
The Zen of WordPerfect

In This Chapter
▶ The importance of file management
▶ Everything you ever wanted to know about backing up
▶ Other important, neat stuff about WordPerfect

*I*n order to truly round out my coverage of WordPerfect's basics, it will be good to thoroughly explore the various aspects of saving files, discuss file exporting, and review some safety tips to keep WordPerfect for Macintosh running smoothly.

Shall we begin?

Saving Files: Your Most Important Step

Saving files might seem like a boring topic, but lose or improperly save a crucial file and you'll soon discover how riveting a subject it can be.

Because this is not *Macs For Dummies* (an excellent book, by the way), I'm going to assume you know the mechanics of what the Mac's file structure is and how it works. If you don't know these things, you'll want to check out that basic Mac text for the details. It's not necessary that you know all of these items, but it does help.

What WordPerfect calls a *file,* you and I might call a letter or document. Drawing on the Mac's innovative file-handling system (innovative, that is, back in 1984 when Windows were nothing more than that which Bill Gates looked out of), a file is stored in a folder, either on the Mac's desktop or the hard disk drive or a floppy disk drive. You can nestle a rather large number of files in a folder, and just about any number of folders can be nested inside one big folder (or hard disk). It seems that this is limited chiefly by disk size, at least in Macs running System 7 or greater. (Frankly, there's no reason on earth why most Macs shouldn't be running System 7 now, but that's for another discussion.)

For most of us, creating a new file is an easy process: we create a new file either by opening the program from scratch or choosing the New command under the File menu and, presto!, the blank "untitled" screen appears and the typing begins.

Closing and saving files is another matter, however. It's virtually impossible to close a WordPerfect file without being asked whether or not you want to save it, as Figure 5-1 demonstrates.

Figure 5-1:
The Save
Changes
to WP
Document
dialog box.

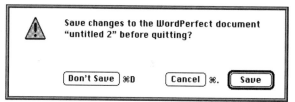

When you try to close a document window or quit WordPerfect outright, you see this dialog box, with the musical question, "Save Changes to the WordPerfect document [document name] before closing?"

At this point, you must answer yes, no, or, if you're from Brooklyn or Queens, "fuhgeddaboutit," which to the rest of the world would be the Cancel button. There are keyboard commands for all these responses. ⌘-Y says, "Yes, save my file, please"; ⌘-N answers with a "Don't Save"; and, as with many other instances in WordPerfect (and the Mac itself), ⌘-. (period) cancels the dialog box altogether, or "fuhgeddaboutit."

If you mistakenly choose Cancel, you can *still* go back and save your work. But click on Don't Save and it's gone forever. Be careful, then, with this dialog box, especially if the file you're working on is the only draft of your Great American Novel. (Oh, and if you sell the screen rights, go for a percentage of the movie's first dollar receipts, not the profits. Just ask Winston Groom, who wrote the novel behind *Forrest Gump* and tangled with Paramount about why the fourth-highest grossing film in history hasn't yet turned a profit.)

When you say, "Yes, save my file, please," you're confronted with another set of choices. Witness Figure 5-2.

```
┌─────────────────────────────────────────────────────────┐
│                        Save As                            │
├─────────────────────────────────────────────────────────┤
│        ┌──────────────┐                                   │
│        │ ▣ Desktop  ▼ │         ▭ Hard Disk Drive         │
│      ┌─┴──────────────┴──┐                                │
│      │◉ Audio CD 1      ▲│      731M Free                 │
│      │▭ Hard Disk Drive  │                                │
│      │▭ Kellner One      │      ┌──────────┐              │
│      │☠ Port Juggler 2.6 │      │  Eject   │  ⌘E          │
│      │⚠ America Online v2.6b20 alias│                     │
│      │▯ CDT Remote™ alias│      │ Desktop  │  ⌘D          │
│      │▨ Chapter 1-4 Illus.│                               │
│      │♫ GraphicConverter▼│      │  New  □  │  ⌘N          │
│      └───────────────────┘      ─ ─ ─ ─ ─ ─               │
│       Save Document As:         ║  Save    ║              │
│      ┌───────────────────┐      ─ ─ ─ ─ ─ ─               │
│      │                   │      │ Cancel   │  ⌘.          │
│      └───────────────────┘                                │
│       Format: │WordPerfect 3    ▼│   □ Password Protect ⌘P│
│       Retain: │Complete Document ▼│                       │
└─────────────────────────────────────────────────────────┘
```

Figure 5-2:
The Save As
dialog box.

The Save As dialog box is where you can do a lot to keep your files safe and well-organized. For one, you'll instantly see where on the hard disk you are located. (The default is within the main WordPerfect directory.) If you want to create a new folder for this document, you can select that option, or you can click on the spot where you see the active folder (or directory) and down will drop a hierarchy of the disk and you can move anywhere to save the file, even out to the desktop.

From the desktop, you can see other logical disk drives attached to your Mac via a SCSI cable or on a network. Select one of these and your file can be saved there.

Saving Choices

One of the great things about the Mac is the wide range of choices it gives in terms of where you can save a file, as you've just seen. WordPerfect adds to this flexibility by offering a variety of formats in which a file can be saved. First, though, let's consider the Macintosh answer to Shakespeare's great question, "What's in a name?"

Picking a name

When saving a file for the first time, you get a couple of additional choices besides location. Along with selecting where to save the file, you also get to choose a name. Here, at least for a while, the Macintosh is way ahead of the PC, and even UNIX systems. You can use up to 31 characters *and spaces* to name a file; the only character not permitted in a file name is the colon (:) because the Mac uses that symbol in its file hierarchy.

The advantage of this should be obvious: Instead of the old DOS/Windows convention of eight characters, a period, and then three more characters (as in the poetic ABC12345.DOC), you can call your file "First Quarter Earnings Report — Unaudited" and instantly know what that document is about. So yes, you can be wild and free and uninhibited — in your file names, that is — without major consequence. Go for it.

The advent of Microsoft's Windows 95 offers the hope of longer file names for users of that operating system. But for now, the only way Windows 3.1 users can have the fun Mac users do is with an add-on program that is not a standard component of Windows. That means your pleasure would be a solitary one. On the Mac, share a file with a long name and everyone can see it.

You've selected a place for your new file and given it a name. How 'bout picking a format, Muriel?

Picking a file format

For most purposes, the standard WordPerfect 3 format is fine. (If you're stuck for disk space, there's a WordPerfect 3 Compressed option that squeezes things a bit.) That's why the standard format is the default choice for file saving. If you plan to use the document as a form or template for other documents, you can save the file as WordPerfect Stationery. (Hold still, Horace: Stationery subjects are explained in Chapter 8.)

But what if you are working on WordPerfect at home and need to transfer the document to a Microsoft Word (ick) system back at the office, or share it with someone who hasn't yet been enlightened about the benefits of WordPerfect? Maybe even someone who uses — gasp — Windows?

If that's the case, you'll want to *pick your format* for this file. Standard WordPerfect options — in addition to older Macintosh and DOS WordPerfect formats — include Word versions 4, 5, and 6; RTF, or Rich Text Format, which can be read by many Mac and Windows word processors; or plain old Text, which lets you save in an ASCII format that just about every computer that has ever existed can use. Figure 5-3 shows the Save As dialog box and the file format options it offers.

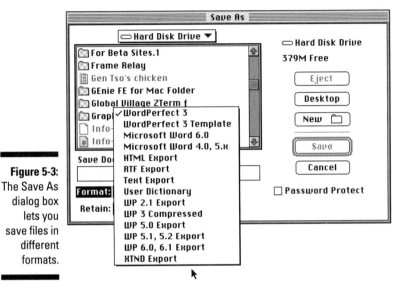

Figure 5-3:
The Save As
dialog box
lets you
save files in
different
formats.

I'm not sure who to blame, but I've found that saving large, complex
WordPerfect files to Microsoft Word 6 format will occasionally cause my system
to lock up, forcing a restart. If you plan on saving a WordPerfect file in Word 6
format, make sure that you save your original file in WordPerfect format *before*
you use the Save As command to save to the other format (so that if you crash,
you won't lose your latest changes to the original file). In addition, save the
translated (Word 6) version of the file to a different folder than the original
file. Doing so seems to cut down on the risk of crashing. And if you do a lot
of file translations, I suggest that you allocate more RAM (an extra 500K or so)
to WordPerfect.

BuG!

Along with the standard translators, WordPerfect is also supplied with several
translators from MacLink Pro, a program produced by DataViz of Stamford,
Connecticut. Buy the whole MacLink program and you'll get a raft of translators
that'll bring your work into just about any PC or Mac format known to mankind,
and it'll also import most of these formats.

You can lose very little — except time — by choosing the most robust format
you can for file exchange. If you're unsure of what a recipient is using, try RTF;
or use the MacLink Translators included with WordPerfect to come even closer
to a format you can use for file exchanges.

Sad to say, few things in life are perfect, and this includes file exchanges in
WordPerfect. Even with the MacLink translators, you might hit a snag every
once in a while. The most practical solution: save a copy of important files
in Text, or ASCII, mode, and know that these files can always be read by
other systems.

There are two other options in the Format drop-down list. One is to save a file as a "User Dictionary," which helps when creating a specialized word list for spell checking. The other sounds like a border radio station just south of Juarez. XTND is the file-changing format developed by Apple Computer and its Claris Corp. software subsidiary. You can select from a variety of XTND formats, some of which are supplied with WordPerfect for Macintosh, and others which can be obtained from companies such as DataViz, which created the MacLink translators program. In short, for now, having the right XTND translators allows you to read — and write — files for the most obscure word processing formats. That might not seem like much until you need it. The bottom line: Get your file translators in order early if you plan to share files all over the place.

This kind of exporting doesn't require a visa or a customs broker at the receiving end, but it can be very profitable. Translating your file into a needed format lets you communicate with other users. Add in the read/write capabilities of most of today's Macs — that is, that you can format, read, and write DOS disks in your Mac's floppy drive — and you've got a winning way of handling documents, no matter where they're going.

The Pane Truth about Mac Windows (ouch)

The windows I'm talking about here are not made by Andersen or Pella, nor do they originate in Redmond, Washington. Instead, these windows each contain a document. You open a document window every time you open, or create, a WordPerfect document file, and you can have a fair number of these open at one time.

Needless to say, the number of document windows you open will depend on the size of your display and complexity of your work. On a 9-inch Mac screen (does anyone still use those?), you don't want to have more than one window open at a time. If you have a 20-inch display, or larger, go crazy. (And since you may be rich, please think about including me in your will.)

Switching between windows is accomplished either by clicking on the various title bars — if the windows are tiled or stacked so that each title bar is visible — or by pulling down the Window menu and choosing the desired workspace. Check out Figure 5-4.

The main thing to remember about windows is that having more than one open won't give you a chill, but it can speed up work. If you're combining notes from several files into one document, having the needed windows open will make the cutting-and-pasting job easier.

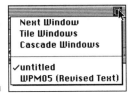

Figure 5-4:
The Window
menu.

Foreign (File) Affairs

Credit Tim Gallan, my book editor and an all-round nice person, with this point:
Working in WordPerfect and sharing the work and graphics of other people will
expose you to foreign file formats. Some of these files come from PCs; others
are created by different Mac programs. A few might even be produced by
people using the UNIX system, Amigas, or even something called *HTML,* which
is the main language of World Wide Web and stands for HyperText Markup
Language. (More on this subject later in Chapter 15.)

While WordPerfect has no problem saving your work in many different formats,
you might have a little apprehension about bringing in a file that WordPerfect
didn't create. In a word, don't worry. (Okay, that's two words, I know.)

This program is smart enough to know when you're opening a file that isn't
native to WordPerfect, and as noted earlier, it can use one of several translators
for both text and graphics files you're importing. Simply drag the file onto the
WordPerfect icon when starting the program, or select the file with the Open
command from within WordPerfect (see Figure 5-5). You'll find that most file
formats read in very, very well, especially if you have a good supply of translators handy.

Now, spare a few moments for some thoughts that will save you much grief, I
promise!

Common-Sense WP Document Management: Keeping Your Data Files Safe

What you're about to read may *never* apply to you. Then again, your car might
never break down or run out of gas, you might *never* have a blackout at home or
at the office, and you might *never* lose your wallet.

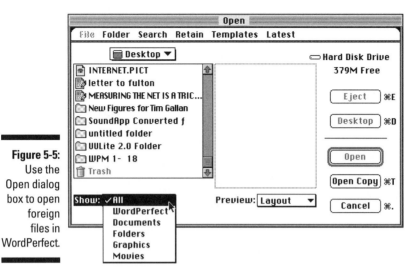

Figure 5-5:
Use the
Open dialog
box to open
foreign
files in
WordPerfect.

Indeed, if you are one of those fortunate few upon whom the sun always shines and into whose life no trials ever enter, please skip the rest of this chapter — go ahead, I'll wait 'til you're gone — and in a few moments, the rest of us will join you in Chapter 6.

OK, gang. Now that the "pod people" are gone (and *you* thought *Invasion of the Body Snatchers* was fiction, didn't you?) let's get serious for a moment.

In Chapters 21, 22, and 23, I deal with all sorts of specific ways to enhance and safeguard your computer, its data, and the WordPerfect for Macintosh program. But let me tell you about some common-sense steps that you should take right now. Today. This minute. And *doubly so* if you're doing what the experts call *mission critical* work on your Mac. (Mission critical is a fancy business term that means work vital to the success of a company, employee, or group. For most of us, that translates to stuff that'll cost you big time if it gets lost.)

After noodling around with computers since 1981 and writing with and about them since 1983, I've learned several important lessons. Top of the list is safety. You just can't be too careful with what you're doing, especially if the work is critical. Some folks will call this paranoia. Others will say I'm "anal retentive." More delicate types will just shake their head and say, "Mark, you're nutso."

Right on. If the whole world calls me screwy and I save my data, ask me if I care.

How my paranoia began

After years of working on PCs (and lusting after Macs), I finally got a Macintosh IIsi with a 40MB hard disk at the end of 1990. Back then, 40 meg was OK as far as disk space goes. By the middle of 1991, however, that hard disk was hurtin'. So was my wallet, which led to using disk compression software in an attempt to squeeze more space from the hard disk. (Disk compression software changes the way a computer writes data to the disk, making it seem to have more space than it does, sometimes as much as twice the space.)

Unfortunately, I forgot the first rule of smart computing, which goes double or triple if you're using compression software or trying any fancy tricks: *Make frequent backup copies of your work, data, and programs.* One day, push came to shove and my disk drive blew up. It blew up totally and completely, beyond most standard recovery measures — and boy, did I try to recover it.

The result: I had to upgrade my hard disk and pray that this disaster wouldn't happen again. Today, I'm working on a borrowed Power Mac 7100 with a 500MB hard disk (thanks to my friends at Apple), while my personal Power Mac 6100 has a 160MB drive. And upgrading to larger hard disks is nowhere near as expensive as it once was: 500MB drives cost around $200 to $250 in most places, one-quarter or one-third of what they cost just a few years ago.

But what is very difficult to replace is your data. There were things on that hard disk I'll probably never see again. Had I made a backup . . . well, you can finish the rest of that sentence.

My new paranoia and what I learned

Simply put, I'm paranoid about losing data and programs. The way to avoid any problems is to make frequent backups of important data, stuff that would be a real pain to recreate, if not totally impossible, should your hard disk get fritzed.

The easiest and cheapest backup is to put your files on a floppy disk. This procedure can be as simple as invoking the Save As command, jumping to the desktop from within the Save As dialog box, and saving your work on a floppy. And this procedure can be as involved as backing up a group of files with Apple's backup software, a shareware backup program, or a more professional backup tool. (See Chapter 21 for details.)

Next up is using a removable storage medium such as a SyQuest cartridge (many Macs used in publishing have been outfitted with these — again, see Chapter 21 for details) or the Iomega Zip drive (yep, Chapter 21 again). These methods cost very little — as low as $200 for the drive and $20 for a cartridge — and offer the capability to store much, much more than the 1.44MB a Mac floppy would give you, for not too terribly much money. Also available now is a similar inexpensive drive from SyQuest, and let's not forget magneto-optical drives, which stuff 230 megabytes onto a cartridge — which is roughly equivalent to 191 copies of the text of the King James, or Authorized, version of the Bible. (Now that's some begetting!)

You may also have the option of electronic backup for your files. If your Mac is connected to an office network where the server — the computer that controls the network and stores critical files — is backed up regularly, then you can also store your work there, again by using the Save As command and shipping the files off there.

Another option, if you subscribe to the CompuServe online service, is to use a *Personal Storage Area* and ship your files there. This method of backing up can be costly, however, and might best be used for truly critical files.

If you've made a backup on floppies or removable media, consider storing a copy off-site, away from your office or home. A safe deposit box might be a good place. For professional work, there are data storage companies who can help you.

All this seems to be like a lot of work and effort. I guess it is. But if you ever lose something that you want to get back and can't, it may seem like nothing compared with the effort required to recreate your work.

As a corollary, keep your WordPerfect for Macintosh program disks safe. If your hard disk blows up, you can reinstall from the program disks and then add your data files.

The bottom line, friend: Your data is very much like that second set of teeth we all got when we were young. Be kind to your data and it'll be kind to you.

Now, where did I put my PolyGrip? (Just kidding.)

The Basic Structure of WordPerfect

Just what is WordPerfect and how is it structured? By now, you've probably seen that WordPerfect is a very capable word processing program; by the end of your journey with this program you will probably find that it can do much much more, including Internet publishing, taking care of your expense account, and even sending e-mail for you.

For the moment, however, let's concentrate on that word processing part and how it the program is structured.

WordPerfect for Macintosh version 3.5 (the latest available as this book goes to press) is supplied on either several diskettes or one CD-ROM. The program stores the bulk of its files in a separate WordPerfect folder on your Mac's hard drive, although the Netscape browser (for Internet users) and the additional typefaces which are supplied with the program are stored elsewhere.

Like many Macintosh applications, WordPerfect interacts with other files on your system to make life easy for you. It uses translators from a company called DataViz to make files created with other programs accessible to you, but it also uses the XTND translators supplied by Claris Corporation with many other applications for the same purpose. And of course, as you'll see in Chapter 11, WordPerfect works with many of the elements found in the Mac operating software, System 7 and System 7.5.

The installation procedure for WordPerfect is pretty much automatic: click on the Installer icon on the first disk or the CD-ROM and you're off and running. The program will do an Easy Install or allow you to select the various elements you wish to install. In either case, all you have to do is make a few simple choices up front, and the program will do the rest. The most you'll need to do is swap out the diskettes if you're using that method of installation. (See the Appendix for details.)

Memory and WordPerfect

On my computer, WordPerfect likes to operate in 3.2 megabytes of RAM. That gives it enough "space" in which to work with open files and to do the other functions it needs to handle. That amount of RAM, by the way, is what WordPerfect assigns itself on systems with 8MB of RAM, or higher.

But for systems with 5 to 7 MB, WordPerfect only takes 2.4MB of RAM, and for Macs with 4MB or less, the preferred RAM size is 1.8MB. You really cannot go lower than these settings and use all the features of WordPerfect. You would also find the system performance to be very, very slow.

Virtual memory is another story. On the Mac, virtual memory assigns a part of disk space as "virtual" RAM, and this feature can make programs work in low-RAM situations. WordPerfect makes good use of virtual memory on Power Macintosh systems. When virtual memory is enabled on a Power Mac, WordPerfect asks for about 3 megs of RAM. With virtual memory off, it wants to hog almost 6 megs. Novell suggests that you use virtual memory. Who am I to argue?

Well, there is something worth mentioning. It seems that with Power Macs, having virtual memory on increases the amount of time it takes to launch *native* applications like WordPerfect 3.5. (By *native* applications, I mean programs written to take advantage of Power Macs' processor capabilities.) I ran some casual tests on a Power Mac 7500, and WordPerfect took several seconds longer to launch with virtual memory on than with virtual memory off. But with virtual memory off, it wants to use almost twice as much RAM. I must say, however, that launching WordPerfect seemed quite zippy with virtual memory off. The situation was the same for other native applications. (Excel takes *forever* to launch when virtual memory is on, and with virtual memory off, it wants to gobble up 10 megs of RAM; it's a lose-lose situation for most users. Thanks, Bill.)

So if you're lucky enough to have lots of RAM (24MB or more), and you launch, quit, and relaunch different native applications throughout a typical working day, then maybe you should keep virtual memory off. If you have less than 16MB of RAM and you work with the same two or three applications all day, then it's probably better to keep virtual memory on. You'll lose a minute or two in the morning when you launch your applications for the first time, but at least you'll be able to run them all at the same time because they all won't want to use twice as much RAM.

If you don't want your applications to eat a lot of RAM but you want to minimize the performance penalty caused by virtual memory, then I suggest that you set virtual memory so that it only gives you an extra meg of RAM. So if you're working on a 16-meg Mac, set virtual memory so that you have 17 megs.

If you are using the Connectix RAM Doubler program on either a regular Mac or a Power Macintosh, you cannot use virtual memory. The up side of this, however, is that RAM Doubler is, in my view, a very good utility for memory management. With RAM Doubler on, native applications don't want to hog twice as much RAM (in other words, they think that virtual memory is on), which is good, and native apps launch almost as quickly as if virtual memory were off. On the down side, judging from my casual tests, a Power Mac 7500 with RAM Doubler was a couple of percent slower overall than the same Power Mac with virtual memory off and no RAM Doubler. In everyday use, however, you will probably never notice this slight slowdown. I, therefore, recommend RAM Doubler over virtual memory, especially when you're not in a position to buy more real RAM.

If you are using a Power Mac 7200, 7500, 8500, or 9500, you need to get RAM Doubler version 1.6 or later; earlier versions won't work with these new Power Macs.

Part II
Becoming a WordPerfect Genius

The 5th Wave   By Rich Tennant

Karl Malden as a young man

Are you gonna keep your nose glued to that screen all day again today?

In this part . . .

By now, you've discovered a good deal about the basics of WordPerfect — or you know these things already and are stopping here to expand your skills. From reports and long documents to graphics, stationery, and the ever-popular mail merge, the intricacies of this program are skillfully unfolded right before your eyes.

OK, OK, you get to judge how skillful, but the information is here, and you'll be able to master these skills, along with WordPerfect's grammar and spelling tools, as well as the Apple software tools that work along with the program.

Chapter 6

Formatting Reports and Long Documents

. . . .

In This Chapter

▶ Setting margins

▶ Inserting page numbers

▶ Creating headers, footers, and footnotes

▶ Creating tables, TOCs, and indexes

▶ Making it fit

. . . .

I Need 15 Perfect Pages . . . by Two O'Clock, Please

Having romped through the basics of WordPerfect, it's time to get down to business. Your business, or maybe your boss's business, but business nonetheless.

After all, when your boss comes in at 9 a.m. — or your client calls around that time — and you find out that a fifteen page report needs to be ready by 2 p.m., it's all business. Of course, without a computer, it would be a real challenge. And with a computer like the Mac and a program such as WordPerfect, preparing a report can be a lot easier than otherwise.

Many of the techniques that I cover here can be used with documents that are much longer than a report, or even in a different format. Some will be useful in preparing newsletters (see also Chapter 12), and others will work in preparing a booklet or even a full book. In fact, it might be worthwhile to see WordPerfect as very close to a desktop publishing program with all its layout and presentation features. This is not your father's Oldsmobile, Binky; it's a really valuable publishing tool.

Setting Margins

When setting up a report in WordPerfect, some of the most basic work is done for you before you even open up a new document. By default, margins are set at one inch on each side of the page, which should be more than adequate for most purposes.

Adjusting margins for special formats (such as reproduction on preprinted corporate paper stock) is easy. Among methods for doing this are choosing the Margins command from the Layout menu or pressing the ⌘-M key combination. Either one will reveal the Margins dialog box (see Figure 6-1); modify your margins as desired and they're set.

Figure 6-1:
The Margins
dialog box.

Margins			
Top	1.0 in	Left	1.0 in
Bottom	1.0 in	Right	1.0 in

Cancel ⌘.   OK

As you can see, this dialog box allows you to enter a range of settings for each margin — top, bottom, left, and right. You cannot preview these changes, but you can use the Undo command in the Edit menu to reverse them. And as mentioned in Chapter 4, you can use the ruler's buttons to change the left and right margins.

For the most basic paragraph formats, such as first-line indents and spacing, flip back a few pages to Chapter 4, where you can review these basics. But what to do if you want to create a different kind of paragraph format?

Indenting Paragraphs

What if you want to start your paragraph with an indent that "hangs" outside the left margin, like the one shown in Figure 6-2? This stylistic device is often used to set off text in a way that calls attention to the information more than a standard layout. To create a hanging indent, as these are known, click on that middle-line triangle in the ruler line above your document and move it as far to the left of your margin as you like. You can either have your cursor within the paragraph you desire to reformat or have that paragraph highlighted.

Figure 6-2:
A paragraph
outdented in
the left
margin.

> Watermark Software Inc., of Burlington, Mass., last week announced a pact with Biscom Inc., of Chelmsford, Mass., to integrate Watermark's $295 Windows imaging software with Biscom's fax server products.

Sometimes, you'll want to set a paragraph off with a bullet, indenting an inch or so from the left margin, as shown in Figure 6-3. You often use this effect in a report when presenting short points summarizing a presentation. To format this sort of paragraph, click on the button bar icon that shows a series of bullet points in the text. You'll see the words "Adds a bullet and indents each selected paragraph" in the Help area on the bottom of your screen, next to the status line. You can apply this style to more than one paragraph by highlighting (selecting) the desired text before clicking on the button bar.

Figure 6-3:
A bulleted
paragraph.

> • Watermark Software Inc., of Burlington, Mass., last week announced a pact with Biscom Inc., of Chelmsford, Mass., to integrate Watermark's $295 Windows imaging software with Biscom's fax server products.

Then again, sometimes you will want your paragraphs *really* indented from the left margin, with maybe just a small dash setting them off (see Figure 6-4). The button to the right of the Bullet button will accomplish that. Just click and watch.

Figure 6-4:
A really
indented
paragraph
with dash.

> – Watermark Software Inc., of Burlington, Mass., last week announced a pact with Biscom Inc., of Chelmsford, Mass., to integrate Watermark's $295 Windows imaging software with Biscom's fax server products.

These neat formatting tricks are brought to you by WordPerfect for Macintosh's button bar, which was detailed way back in Chapter 3. It's worth repeating, however, that these basic formatting tricks — and a couple of others — are nice to have within easy reach, which is what the button bar does for you.

Page Numbering Made Easy

One of the things we all like to do with reports is keep track of how many pages the report contains. A simple press of the Option-F8 key combination, which you'll find on extended Mac keyboards, or a selection of the Page Numbers command on the Layout menu will reveal the Page Numbers dialog box, shown in Figure 6-5.

In the Page Numbers dialog box, you get to select which number to place on a page (useful when planning to string several files together as a single document). If you invoke the command on what is physically page one, the number will show as one; on subsequent pages, the current number will be displayed. Because it's a dialog box, however, you can change that number to any digit you like.

Page Numbering	
Number: 3	Type: Arabic (1,2,3)
Position: No Page Numbers	
Font: Geneva	Size: 12
Force Page: As Is	
☐ Place Number At Current Position ⌘P	
Cancel ⌘.	OK

Figure 6-5:
The Page
Numbering
dialog box.

This method of page numbering can be a really neat feature for you in WordPerfect. If your preference is to have unnumbered pages for the title page and table of contents, for example, you can start the numbering on what is really page 3 but number it as page 1.

You can also choose the style of numbering for your pages here. Arabic numerals — 1,2,3 — are the default here, but a simple click will change them to Roman numerals — I, II, III, and so forth.

In addition, you can choose the position of the numeral, and there are eight options here covering just about every place you'd want to place a page number, including top, bottom, center, left, right, and alternating corners on left and right pages, top and bottom. And if those choices aren't to your liking, WordPerfect lets you place the page number wherever the cursor (insertion point) is located on the page. If you want a different font or point size for the page number, you can select those here as well.

One of the nice things about placing page numbers in WordPerfect is its capability to number pages so that they appear on alternating sides of the page. That's *alternating* good for preparing masters for printed newsletters, reports, and even books if you're into self-publishing. But what do you do when you need to have page 7, which would normally appear on the left side, appear on the right because it *starts* a chapter? That's where the Force Page button in the Page Numbers button comes in. Click on it, and you can force the page number to appear on the "front" or right-hand side, or the "back" or left-hand side. WordPerfect will even insert a blank page in a document in order to get the page numbers right.

When you've made your page numbering choices, click on the OK button and WordPerfect will carry out your wishes. (Don't you wish everything in life was that simple?)

Don't Lose Your Head (er)

As we leave the pleasant valley of page numbering, let's take a header, if you will. In fact, let's create a header. To start, go to the Layout menu, move your curson onto the Header/Footer command, and from the submenu, select the New command. From the resulting dialog box, select Header A and click OK. Now watch the Header screen appear. It's shown in Figure 6-6.

It looks very much like the normal screen you type on. In fact, the title bar shows your document's name and the words "Header A" (or whichever header you're working on), and there are several ribbon bars available for your editing pleasure.

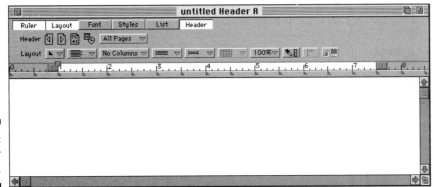

Figure 6-6:
The Header
screen.

Unique in the Header screen is the Header ribbon bar (see Figure 6-7). Here, you can move through the headers you've already assigned to the document in question, both forward and backward. This feature allows you not only to check your work, but to easily select and copy elements from one header to another in order to maintain consistency.

Figure 6-7:
The Header
ribbon bar.

< change if needed

If you're preparing a super-long document and want consistent headers across all chapters, simply open an earlier chapter and the header you want. Select all the text and formatting in that header, copy it, and paste it in the header window of your new document. Then you can change those elements that need revision, such as renaming a header "Chapter 4" instead of "Chapter 3." Neat, huh?

In the body of the header, you can type whatever you want. The text can be just a chapter or section name, standard words such as "Company Confidential" or ... well, just pick something. As with a standard document, the ribbon bars allow you to select fonts, type style, and positioning. Unlike a standard document, however, the Header bar allows you to also insert a date, a page number, and the time, as well as specify on which pages the header will appear, whether it's all pages, or just odd or even ones.

When you're finished with your header, just close the window by clicking the close box in the upper-left corner of the title bar. The header won't appear as part of your text display, but it's lurking there, in your document, ready to appear when you print or when you hit the Print Preview button. Then your header will appear in all its glory.

You can have as many as two headers per page, and they'll each appear below the top margin. Want a header that's higher on the page? Simply adjust your margin to the position you want.

Fabulous Footers (Not Footnotes!)

Let's be clear: As you probably know, a footer is not a footnote. Footnotes, which I will cover in the next section, are usually specific to a given part of text. Footers are the words we choose to place at the bottom of each page in a document.

In business today, a footer usually includes the date, page number, and that "Confidential" word the lawyers love, the one that protects you if someone you give a report to violates confidentiality and spreads your work around. If it's a term paper you're preparing (more on that in Chapter 14), a footer could include your last name, student I.D. number, or other details.

Whatever you choose to put in a footer on your report, creating and editing one is marvelously easy. Go to the Layout menu, move your cursor onto the Header/Footer command, and from the submenu, select the New command. From the resulting dialog box, select Footer A and click OK. The Footer screen appears. It's shown in Figure 6-8.

All the procedures you used in creating a header (see the preceding section) apply here. That's nice, I believe, because you don't have to learn separate steps to create a footer; if you've done a header, you've already learned it.

If you've turned here without having created a header and just want to place footers in your documents, a brief reprise: The footer window is much like your text window, with the addition of a Footer ribbon that lets you add the date and page number, as well as fast forward through available footers. Type your footer in just as you would regular text and be sure to specify (using the buttons) whether you want it on all pages, the odd ones, or the even ones.

How long can a footer be? Well, it really could be 12 inches (get it?) or even longer. WordPerfect allows you to insert as much text in the footer (or header) window as you like. As an experiment, I copied about half a page of text, pasted it into a footer window, and closed the window. Upon inspection with Print Preview, there was my monster footer, taking up about half a page. In most circumstances, however, you don't want your footer to be longer than a couple of lines, but your mileage may vary with your driving style and road conditions.

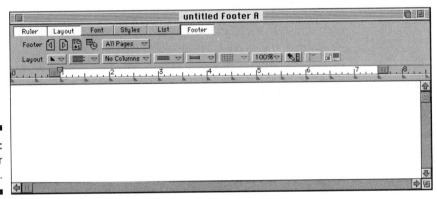

Figure 6-8:
The Footer
screen.

Just as headers appear just below the top margin of a page, footers appear just above a page's bottom margin. If you want to see your footer lower than the default one-inch bottom margin, then you'll need to adjust that margin.

With your headers headed and your footers footed, what else is left to a report? Yes, friends, it's time for . . . footnotes.

Friendly Footnotes (Not Footers!)

Putting a footnote in a report is often necessary, especially when you're citing the work of others. Professors and teachers like to see them, and so do some clients. And if you're preparing a formal report for the government, you'd better have those footnotes in place — Washington types just love 'em. (Those who like their footnotes collected in one place at the end of a document require, not surprisingly, *endnotes*. I'll get to those in a minute.)

Creating footnotes isn't difficult in WordPerfect, however. In fact, if you remember the old typewriter-and-white-out days, it's almost totally fun!

To begin, place the insertion point at the spot where you want to place the footnote. Once there, select the New command from the Footnotes submenu under the Layout menu. In practice, this means pulling down the Layout menu item, dropping down to Footnotes, and dragging your cursor over to the New command. When you select this command, you see what appears in Figure 6-9.

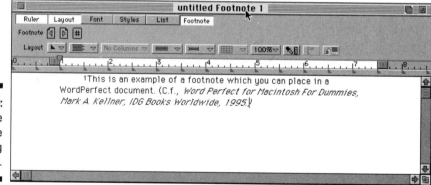

Figure 6-9:
The
Footnote
Editing
window.

Yes, Matilda, it's another editing window, complete with ribbon bars. This time, the extra one worth considering is the Footnote bar, which will move you forward and backward through the footnotes in your document (a great way to recall how you expressed yourself before); you can also use it to add a footnote number if one isn't there, that is, if you've deleted it. Note that the window will open with a footnote number and a default indentation. You can change these settings as you like to suit whatever footnoting style (Chicago Manual, American Psychiatric Association) you desire.

Generally, you'll want to set footnotes in a smaller type size — and perhaps a different typeface — from the body of your text. You can use WordPerfect's editing features here to great advantage. Select (or highlight) the desired text in your footnote, pick the size and font you want, and make the changes in the Font bar.

When you've finished the footnote of your choice, click the window closed. You'll see just a small number in superscript at the point where you've inserted the footnote, which, like headers and footers, will appear in the Print Preview screen. Figure 6-10 shows a header, footer, and a footnote on a page.

Another nice feature here is the capability to change your mind and delete a footnote. Simply backspace over the footnote number and, poof!, the footnote disappears. Any subsequent footnotes are renumbered so that you don't have to worry about that task.

Turning Out a Table

Grab a stopwatch, if you will, and see how long it takes to create a table in WordPerfect for Macintosh. I timed it at under three seconds. Here's what I did:

I moved the cursor to the Table button in the Layout ribbon bar and clicked on it (see Figure 6-11). I dragged the mouse pointer across the number of columns and rows I wanted the table to contain — up to eight columns by twelve rows. I released the button and up popped my table on the screen.

That's the basics of (ahem!) setting your table. Once open, however, your options are relatively limitless. Creating and editing a table here is a phenomenal experience.

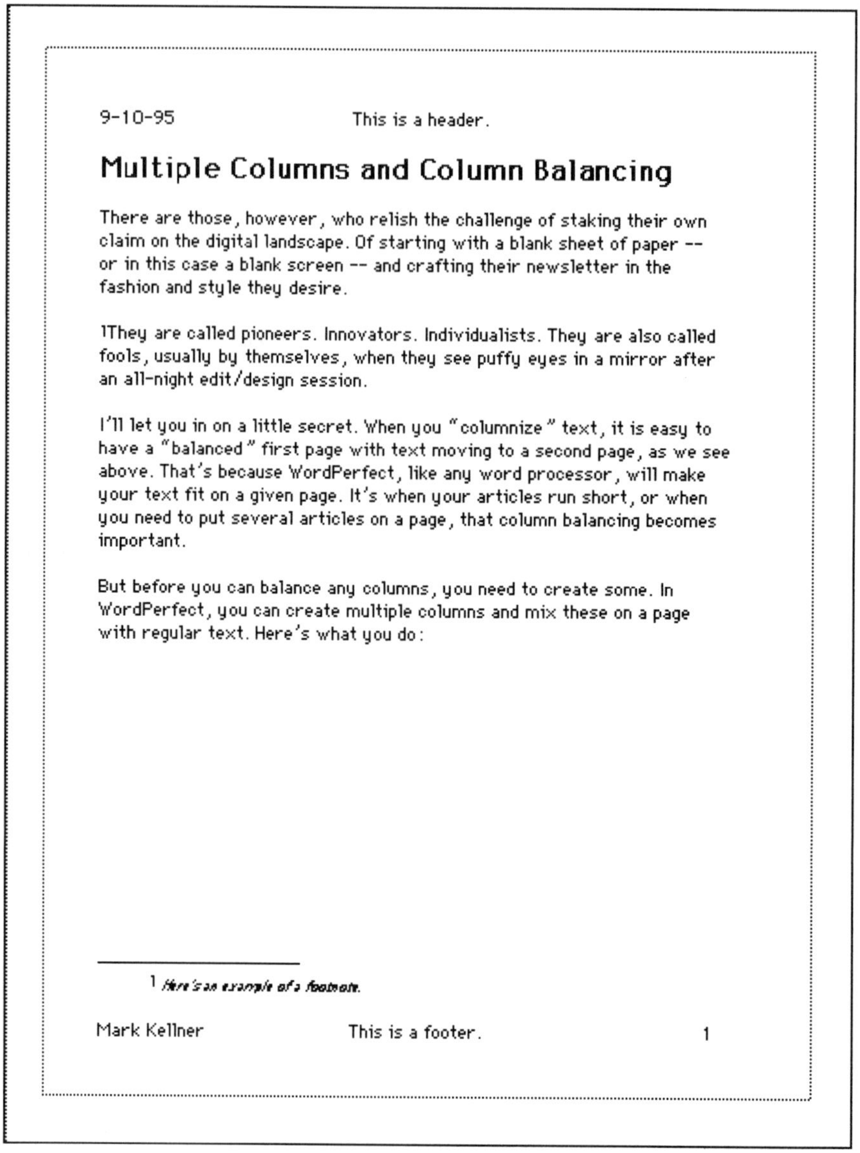

9-10-95   This is a header.

Multiple Columns and Column Balancing

There are those, however, who relish the challenge of staking their own claim on the digital landscape. Of starting with a blank sheet of paper -- or in this case a blank screen -- and crafting their newsletter in the fashion and style they desire.

1They are called pioneers. Innovators. Individualists. They are also called fools, usually by themselves, when they see puffy eyes in a mirror after an all-night edit/design session.

I'll let you in on a little secret. When you "columnize" text, it is easy to have a "balanced" first page with text moving to a second page, as we see above. That's because WordPerfect, like any word processor, will make your text fit on a given page. It's when your articles run short, or when you need to put several articles on a page, that column balancing becomes important.

But before you can balance any columns, you need to create some. In WordPerfect, you can create multiple columns and mix these on a page with regular text. Here's what you do:

1 *Here's an example of a footnote.*

Mark Kellner   This is a footer.   1

Figure 6-10:
Putting it together — header, footer, footnote on screen (in the Print Preview window).

Figure 6-11:
The Table
button in
action.

The Table ribbon

Let's start with the Table ribbon as a tool for getting your tables generated and formatted. (Note: You can access most of these commands from the Table menu, but I'll examine the Table ribbon as a faster means of accomplishing your goals.) Figure 6-12 shows the Table ribbon.

Moving from left to right, the first two buttons allow you to add rows and columns to a table you've already defined. Just place the insertion point at the spot where you want to add space, move the cursor to the appropriate button, and click. Next over is the Delete button, which will clear out a row or column you've selected. Highlight the desired area, click, and hasta la vista, baby!

Figure 6-12:
The Table
ribbon.

Next up comes a button with which you can modify the border of your table. The standard WordPerfect border for a table is a double-lined thing which reminds me of nothing as much as an old school composition book. Press this button and up pops a wide range of choices for the border around the table and the lines within the table as well.

WordPerfect will create your table with cells of uniform width and height, but changing these is easy, sort of. Position the cursor on the edge of the cell you want to change, click on it, and when you see a dotted line across the screen, move the edge in the desired direction. In order to keep all cells in a row or column equal, the width or height of all cells in a row (when changing height) or in a column (when changing width) will be changed to the same dimension (see Figure 6-13).

Features	Benefits	Cost	Available
133 MHZ PowerPC Chip	Super-Fast Operation; Lots of Processing Power	$150 extra per unit	August 1995
200 MHz CPU Chip	Smokin'	$500 extra per unit	Summer 1996 if we're lucky

Figure 6-13: A table set with variety.

There are four other formatting options you can use on your table. Two of these can be applied to a single cell or to a group of cells.

> The first option is a *fill pattern*, which is accessed with the No Fill button on the Table bar. Click on it and you'll see a range of choices from leaving the background blank (No Fill) to various shades of black up to 100 percent. There are controls to change the color of the fill or to use one of 64 different patterns. Use these controls to highlight certain aspects of your table's text, even in black and white (see Figure 6-14).

The second formatting option aligns text within a cell along the top or bottom edge of that cell or centered between the two points. Highlight the cell you want, click on the button, and the job's done.

Combine
Split

As you lay out your table, you might get the urge to combine information in several cells into a single cell. This can be done with the (surprise) Combine Cells button. When applied, this command erases the border between selected cells and brings the text together. Conversely, the next button over splits a combined cell back into its original elements.

Lock cell

If you want to keep certain elements of a table static — say as a template you wish to reuse periodically — you can protect certain cells by highlighting them and clicking on the Lock button in the Table bar. To remove this protection, however, you'll have to go to the menu bar, pull down the Tables menu, and choose the Protect Table command.

Features	Benefits	Cost	Available
133 MHZ PowerPC Chip	Super-Fast Operation; Lots of Processing Power	$150 extra per unit	August 1995
200 MHz CPU Chip	Smokin'	$500 extra per unit	Summer 1996 if we're lucky

Figure 6-14: A table with a fill pattern.

The Math ribbon

Because it includes mathematical capabilities, WordPerfect's table editing will let you do math in a cell. Click on the Math button and down pops an extra Math ribbon bar (see Figure 6-15) where you can select a formula to either average a given set of numbers or to sum up a series, which is inserted between parentheses in the formula. A Sigma button, so called because of the Greek alphabet letter it bears, can also be used to sum up your figures. It's not a spreadsheet, but it is a handy way to add numbers to your table.

Creating tables in WordPerfect can be as simple or complex as you want. But the effort required can give you great rewards with a fine looking addition to your report.

With all of this, you might wonder about importing tables from spreadsheets. Using publish and subscribe, you can import such information and export it as well. But for truly customized displays, you'll want to use these table editing features to get the job done.

Figure 6-15:
The Math
ribbon.

Of Text and Tables

If you have text which has been set up (or delimited) with tab stops, you're ahead of the game in getting WordPerfect to make a table from that text. Highlight the tab-delimited text, go to the Table menu, select the Text to Table command, and you can automatically convert this text into a table. This method also works for straight text, comma-delimited text, and text that is set up in either a merge format or columns.

And if you have done a table that you want to convert to regular text, highlight the entire table and select the Table to Text command from the Table menu.

Setting Your (Other) Table (of Contents)

A report of more than, say, five or seven pages — and certainly one that runs more than ten pages — will probably benefit from having a table of contents. With a little planning and forethought, generating a TOC (as it's called) can be a piece of cake. Figure 6-16 shows a TOC.

When you begin your document, designate a location for your TOC and set the insertion point there. You now need to tell WordPerfect that here is where you wish to generate a table of contents.

There are several ways of getting to this point. For our purposes, I'll concentrate on the List ribbon bar because it does a great job of putting commands within reach, as you can see in Figure 6-17.

On the List bar you'll see a button next to the words "Table of Contents" that reads "Define." Click on this button and you'll see the phrase "«Table of Contents Generated Here»." From now on, as you move through your report and indicate what should be included in a TOC listing, the result will be in this location.

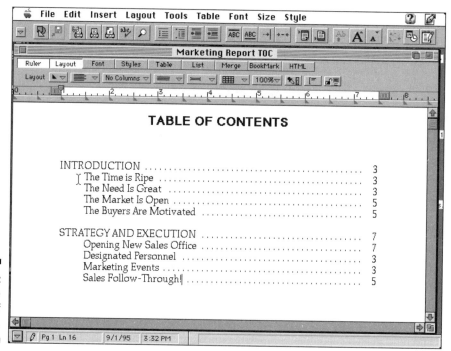

Figure 6-16: A sample table of contents.

Figure 6-17:
The List
ribbon.

Marking off TOC items

As you write your report (or edit the copy imported from other files) you'll come across items you want to place in your TOC, such as chapter headings and subheadings. When you come across one of these, assigning them a place in the TOC is easy.

If it's a subhead, like the one above this section, simply highlight the text and move your cursor to the TOC section of the List ribbon bar. A primary reference is indicated by clicking on the button with the number 1 in it; subsidiary references — say section headings under a chapter listing — are indicated with the button containing the number 2. Make your choice and WordPerfect will remember each one as you move on.

WordPerfect's TOC generator will also remember on which page your entries are located. Should they shift as other blocks of text are added or deleted, your TOC will adjust automatically when it is generated.

Generating a TOC

You're at the end of your report or book or term paper. (And aren't you glad!) Now it's time to generate your TOC. From anywhere within the document, click on the Generate button and sit back.

Within seconds, your TOC will appear in the place where you wanted it generated. The result really looks nice and professional, and with far less effort than any manual system I've ever heard of or tried.

The default settings for generating a TOC include the use of dot *leaders* to indicate the space between the end of a TOC entry and the number indicating its location. However, you might want blank space or something else to do this for you. Clicking on the Other button in the List bar brings up a dialog box where you can define the attributes of the TOC, including the kind of leader it uses (see Figure 6-18).

```
┌─────────────────────────────────────────────────────────┐
│ ▦                           List                          │
│   Type: │Define Table of Contents        ▼│               │
│  ┌─Attributes────────────────────────────────────────┐   │
│  │   Page Numbers: │Dot Leaders        ▼│ ☐ Wrap Last Level │
│  │   Level Format: │1 ▼│              ☐ Allow Underlining │
│  │      Max Level: │5 ▼│              ☒ Line Between Entry │
│  │   Concordance File ┌──────────────────────────────┐ │   │
│  │                    └──────────────────────────────┘ │   │
│  └────────────────────────────────────────────────────┘   │
│              │Generate│ ⌘G   │Find File│     │Define│      │
└─────────────────────────────────────────────────────────┘
```

Figure 6-18:
The List
dialog box.

Among the other options in the TOC dialog box are the means to set several attributes. You can set the kind of leader or spacing filler between the end of the entry and the page number, the style such lists are to follow, and the number of levels you can set for a TOC. This can be useful when preparing several versions of a key document: one with great detail, let's say, and another that acts as an executive summary.

Indexes without Tears

Generating an index is very much like the process used to generate a TOC. One key difference is that your index usually appears at the end of a document — for most of us, this means adding a page break at the end of our current document and defining the index location from the List ribbon bar.

To define an index location, one method is to add a page break at the end of your document, go to the new page created by that page break, and click on the Define button (see Figure 6-19) in the List ribbon.

Figure 6-19:
Some index-
related
buttons in
the List
ribbon.

 —— Define Index Entry button
—— Define button

Then, as you move through your document, you highlight items for inclusion in the index and then click on the Define Index Entry button (shown in Figure 6-19) next to the Define button to mark an item as an index entry. The act of marking index items will do nothing to your text as it appears in print, but you will see a small marker on the screen, as shown in Figure 6-20.

When finished with your writing and editing, click on the Generate button in the List bar. WordPerfect will then do its magic and whip up an index you'd be proud to call your own.

Figure 6-20: Text marked for an index.

imaging software

Make It Fit!

"Here's a needle. Here's a thread," Captain Jean-Luc Picard said to his tailor. "Make it sew."

Sorry. This section isn't about bad puns, but rather about what to do when you have a document that *should* fit on two pages, but just a little bit edges over to page three. Not only might this situation *look* unattractive, but it wastes paper and, in the case of overseas airmail, it can waste money because every sheet of paper can add to your postage tab. (That is, of course, if you still *use* overseas airmail. For many of us, e-mail has replaced the post office, but that's another story.)

You can make a document fit the space you desire by manually adjusting this margin, changing the type size, fidgeting here and there, but why bother? Why, George, when WordPerfect will do almost everything for you? The key lies in a simple command on the Layout menu: Make It Fit. Take a gander at Figure 6-21.

Figure 6-21: The Make It Fit command on the Layout menu.

When you make the decision to make it fit, WordPerfect will present you with a variety of options to select so it knows what to adjust in order to achieve your goal (see Figure 6-22).

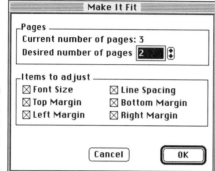

Figure 6-22:
The Make It Fit dialog box.

At the top of the dialog box, specify what you want to adjust — in Figure 6-22, turning three pages into two. WordPerfect will adjust the size of a given font, the margins on all four sides, and the line spacing of your pages in order to make things work (so long as you leave these options checked in the bottom part of the Make It Fit dialog box, as they are by default).

Click the OK button and WordPerfect goes to work. The good news is that WordPerfect can often accomplish this task for you. The bad news is that, as in real life, you can't truly stuff 10 pounds of flour into a 5-pound sack. In the digital equivalent, WordPerfect offers you the message shown in Figure 6-23.

In a situation like this, you'll have to fend for yourself. My best advice: make some of the adjustments WordPerfect won't make for you, like changing the typeface. If you go from Geneva to Times, you'll likely be able to get a lot more text in a smaller area. Trust me.

Figure 6-23:
Sorry! No can do.

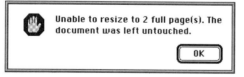

Chapter 7

Graphics Explained

. . . .

In This Chapter

▶ Inserting graphics

▶ Positioning and sizing graphics

▶ Creating your own graphics

. . . .

Not Just Words, Pictures

Imagine this book, which uses words and images to show you the basics of WordPerfect, without any pictures. Not even the cute guy on the cover, for which I was the model (not!).

You might be able to imagine it, but you might also imagine that it wouldn't be as much fun or as helpful.

A picture is worth a thousand words, as the saying goes, but in many documents, it can be invaluable. Just think of any time you've tried to assemble something and the instructions lacked clear pictures.

Fortunately for you, *WordPerfect 3.5 For Macs For Dummies* is here *with* illustrations, and, equally fortunately for us all, WordPerfect lets you include graphics of all sorts in your documents. These images can range from photographs to corporate logos and symbols, to that great gift of the 1980s and 1990s — clip art. You'll recall that there is a Graphics ribbon bar in this program; now you get to see how it works and what graphics can do for you.

First, though, some background and explanation. (Hang on for this section; it'll help you, I promise.)

Why Import (or Use) a Graphic?

Why use graphics? Because they help us say things. More than almost any time in history, this is a society and culture that relies on visual cues as well as verbal ones. Street signs that once read "No Left Turn" are now replaced with signs showing a left turn overprinted with a circle and a bar through the center. And we all know what that means.

Similarly, you can probably dress up many documents with the judicious use of graphics. No, you won't want to add a smiley face to a legal letter threatening eviction because a tenant is overdue on rent (not unless you have a real mean streak), but if you're preparing a less formal document, it mightn't hurt to add a graphic or two.

Graphics can come from many sources. One of the first you'll find on any Macintosh is in the Scrapbook, a little application program on the Apple menu (found in the left corner of every Mac menu bar). So pull down your Apple menu and choose the Scrapbook. Opening the Scrapbook takes you out of WordPerfect, but because the Scrapbook program requires only 20 kilobytes of memory, running both at once should not tax most systems.

In the Scrapbook, by default, are several standard graphics that illustrate its capacity to hold (like a real scrapbook) all sorts of things. The difference between a paper scrapbook and this one, however, is the capability to copy something in the Mac Scrapbook and then paste it in a document.

For example, I copied a graphic for the word "memo" from the Scrapbook as I started writing. This seems like a good place to introduce this item, so take a look at Figure 7-1.

Figure 7-1:
The memo graphic from the Scrapbook.

With the graphic on the same page as my text, I can do several things:

- ✔ I can move it anywhere on the page I desire, within the predefined margins of that page.
- ✔ I can resize it to make it smaller or larger.
- ✔ I can go to the graphics editor and enhance it in several ways.

The graphic item, then, is an *object* that a WordPerfect user can manipulate so that it appears in print as desired. You can color it, draw a frame around it, or stretch it in any way you desire. With all of the options, you should have no trouble using graphics to enhance your written content.

If you have never used a graphic before in your word processing, think about adding some. Like a dash of Tabasco in the right place, it can really spice up your work.

Clip Art, Not a Clip Job

Along with the Scrapbook, where graphics can be stored for future use, you may want to use what's known as *clip art*, predrawn sketches and other elements, which nowadays are supplied on floppy disks and CD-ROM discs. Many of these images can be integrated right into WordPerfect using a couple of methods.

- ✔ You can open a piece of clip art with the viewer program normally supplied with clip art programs. (You can oftentimes use a typical paint or draw program as well.) From whatever program you use, you can copy and paste images directly into your document, or you can store them in the Scrapbook for future use. (More info on such procedures comes later in the chapter.)
- ✔ You can import the clip art as a file and insert this into your document. The advantage here is that WordPerfect will convert the image into a format it can best use.

Either way, bringing clip art into a document is not a difficult task. Indeed, being able to add illustrations enhances the capability of WordPerfect to do more than just word processing. If one of your goals is to create a newsletter or brochure with this program, you'll find the capability to add graphics a great help.

Graphic Formats

There are a whole bunch of formats from which WordPerfect can import graphics. Among the most popular are

- ✔ **PICT:** Picture resource, a native Mac graphics format.
- ✔ **GIF:** Graphics Interchange Format, a popular graphics file format, especially for images distributed online.
- ✔ **JPEG:** Joint Photographic Experts Group, which is another widely supported picture compression format in the online world.
- ✔ **TIFF:** Tagged Image File Format, a standard file format for bit-mapped graphics, including those created by scanners.
- ✔ **.BMP:** Bitmapped, a graphics file format used by Windows.

Some of these — most notably PICT and TIFF — can be imported by WordPerfect itself. The others might require the use of either a file translation program such as MacLink or a graphics editing/conversion program such as Adobe Illustrator or a shareware program such as GraphicConverter (which is incredibly useful and well worth the shareware fee). Once so converted (to a PICT or TIFF format), the graphic can easily be imported into your document.

Most commercially supplied clip art for the Mac is in either the PICT or TIFF formats, so these files need not be converted.

Placing Graphics within a Document

You can insert graphics into documents using three different methods: (1) copying and pasting, (2) importing, and (3) publishing and subscribing.

Copying and pasting step-by-step

1. **In an open WordPerfect document, find a spot for your graphic and place the insertion point there.**

2. **Locate your graphic.**

   If it's in the Scrapbook, open that program from the Apple menu. If it's in another program such as, say, Photoshop, open the graphic within that program. (Unless you're short on RAM, you should be able to open other programs while WordPerfect is running.)

3. **From within the graphics program or Scrapbook, select (highlight) the graphic and choose the Copy command from the Edit menu (⌘-C).**

4. **Switch back to WordPerfect.**

   You can switch between open applications via the Applications menu on the right side of the menu bar. This menu is represented by the icon of the currently active program and contains a list of all open programs.

5. **From within WordPerfect, choose the Paste command from the Edit menu (⌘-V).**

   The graphic you copied appears at the insertion point within your WordPerfect document.

Importing step-by-step

1. **In an open WordPerfect document, find a spot for your graphic and place the insertion point there.**

2. **Choose the Insert File command from the File menu.**

   The Insert dialog box appears. It looks and functions just like a standard Open dialog box.

3. **Using the Insert dialog box, locate the graphic file you wish to import.**

   Note that WordPerfect may not display graphics files within the lists of this dialog box unless you choose the All option in the Show drop-down menu near the bottom of the dialog box.

4. **Once you locate the graphic file, click on it to select it and then click the Insert button.**

   WordPerfect may ask you to confirm the translation of the file if it's in a format that WordPerfect can't readily read (see Figure 7-2). If all goes well, the graphic will appear at the insertion point within your document.

Using publish and subscribe

Along with copying and pasting and importing, there is one other method for putting graphics into your document, and that is Publish and Subscribe, which is fully discussed in Chapter 15.

Briefly, Publish and Subscribe are tools Apple provides to let you create (or *publish*) an item on your computer or your network, which other documents can use (or *subscribe to*). In the case of a graphic — one created with a drawing

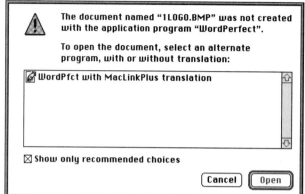

Figure 7-2:
WordPerfect
helps you
translate
files.

program, perhaps, or one downloaded from an online service — you can use the external graphics program to publish it and then subscribe to the graphic in your WordPerfect document.

The chief advantage of Publish and Subscribe is that when the published item changes, the subscribed copy changes as well. This feature works well with text, as you'll see in Chapter 15, and can also work with graphics that change from time to time.

Before you can use the following set of steps, you will have to have published a document from within a graphics program.

1. **Select the location for the subscribed item in your document.**

2. **In the Edit menu, highlight the Publishing command. From the resulting submenu, choose the Subscribe To command.**

3. **In the resulting dialog box, locate the desired file.**

4. **Select the format desired (WordPerfect format is usually best).**

5. **Click on the Subscribe button.**

   The file appears in your document at the location you specified.

You can only subscribe to items which have been published; Chapter 15 will detail that process for users of graphics programs. You'll need to consult that program's documentation to learn its publishing procedures.

That's all there is to it! Use one of the three procedures I just discussed, and a graphic of your very own will appear where you want it in your document.

Positioning and Sizing Graphics

Putting a graphic in its place is a simple task. Click once on the graphic and a frame appears around your graphic (see Figure 7-3). Click and hold down the mouse button and you can now move that graphic anywhere on the page you desire.

This same border is also your key to *sizing* graphics — making them either larger or smaller than they are currently. You'll notice small boxes in each of three corners of the graphic border. Click on one of these and hold the mouse button. Then drag the border either away from or closer to the opposite corner. You'll see the graphic's size change, proportionally, either smaller or larger.

Your limits for making a graphic larger or smaller are, essentially, the size of the page. It's possible to shrink a graphic to microscopic size or stretch a graphic to large proportions.

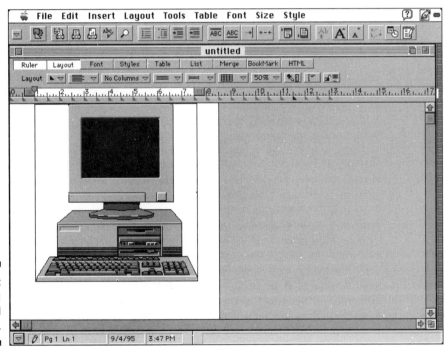

Figure 7-3:
A graphic surrounded by a border.

Wrapping Text around a Graphic

As you position your graphic on a page, it's possible to have text wrap around it. Simply position the graphic in a desired text location using the technique discussed in the preceding section and watch: the text will reflow around the graphic.

This text wrap, as you'll see in Chapter 12, is very useful in producing brochures, newsletters, and other publications. Because graphics are so easily moved around on a page, wrapping text is not a difficult task.

Creating Your Own Graphic

You might be more artistic than I am; on a good day, and with the aid of a computer and much practice, I can draw a straight line. More or less.

But if you are the kind of person for whom drawing is a natural thing, take heart. WordPerfect offers a rather nice suite of drawing tools for you to work with.

To find them, click on the Graphics icon in the Button bar. You'll see a screen of very small dots on which a tool bar is superimposed (as shown in Figure 7-4).

With WordPerfect's graphic tools, you can create just about anything you want. There are tools for drawing text boxes, rectangles and other shapes, as well as tools for filling in those boxes and coloring them. Figure 7-5 shows a straight line; Figure 7-6 shows a rectangle, and Figure 7-7 shows a rectangled filled with a pattern.

Creating a graphic in WordPerfect starts with a box (or oval or circle or whatever shape you choose) in which you can color, add text, or do whatever you like. Elements can be layered upon each other for different effects (such as placing a text box inside an oval so that lettering appears in the final version).

As I'm *not* an artist, I won't (necessarily) fake instructions on how you can become one. My best advice here is to play around — liberally — with the drawing and painting tools provided. You'll likely stumble on *several good* strategies for doing what you want artistically, which as you'll see is just about anything.

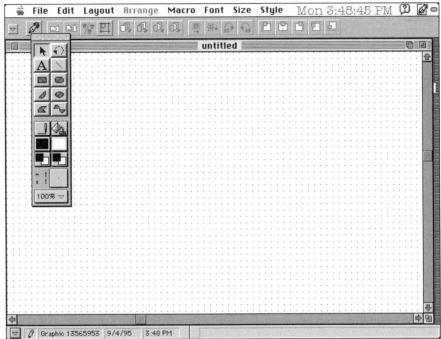

Figure 7-4:
The
Graphics
Editing
screen.

Figure 7-5:
A straight
line.

Figure 7-6:
An unfilled
rectangle.

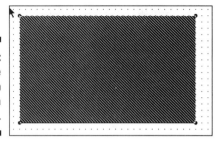

Figure 7-7:
A rectangle
that's been
filled with a
pattern.

Colorizing Your Art

Any graphic you place in a WordPerfect document, whether it's imported or created, can be colored using the graphics tools, notably the Fill buttons, one of which selects the color you will use and the other paints it in. First, you need to select the graphic you wish to change.

Then click on the Fill Color button and hold the mouse button. You'll see a palette of colors from which to choose (as Figure 7-8 shows in black and white). You can then "fill" your graphic with that color by moving your mouse pointer to the desired color and letting go of the button. You can also fill a graphic with a pattern. Figure 7-9 shows the Fill Pattern button.

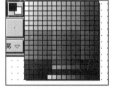

Figure 7-8:
The Fill
Color button.

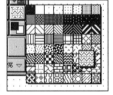

Figure 7-9:
The Fill
Pattern
button.

Of course, adding color works best only on a color Mac display. Don't forget that WordPerfect can display and print graphics that are already in color and have been imported into a document.

Don't Overdo It

There can be a temptation, once you start using graphics, to overpopulate a document with them. This overuse can lead to pages looking as if they had acquired a bad case of chicken pox, littered with graphics to an incredible degree.

In my opinion, simple is better. Use your graphics sparingly and for a purpose (to show the company logo or to help make a point). And think of who will *see* the graphics you use. Make sure the pictures you select are easily understandable, and you'll have an even greater chance of getting your message across.

The 5th Wave By Rich Tennant

"Of course graphics are important to your project, Eddy, but I think it would've been better to scan a picture of your worm collection."

Chapter 8

Stationery Subjects

. . . .

. . . .

At Last! Do-It-Yourself Letterhead

One of the great features of WordPerfect is the capability to create and use one's own stationery.

Gone are the days, or so it would appear, of going down to a printer — or getting a mail order catalog from a place such as The Drawing Board (remember them?) — and waiting a month or so for letterhead to arrive. You can now have letterhead ready in as little as 30 seconds or so. Need to change one aspect of it or another? Just key it in and it's done.

This kind of freedom makes WordPerfect for Macintosh a great boon to entrepreneurs and those of us who either work at home full time or run a side business. If you're active in civic affairs, work in a hobby group, or do other things for which a letterhead is regularly required, you can get yourself set up in a jiffy. And as I describe in this chapter, you can save that letterhead for reuse time and time again.

But wait, there's more! Yes, friends, for an unlimited time — for as long as you use WordPerfect — you can use the *same* techniques for creating letterhead to develop memo forms, report forms, surveys, quiz forms for classes, invoices, expense reports, you name it.

In short, the stationery-creating capabilities you'll find here have a range of applications as varied as your imagination.

Now just in case you're not feeling too creative this morning, the folks at WordPerfect have come up with some stationery designs of their own. I'll start with these and see where they can take us.

Using WordPerfect-Supplied Stationery

To open a stationery file from within WordPerfect, pull down the File menu and highlight the Template option. A list of stationery files appears to the right in a submenu (see Figure 8-1).

The list of available stationery files includes those supplied by WordPerfect as well as those you create. For now, pick one that the program has made up, the Letter form.

When you select it, WordPerfect automatically fills in key spots in the letter, including your company or organization name, address, and phone number. Take a look at Figure 8-2.

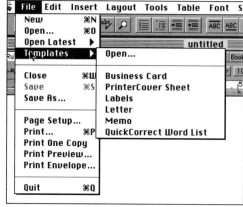

Figure 8-1:
The
Stationery
submenu in
the File
menu.

Figure 8-2:
A basic
letterhead.

INTERNATIONALWIDGETS, INC.
5555 MAIN STREET
ANYTOWN, VA 22043-9999
(703) 555-1234
Fax#: (703) 555-6789

Opening this document also prompts a dialog box that asks you to fill in the recipient's name, address, city, state, ZIP code, and a salutation ("Mary" or "Dr. Smith" or whatever). As you answer these questions, the macro that accompanies the Letter stationery will fill in the appropriate places in the body of your letter. Today's date will be inserted as well, and when finished, you'll be ready to type the body of the letter, print, and mail.

Of course, all these elements can be edited on screen, but the idea behind the stationery is to save time and trouble by putting it all together for you.

This new version of WordPerfect includes a variety of stationery forms for you to use, including a fax cover sheet (labeled "Printer Cover Sheet" in the Templates [Stationery] menu for reasons I can't fathom).

When you open a stationery file, it opens as an *untitled* document. In order to keep a copy, be sure to use the Save command and give the document a name. If you're creating this stationery for the first time, save it as a stationery file (see below); if you're using existing stationery, give it a sensible name such as "Letter to Joe re Money Owed."

Creating Your Own Stationery

Creating your own stationery form is simple, and it can be fun. After you open a new file, put the insertion point at the spot where you want your text to appear and start typing. If you want to include a graphic — either some clip art or something you've scanned in or drawn — use the steps you learned in Chapter 7 to either paste or insert the graphic.

So far, so good. Now the fun begins.

Play with your text and graphics elements as much as you like. In creating the letterhead shown in Figure 8-3, I positioned the graphic carefully and shifted it around before deciding on a final location. In one trial, I put the main title (*The Philatelic Communicator*) in red, using the color button in the Font ribbon bar; when using a monochrome laser printer, the letter prints as black.

Figure 8-3:
With this
letterhead, I
added an
automatic
dating
function.

The Philatelic Communicator
Quarterly Journal of
Writers Unit 30, American Philatelic Society.

Mark A. Kellner, Editor
5555 Carina Lane • Foster City, CA 94404-9999 USA
Telephone: (415) 555-5555 • **Fax**: (415) 555-5555
Internet: *MarkKellner1.com*

September 4, 1998

I then inserted a date function at the appropriate point, just above where I put the inside (recipient's) address and begin the letter. Because I like to use the Dateline font, I've specified that as part of the stationery form. The result: I can launch into letter-writing faster than before. And now, so can you.

Don't forget color

When creating letterhead, remember that you can use color to highlight text in WordPerfect. The low cost of many of today's inkjet printers and the falling prices for color lasers will, I believe, mean an increase in colorful communications in print (see Chapter 17).

There are basically two steps to adding color to a spot of text:

1. **Highlight the text.**
2. **Click on the Color button in the Ribbon bar and select the color you want from the palette.**

   Once you make your choice, the highlighted text appears in the new color.

Best of all, you can always change your mind and undo (⌘-Z) your color choice or make another one.

Matching envelopes

You know, I thought making my own letterhead was fun. Then I saw how *easily* this new version of WordPerfect creates envelopes. I don't believe there's anything better on the market today, especially working within the application, than this nifty little feature.

All you have to do to begin the envelope process is click on the Print Envelope button in the button bar, or choose the similar option from the File pull-down menu. This will bring up the Envelope dialog box, which looks suspiciously like Figure 8-4.

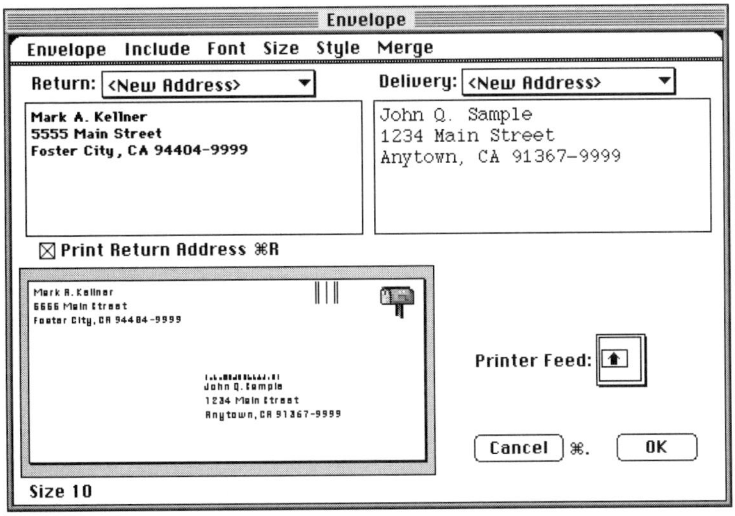

Figure 8-4:
WordPerfect's
powerful
Envelope
feature.

Because you've already entered your "Personal Information" when you first used the letterhead template (stationery) form, WordPerfect reads in that data when creating your return address. (Note: For some odd reason, WordPerfect didn't pick up the "International Widgets" when creating this address. You can move your cursor in the return address field and add a company name if you desire.)

If you've been typing a letter, say to our good friend Fred Schmidlap of Global Widgets, WordPerfect will grab that address and place it in the address block. Now the fun begins: Look at the lower-left corner of Figure 8-4. You'll see a representation of how the envelope will look, and I've got a close-up right here in Figure 8-5.

Figure 8-5:
WordPerfect
shows how
your
envelope
will look
when
printed.

You'll notice, I'm sure, the funny little lines at the top of the envelope and just above the name. These are, respectively, a FIM (for Facing Identification Mark) bar code and a ZIP+4 bar code. The FIM will tell the machines used by the U.S. Postal Service that there's postage on this envelope; the second will help those machines sort mail for delivery. Using a ZIP+4 bar code should get your letters to recipients faster and more accurately. It also identifies you as a professional who knows how to use the latest mail-addressing techniques.

WordPerfect will also print bar codes if you have only a five-digit ZIP Code for a recipient, and this, too, will help speed your mail.

Before we leave envelopes, let's take a look at some of the other, useful customization features you can use when creating the carrier for your latest letter, mash note, or payment request.

Most of the time in business, you'll use a Size 10, also known as a Number 10, envelope for your correspondence. WordPerfect's envelope creator defaults to this size, but as you see in Figure 8-6, you can pick a range of sizes, so long as they are compatible with your printer.

If you're a writer sending out query letters to editors, or a faithful Dear Abby reader who is asked to send in a self-addressed, stamped envelope, the Size 9 envelope will hold paper that's 8 1/2 inches wide (that is, a letter sheet, folded) and fit in an outgoing Number 10 envelope. You can use WordPerfect's envelope creator to personalize your return envelope so that the acceptance letter from Steven Spielberg arrives with no great delay. (And by the way, it really should be called an "addressed, stamped envelope." Show me an envelope that *really* addresses itself and I'll give you $100.)

How WordPerfect's envelope feature might save you money

Ever since the 1991 postal rate hike, the one that took us to 29 cents, mailers — the Postal Service and the independent Postal Rate Commission — have tangled over the notion of a "Personal Automation Rate," which would let consumers and small business mailers save a penny or two off the first ounce of a first class letter if the envelope had a FIM and bar code. Advocates say that if a "small" mailer is doing much of the USPS' automation work, they should get a discount just like the "big" mailers such as Sears and the phone company.

Neither in 1991 nor 1995 did the Personal Automation Rate survive the rate-setting process. But there's always hope for the future, and the capabilities of a program such as WordPerfect might help convince postal officials and rate setters that such an automation discount is timely and right and fair.

Figure 8-6:
Envelope
sizes can be
selected
here.

What else would you want to specify on the envelope trail? You can use the
built-in Font, Size, and Style menus to determine the way you want your
envelope to look. Go to the Include menu and these choices present themselves, as shown in Figure 8-7.

From this menu, you can choose whether or not to include the bar code and
FIM marks discussed earlier. In fact, you can decide whether to put the bar code
above or below the recipient address, as well as choose among the three kinds
of FIM bars the Postal Service uses. (Ask your local post office for guidance;
they have a booklet on the subject.)

You can also elect to omit a return address if you so desire; simply check on the
Print Return Address box to deactivate this feature.

Figure 8-7:
The Include
menu
lets you
customize
envelopes.

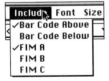

Saving Stationery

When you've created your stationery file, use the Save As command to store it.
In the Save As dialog box, be sure to select the WordPerfect 3 Template option
from the Format drop-down in order to save the file properly (as shown in
Figure 8-8).

You need to save your document as a stationery file in order to both access it
from the Stationery list and open up new versions as untitled documents.
Saving it as a regular file won't lose any data, but it won't appear in your list.
Should you save your stationery file as a regular document file by mistake,
simply open the file and resave it as a stationery document.

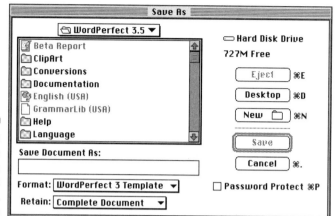

Figure 8-8:
Saving a file
as a
template
(stationery).

Using your new stationery as the basis for a merge file is a great idea. To do this, save your document as stationery, open a copy, and do your merge thing. See Chapter 9 for the full scoop on "Mail Merge Made Easier."

Creating Watermarks

Something that's very popular with users is placing a faint subprint in the center of a page that represents either a logo or other design. This element is called a *watermark* after the image impressed in sheets of finer papers.

Adding one in WordPerfect for Macintosh can be fast and simple. Select the Watermark command from the Tools menu and you can be on your way. Figure 8-9 shows the Tools menu and Figure 8-10 shows the Watermark dialog box.

When you select this command, you are asked if you want to create a new watermark or edit an existing one. For now, select New and you're asked whether this will be Watermark A or Watermark B, as shown in Figure 8-11. By the way, "Watermark A" and "Watermark B" are just ways of naming your watermark.

The graphics workspace appears, as shown in Figure 8-12.

If you're pasting in a graphic that is already selected, simply choose the Paste command from the Edit menu. Otherwise, you can insert a graphic file using the Insert File command in the File menu.

Figure 8-9:
The
Watermark
command in
the Tools
menu.

Figure 8-10:
The
Watermark
dialog box.

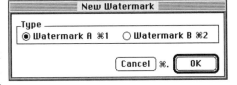

Figure 8-11:
Make a
selection
and click
OK.

Once you've imported a graphic or drawn your own using the graphic tools
supplied (see Chapter 7), you can size and position it anywhere on the page.
When finished creating the watermark, close the window and your watermark
will appear behind your text.

To lighten your watermark so that it doesn't overwhelm your text, use the Pen
and Fill Color drawing tools to select a shade of gray. With practice, you'll easily
create the right watermark.

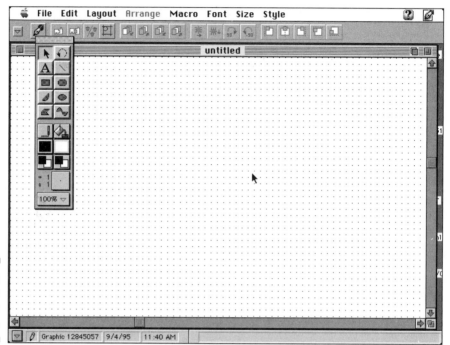

Figure 8-12:
The
graphics
workspace.

Chapter 9
Mail Merge Made Easier

. . . .

In This Chapter

▶ Creating or importing the data

▶ Creating the merge document

▶ Performing the merge

▶ Doing envelope merges

. . . .

*I*t'll happen sooner or later, particularly when others find out you have a Macintosh *and* WordPerfect. You'll be asked to do a mailing that sends the same letter to a bunch of people. They could be members of the P.T.A. or the garden club. Or they could be a group of suppliers to your firm. Or maybe you need to send a batch of résumés to prospective employers, and using mail merge is a great way to answer a group of classified ads.

Quick and easy is a good way to describe the mail merge process. You type a letter once, and with a list of addresses in your computer, you can send that letter to dozens, or even hundreds, of people, and each will get a personalized letter — even though you only typed the text once. To personalize messages even further, you can tell WordPerfect to pause when creating each letter so that you can enter special information.

WordPerfect for Macintosh makes this process even easier by placing the tools for mail merges at your fingertips. The ribbon bar at the top of your screen includes a Merge button. Click on it to reveal the Merge ribbon where you can access the most-used mail merge features, each available with a simple mouse click (see Figure 9-1). This ribbon will save lots of typing and help you to avoid the errors you might encounter with other programs that require you to enter these fields manually.

You begin by creating an address list.

Figure 9-1:
The Merge
ribbon (not a
singles
place).

| Merge | End Of Field | End Of Record | Field... | From Keyboard | Other ▽ | Merge... | Markers |

You Make a Little List (and a Letter)

Call it one of the undeniable truths of life, but you need two important elements to make a merge letter work. One is a "form" letter, that is, one into which data is merged at the points you indicate. The other is a mailing list which contains the data you need.

As the late songwriter Sammy Cahn would say, "You can't have one without the other." And as Ed Bundy would later say, "A computer? What's that?"

Be that as it may, our journey into mergedom has to begin with this understanding. It's also important to know that the fields in both files have to line up, so that names and addresses appear in the right spot. (As you'll see, however, you can "skip" a variable as long as you have a placeholder for the omission.)

It's kind of like balancing a ledger: what's on one side (the form letter's spaces) must match what's on the other side (the number of fields in a merge record) in order for your mail merge to be a success.

Start with a new file, having selected the New command from the File menu, or by using the names and addresses of the people you want to contact. (Make sure you've got all the ZIP codes or postal codes you need to speed delivery.) Unless they're already in a database program, or another electronic form, you'll probably need to type these in. (If you have a database file already stored on your Mac, skip ahead for instructions on how to use those names, but be sure to read the section on "Putting It Together: Creating a Merge Document.")

Creating a List from Scratch

The first step in creating a mail merge list is to open a new file in which you can type the names and addresses. You need to tell WordPerfect about the elements it finds in the merge file, however. And you do this by creating a mini-guidebook to your list, which becomes the first record in your mail merge file. WordPerfect then reads this record and knows that the first line is the courtesy title, the second is the name, and so forth.

To create this introductory record, go to the Merge ribbon and click on the Other button; then select Define Names from the list of options (see Figure 9-2).

Figure 9-2:
Define
Names,
from your
friends at
the Merge
ribbon,
Other button
division.

What do you create by doing this? A Define Names record, and it looks like Figure 9-3.

Figure 9-3:
A Define
Names
record.

What you've done in this entry is tell the program that the first item in a given record is the name, the second is the title, and so on. Because I may address one person as Mr. Smith, but another as Bob, I included a salutation line. At the end of the <Define Names> statement, you'll want to insert <End of Record> to tell WordPerfect you're finished with the definition. You do this by going to the Merge ribbon and clicking on the End of Record button.

Now that you've defined what WordPerfect will find in the address list, you need to enter it by typing in each name and address, following the pattern in this initial record.

For each record, enter the appropriate data, along with a marker telling the computer where each segment of that record ends. This marker is called End of Field and it's used so often, you'll find a button for it on the Merge ribbon. (Click the button and the program inserts a hard return, too, saving even more time.)

After each record is completed, use the End of Field button to insert this marker (and another hard return) and repeat the process until your list is complete.

Enter each name like this:

> Mr. Tom Jones
>
> Jones International Corporation
>
> 25 West 43rd Street
>
> New York, NY 10036-0123
>
> Mr. Jones

Typing in a long list of names isn't the easiest work in the world or the most fun. But using the Merge buttons in WordPerfect makes a tough job easier, particularly if you have bad memories of doing this in MS-DOS, or even Windows.

Once you're done creating your data file, be sure to Save the list on your hard disk or a floppy disk (using WordPerfect's usual document format). Few things can be more frustrating than to have worked hard on a list of 100 names only to lose it by not having saved the file!

Putting It Together: Creating a Merge Document

After saving your data file, it's time to create a *merge document* to use with your mailing list.

Start by creating a new file using the New command in the File menu or the ⌘-N key combination on your keyboard. (If you have a stationery file, you can open one of these for a letter-based merge if you so desire.)

When you get to the place where you want to insert the necessary fields, go to the Merge ribbon again and select the Field button. You'll be presented with the Merge Field Number dialog box, as shown in Figure 9-4.

Here, the choices may look bewildering, but they're actually quite simple. You can define fields by number or name. Using names is easier. Just click on the blank box in the Field Name area and type in the name of the field you want placed there. Repeat this for each field you need, inserting the desired field names and placing the fields wherever you want in your document.

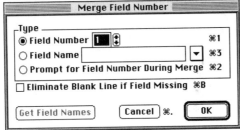

Figure 9-4:
The Merge
Field
Number
dialog box.

If your data list has a variety of addresses — some with company names and some without — check the Eliminate Blank Line If Field Missing box when creating a field. It will then end the field with a question mark and skip it if the information is missing from a given record.

What if you want to enter specialized information in your merge letter, such as a date for a meeting or (if you're collecting money) the balance due? There are two ways of accomplishing this.

✔ One is to include the specific data in your merge file and then create Merge fields to handle them. That's quick, but it makes your carefully crafted mailing list a one-time venture, unless you want to go through those 500 records, one by one, and make the changes.

✔ A better way, you might find, is to insert a Keyboard Merge field at the appropriate place in your document. This stops the computer until you've typed in the necessary information. Using the From Keyboard button on the Merge ribbon inserts a field into your file.

If someone else will run the merge operation you set up, or if you think you'll need a reminder of what to place in the field, you can add a Keyboard Response message at this point. The Merge Message dialog box will appear on the screen when the merge is run and offer instructions on what to do (see Figure 9-5).

When you've filled in the required data, click on the OK button to continue the merge process. After you've inserted the field names you want, your merge form should look something like Figure 9-6.

The fields that are enclosed between the < and > symbols will be replaced by the appropriate items in your data file when you do your merge, something I'll get to in a couple of pages (promise!).

Before you do an actual merge, however, save the merge file using the Save command.

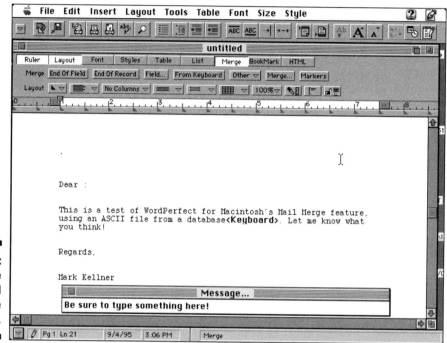

Figure 9-5:
The
Keyboard
Response
message.

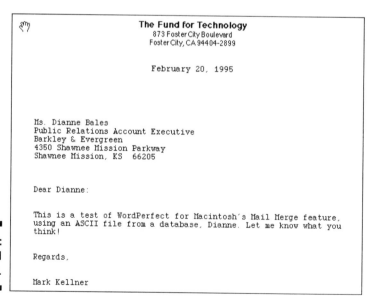

Figure 9-6:
A completed
merge form.

Importing an Existing Data File

What if you've got those names and addresses in another program, a database such as FileMaker Pro or an address book such as Now Contact? You can use this data without having to retype it. You can even take a file from a Windows or MS-DOS database and use it for your mail merge, provided your Mac can read a DOS-format disk.

From each program, export the list and elements you need into an ASCII (text) file that is either comma-delimited or tab-delimited — that is, where the elements are separated by commas or tab marks. The files will include a header record that describes what each record contains.

As you might guess, you will want to use the Save As feature in whichever program from which you are exporting data and make sure it saves the file as ASCII or a similar format. If you have never done this before, checking the program's documentation is a good idea.

You don't have to add the end of field marks that you would add to a file you create manually. The commas or tab marks take care of the delimiter, while the hard return at the end of each record is equal to the end of record mark.

The big plus is not having to retype those names in a WordPerfect format. The big minus is that you have to *be sure* that the records in that "foreign" file exactly match the merge codes you've set up.

One key way to assure this is by careful editing of your source file. The other, frankly, is by trial-and-error. Take a sample of your list, say the first 10 or 15 names, and save this list as a separate file (such as "Mail Merge Sample") and test this file against your mail merge form. If you're not satisfied with the result, review your source file again and see where you might not have matched fields in the list with those of your merge file.

Merging and Printing Your Letter

You've got your list — homemade or imported — and you've created your merge document. Now it's time to bring the two together and then print the result.

Move your mouse pointer to the Merge ribbon and click the Merge button. You'll be greeted by the Open Form dialog box, which is shown in Figure 9-7.

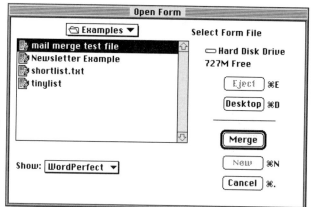

Figure 9-7:
The Open
Form dialog
box.

Here, you can select the file needed by highlighting it and clicking on the Merge button. After selecting your Merge file, you'll be asked to choose a data file in the Open Data dialog box, as shown in Figure 9-8.

Here, a file created in an ASCII format (shortlist.txt) is highlighted. To select it, click on the Merge button.

Now comes the easy part: WordPerfect will merge the data into your form. If you don't have a Keyboard request command requiring your input, you can step away from the computer, wait a few minutes, and come back to a new, untitled file containing all the merge letters you desire. Or you can sit in front of your computer and watch the merge process speed by.

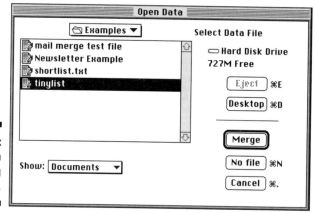

Figure 9-8:
The Open
Data dialog
box.

Of course, if you have the Keyboard field in your document, you'll need to stay by the computer and enter the appropriate information as requested.

However you end up working with the Merge process, you'll find that it's easier and faster than other methods of creating this kind of letter. Your work will be completed faster, and the people who receive your letter won't know they've received a "form" letter — unless you tell them.

Doing Envelope Merges

You were probably thinking that after my gushing over WordPerfect's envelope-creating capabilities back in Chapter 8 (remember the thrilling discussion of postal bar codes?), there wouldn't be anything *else* to say.

Au contraire, postage-stamp breath! Take a quick glance back at the Envelope dialog box and you'll see the Merge menu. Choose the To Destination Address command to open a merge form and data file.

You'll want to create a separate merge form for envelopes that positions the address in just the style you want, perhaps name and title on one line, for example.

Once you've created your envelope merge form and matched your data to it, you should have a batch of envelopes ready for printing. Neat, huh?

Other than creating that separate envelope merge form, the process for merging envelopes is the same as for letters, but with one very important exception: Be sure you know how your printer handles envelopes and follow the instructions for loading them properly.

One way to work around the envelope printing problem is to print addresses on peel-and-stick labels. You create a label merge form for this task using the Label template (see Chapter 13) and print accordingly. Be aware that in some circles, a label-addressed letter is viewed as junk mail and might not command the attention you want your missive to receive.

Chapter 10
Language Lessons

Under a Spell (er)

Ouch. Don't you just *hate* section headers that are puns? You don't? Good, you're my kind of person. (To the rest of you, be assured I will suffer some punishment for my verbal excesses!)

Anyway, the spell checker in WordPerfect is one of those great modern inventions that will save you grief, tears, and heartache. Remember the scene in the movie *Rising Sun* where the operative of the Tokyo-based conglomerate is bent over, crying, in front of the chairman when a failure is revealed? Well, the way the script was actually written, the failure wasn't a horrible crime but rather the poor use of a spell checker. But the producers thought nobody would believe people today wouldn't use a spell checker.

After all, Preston, you just *know* that Murphy's law has been known to strike with a vengeance when your hands hit a computer keyboard. And even if you're using voice recognition software to dictate your writing directly to the computer (wish I had some about now), you can be sure a misspelling or two will pop up.

All this blather is meant to emphasize how important spell-checking is to a document. Every time I've used a spell checker correctly, I've gained. And almost every time I skipped over that feature, I've caught you-know-what for my neglect.

As you'll see in a few moments, the spell check in WordPerfect is less necessary than it might have been, thanks to a feature called QuickCorrect. Type "teh" instead of "the" and WordPerfect will automatically correct it for you. However, QuickCorrect is *not* a substitute for a good spell check. And, frankly, neither feature will replace human-eye inspection of a document.

Performing a spell check

To do a spell-check, put the insertion point at the place in your document where you want to begin checking. Usually, this would be at the beginning, but if your file is 50 pages long, and you've already spell-checked the first 40, starting at page 41 is no sin. Nor is highlighting a certain portion of text and merely spell-checking that portion.

Once you're at the place you desire, either click on the Spell Check button in the button bar or press the ⌘-E keystroke combination or click on the Tools menu and select Speller (see Figure 10-1).

However you invoke the spell checker, WordPerfect will present you with the dialog box shown in Figure 10-2.

As you meander through your document, you will get to know this dialog box rather well. Here, you'll see any misspelled words WordPerfect finds, along with suggested corrections. First, however, some basics about the miniature menu bar you find in this window.

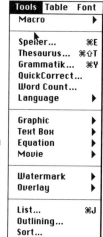

Figure 10-1:
The Speller
command
from the
Tools menu.

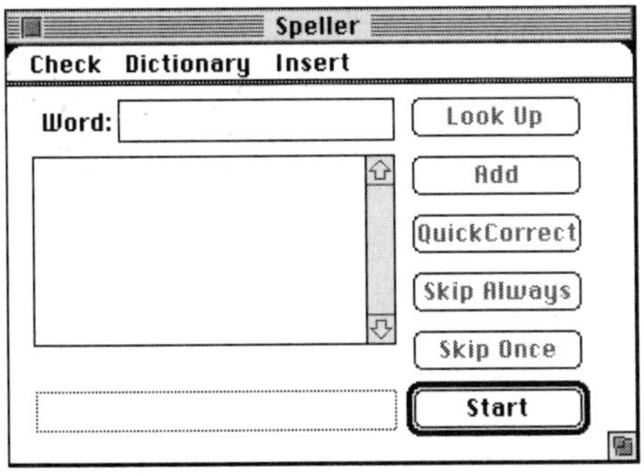

```
┌──────────────────────────────────────┐
│▤▤▤▤▤▤▤▤▤▤▤ Speller ▤▤▤▤▤▤▤▤▤▤│
│  Check   Dictionary   Insert          │
│──────────────────────────────────────│
│  Word: [            ]   ┌──────────┐  │
│                         │ Look Up  │  │
│  ┌─────────────────┐▲   └──────────┘  │
│  │                 │     ┌──────────┐  │
│  │                 │     │   Add    │  │
│  │                 │     └──────────┘  │
│  │                 │    ┌────────────┐ │
│  │                 │    │QuickCorrect│ │
│  │                 │    └────────────┘ │
│  │                 │    ┌────────────┐ │
│  │                 │▼   │ Skip Always│ │
│  │                 │    └────────────┘ │
│  └─────────────────┘    ┌──────────┐  │
│                         │ Skip Once│  │
│  [             ]        └──────────┘  │
│                         ┌──────────┐  │
│                         │  Start   │  │
│                         └──────────┘  │
└──────────────────────────────────────┘
```

Figure 10-2:
The Speller
dialog box.

The Check pull-down menu (see Figure 10-3) lets you boss WordPerfect around, telling it just where to check and what to look for. You can check the entire document, a selected portion of text or from the insertion point to the end of the document. Here, too, you can tell WordPerfect to either check or ignore words which have numbers in them (like, ugh, Windows 95) or duplicate words (such as "had had"). You can also ask the speller to phonetically look up correct words and to automatically replace words.

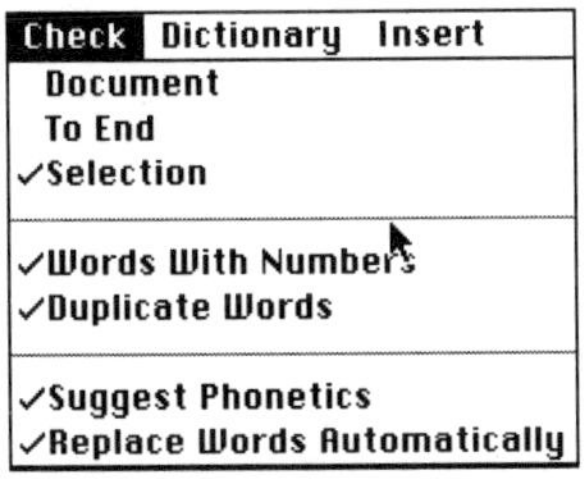

```
┌──────────────────────────────────┐
│ Check │ Dictionary   Insert       │
├───────┴──────────────────────────┤
│   Document                        │
│   To End                          │
│ ✓Selection                        │
│                                   │
│ ✓Words With Numbers               │
│ ✓Duplicate Words                  │
│                                   │
│ ✓Suggest Phonetics                │
│ ✓Replace Words Automatically      │
└──────────────────────────────────┘
```

Figure 10-3:
The Check
menu.

To the right of this menu bar item is Dictionary, which allows you to select the dictionary that you want the program to use (see Figure 10-4). For most of us in the U.S. of A., it will be the default Dictionary (USA) supplied with WordPerfect. For others, it might be a legal or medical or biblical dictionary available online from user groups (see Chapter 21) or purchased commercially. It might even be a dictionary you create and edit yourself. Either way, click on the available dictionary and away you go.

Figure 10-4:
Select your
desired
dictionary
here.

```
┌──────────────────────┐
│ Dictionary │ Insert   │
├────────────┴─────────┤
│ ✓Dictionary (USA)     │
└──────────────────────┘
```

Finally, the last pull-down menu allows you to make very good use of the Speller as a look-up tool. (This is also great for solving crosswords!) You can enter "w*ing" and find every word the WordPerfect spell checker has between "wadding" and "Wyoming," about 397 of them, one of which might be perfect for your next sentence.

To do this, you type the "w" and then click on "Insert" to either insert a single wild-card character (the asterisk) or one to match multiple characters (an ellipsis). Then click on "Look Up" and presto!, your word options appear.

Once you've set the criteria for your search (the default settings are searching the entire document, looking at words with numbers, suggesting replacements, and using the default dictionary), then you can begin the spell check in earnest (see Figure 10-5).

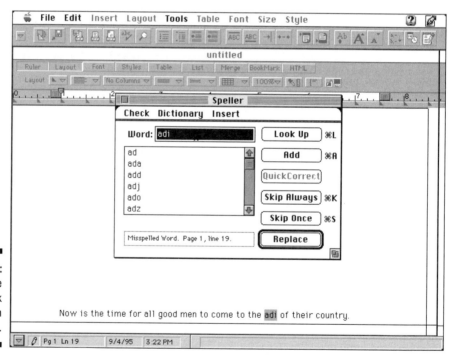

Figure 10-5:
An active spell check finds an error.

How spell checkers work

As with most programs, WordPerfect is supplied with a list of several thousand words, and when a spell check is run, it looks through a document for all the words it does not recognize. These are flagged by the system and displayed in the dialog box with any alternatives the program can find.

When WordPerfect flags a word with the Speller, it's not necessarily an incorrect word. It may just be one that the dictionary doesn't recognize, such as a proper name. If that's the case, or if it's another kind of spelling you wish to accept, even if the dictionary doesn't, simply click on the Skip Once, Skip Always, or Add button. The first will skip the unrecognized word once; the second will skip the word throughout the present session with that file. When you "Add" an unrecognized word, WordPerfect will then recognize it forever and ever until you remove that word from the list.

Another neat feature of WordPerfect is that it will add a commonly misspelled word (common to your typing, that is) to the QuickCorrect list. Any time it's typed, WordPerfect will automatically correct it, as discussed later in the chapter.

You can move at your own pace through the Speller, but know that the program itself can run quickly. In fact, this Speller is one of the fastest I've ever seen on any computer platform.

A Way with Words — Creating, Editing, and Selecting WordPerfect Dictionaries

Most of us will only need one basic dictionary with which to work, and that is the basic WordPerfect dictionary, augmented perhaps with some words in the User Dictionary that we create by clicking on the Add button during a spell check. Others will need custom word lists, some of which (as mentioned) are dicussed in Chapter 21.

But what can you do if you need to create a dictionary list or edit an existing one? WordPerfect has a couple of options for you. One of these involves creating and editing a list of words from within the program; another option is the little-known ST Utility, which I'll visit in a moment.

Creating a WordPerfect dictionary

1. **Open a new file in WordPerfect (⌘-N).**

2. **Type in each word you wish to add on a separate line, with a carriage return at the end of each line.**

3. **When finished, select Save As from the File menu.**

   The Save As dialog box appears.

4. **Open the Language folder in the WordPerfect folder to save your dictionary.**

5. **From the Format pop-up menu, select User Dictionary.**

6. **Click on the Save button.**

Editing a dictionary

Once you've saved a dictionary, you can edit it using the ST Utility. To get to this utility, however, you need to go outside of WordPerfect to the Mac operating system and into the Language folder, which is nestled in the WordPerfect folder. There, you'll find an icon for the ST Utility. Double-click on it and you'll see the startup screen shown in Figure 10-6.

From here, you get the opportunity to select and open a dictionary file. For this example here, I'm going to open the User Dictionary (see Figure 10-7).

Figure 10-6: The ST Utility startup screen.

```
Speller/Thesaurus Utility
    Version 3.0.3

Copyright ©1992
WordPerfect Corporation
1555 N. Technology Way
Orem, Utah 84057
```

Figure 10-7: The Open Dictionary dialog box.

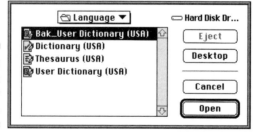

Once open, the given dictionary represents each word in lower case (see Figure 10-8). But don't worry: If you have included a proper name (like "Kellner," for example), WordPerfect will recognize the proper capitalization, even though it doesn't show up in the word list that way.

If you want to add a word, simply type it in the box as shown in Figure 10-9. Click the Add button and the word will jump to the word list.

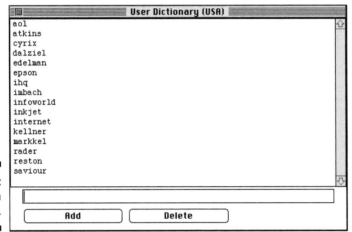

Figure 10-8:
An open
dictionary.

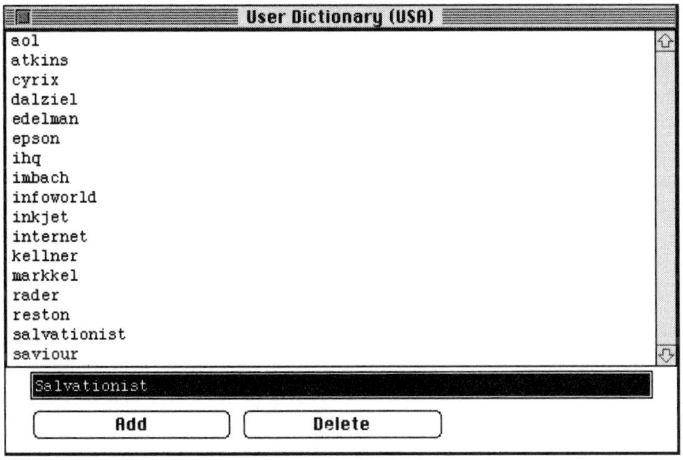

Figure 10-9:
Adding a
word.

When running a spell check, you can tell WordPerfect which dictionary to use by clicking on the Dictionary pull-down menu in the Speller window (see Figure 10-10).

As you can see, the Dictionary features in WordPerfect make it possible for you to not only select the right word, but add special lists for special needs. It's a helpful feature that can streamline and speed your spell checking, as well as make it more accurate.

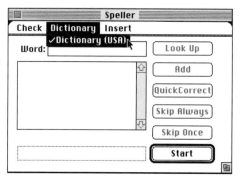

Figure 10-10:
Selecting a
dictionary
from the
Speller
window.

How's Your Grammar?

And, no, I'm not talking about your mother's mom. I'm speaking about the way we use words and language. It's important, particularly in business and professional circles.

Some of you mastered the details of English usage back in, of all places, grammar school, also known as grade school, and those lessons have remained fresh for years. Others (me included) still have trouble with certain aspects of word usage and grammar, at least from time to time. Even if you consider yourself a good grappler with grammar, you have to admit that we all make mistakes from time to time.

Checking grammar, however, can be laborious in a long document. If you're unsure of a rule (I always have to watch my use of which and that), it can be frustrating: How do you know you're in error if you don't know all the rules?

Fortunately, WordPerfect for Macintosh is here to help you. Enter Grammatik, the grammar checker *par excellence* — although the program will probably "flag" me for using a foreign language phrase when simple English would do.

Grammatik — what a feature!

One or two sessions with Grammatik (which is a subset of the full Grammatik 6.0 program available separately) will, I believe, convince you that it is a powerful, helpful adjunct to your word processing efforts. Grammatik simply works better in flagging grammatical errors than does the grammar checker built into Word 6 for Macintosh; it also can measure your writing against several established styles.

Grammatik is not an invention of WordPerfect, but instead was the product of some creative programmers at a firm once known as Reference Software, Inc. The Grammatik program had been out for a couple of years before the WordPerfect folks snapped it up (along with the company's programmers and product marketing experts), incorporating it into WordPerfect for Macintosh and other flavors of WordPerfect and selling Grammatik as a stand-alone program.

The basic grammar check is quite formal: no contractions allowed, for example, and forget about using the word "you" as a reference in a sentence. It strictly enforces other rules, and watch out for passive voice — it will not be approved. Grammatik compares your work against the predominant rules for specific styles of writing: advertising copy, business letters, documentation (such as user manuals), fiction, journalism, memos, proposals, reports, or even technical writing. If none of these styles match your writing requirements, you can define a special grammar-checking style, something I cover later in this chapter.

Having these all these different styles to check against is a tremendous plus. As a user, you might need to speak in different "voices" depending on who will read your work: A report to the boss is different from the draft of a short story, for example. Having a grammar checker look not just for subject and verb agreements, but keeping an eye on where your words are to be read is a real plus you just don't find in other Mac word processors. (I know because I've looked.)

Let's begin at the beginning, with a "basic" grammar check.

Basic grammar checking with Grammatik

OK. You've written that memo to the boss asking for a $5,000 raise. You've worked hard, you brought in the hard-to-get Ingols account, and you've made your mark in the company.

The boss, however, is a stickler for grammar who'd rather chip a tooth than let a participle dangle. Ending a sentence with a preposition is not something he relates to. Yes, Horace, you've got to get the ol' grammar checked.

Here's how to do it: While your document is still on the screen, select the portion of it you'd want Grammatik to check. (If you've written a letter or memo, for example, you might not want or need a grammar check on the letterhead or the inside address.) Then pull down the Tools menu, choose the Grammatik command, and watch the fun begin.

Keyboard-command fans can zap into Grammatik by pressing the ⌘-Y key combination. The Grammatik window is shown in Figure 10-11.

When it opens, Grammatik will invite you to tell it where to check (the selection or the whole document) and which rules to check by, both with pull-down menus. Once you've decided, click on the Start button to begin.

You'll see that the Grammatik dialog box is rather like that for the Speller. You can specify checking of a document, selected paragraphs, or go from the insertion point to the end of a document.

Along with the Check options, you will note here that Grammatik has ten — count 'em — ten basic checking styles, as shown in Figure 10-12. You might select one of these or none and create your own using the Custom options on the next menu over.

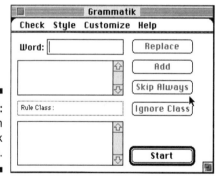

Figure 10-11: The main Grammatik window.

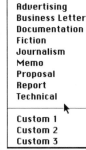

Figure 10-12:
Pick a
(grammar
checking)
style, any
style.

Customized grammar checking

I've noted that Grammatik's rules are somewhat broad-based; they're designed to fit a wide range of writing styles and editorial needs. Your company or school might have different rules or special usage guidelines, such as spelling out all numbers or only those below the number ten.

If you want to have WordPerfect and Grammatik keep track of these rules on a regular basis, you can create your own grammar-checking style. To do this, start by revving up Grammatik.

Pull down the Customize menu in Grammatik's menu bar and you'll see three potential custom entries, numbered 1 to 3. Select one, and you'll see the dialog box shown in Figure 10-13.

You can leave the name as Custom 1 (or whichever number is visible), or you can change the name to something more descriptive: Annual Report, Term Paper, or Law Review.

You also get the opportunity to *pattern* your new style after an existing one. Click on the Pattern After pop-up menu and you'll see Grammatik's predefined styles as well as the other two custom options (which may have been re-named). If you want to follow, say, the Journalism style but with a few modifications, select that choice and you're more than halfway there.

Figure 10-13:
Define your
customized
style.

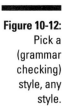

Once you've selected a writing style to pattern your custom style after — or if you want to create a style that is totally your own — click on the Edit button to start setting the rules your way. Once you've done this, click on the Save button to add the finishing touches (see Figure 10-14).

Here, you can select various criteria for the Grammar checker to flag sentences. If you don't like a lot of passive sentences, then you might want to use the default setting which says one out of ten sentences in the passive voice is the limit. The other settings also allow you to set numeric criteria for correction.

Click on the Rules button here and you can specify which rules to accept or reject in your grammar checking. Some you might wish to accept, others you might want to ignore. The choice here is yours, but have a copy of *The Elements of Style* by Strunk and White handy before you make a rash choice.

The first section of the dialog box asks you the level of *formality* that you want assigned to your writing. This setting can be Informal, Standard, or Formal. The Thresholds options let you define the rules under which Grammatik will flag errors involving consecutive nouns or prepositional phrases, long sentences, passive sentences, number spelling rules, and the number of words allowed in a split infinitive.

Having decided on these points, you can now click on the Rules button to select specific rules that apply to your situation (see Figure 10-15).

Merely select — or deselect — the rules you want or don't want in your grammar checking. When finished, click OK and you'll return to the Edit dialog box. You can then click on the Save button to store your work. Now you have a customized grammar checking routine designed to fit a specific task.

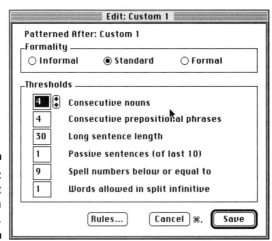

Figure 10-14:
The Edit
Custom
dialog box.

```
╔══════════ Edit Rule Settings: Custom 1 ══════════╗
║                                                    ║
║  Patterned After: Custom 1                         ║
║                                                    ║
║  Style, Grammar/Mechanical Rules:                  ║
║  ┌─Style────────────────────────────────────┐ ▲  ║
║  │ ☒ Abbreviation                            │    ║
║  │ ☒ Archaic                                 │    ║
║  │ ☒ Cliche                                  │    ║
║  │ ☒ Colloquial                              │    ║
║  │ ☒ Commonly Confused                       │    ║
║  │ ☐ End-of-Sentence Preposition             │    ║
║  │ ☒ Foreign                                 │    ║
║  │ ☒ Formalisms                              │    ║
║  │ ☒ Gender-Specific                         │    ║
║  │ ☒ Jargon                                  │    ║
║  │ ☒ Long Sentence                           │    ║
║  │ ☒ Overstated                              │ ▼  ║
║  └───────────────────────────────────────────┘    ║
║                                                    ║
║                      ( Cancel ) ⌘.  (   OK   )    ║
╚════════════════════════════════════════════════════╝
```

Figure 10-15:
The Edit Rule
Settings
dialog box.

The actual act of checking grammar

Once you've defined your checking style — or accepted one of the ones already contained in WordPerfect — it's time to begin the checking. Like the spell checker, Grammatik will move through the document reading a sentence at a time. It will flag something questionable and alert you to a potential problem.

Unless you click and bypass the option, Grammatik will perform a spell check of your document while it checks grammar. But the spell-check list used here is *not* the WordPerfect spell checker to which you may already have added words unique to your organization. To make sure you get the spell check you want, bypass the Grammatik spell check and run your document through the WordPerfect spell check, accessed via the Tools menu.

Grammatik works based on various rules, such as the avoidance of double negatives. When it finds a sentence that violates the rule, it calls your attention to that violation (see Figure 10-16).

Along with catching an error (or something that it doesn't recognize, such as a spelling question), Grammatik suggests a fix or two that will put your work in accordance with its checking rules. Along with the suggested correction, you'll also see a brief explanation of why a given phrase or word use is being questioned by the checker. This way, without even being a grammatical genius, you can see what to look for in future compositions and understand why the program called something to your attention.

Again, as with the spell checker, you can accept the suggested correction (or one of the options suggested, if more than one are presented) or skip to the next sentence by clicking on the Next button.

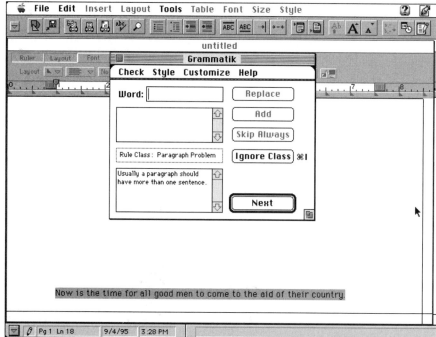

File Edit Insert Layout **Tools** Table Font Size Style

untitled

Grammatik

Check Style Customize Help

Word:

Replace

Add

Skip Always

Rule Class: Paragraph Problem

Ignore Class ⌘I

Usually a paragraph should have more than one sentence.

Next

Now is the time for all good men to come to the aid of their country

Pg 1 Ln 18   9/4/95   3:28 PM

Figure 10-16:
Oops! I broke the rules!

You can tell Grammatik to skip over violations of an entire rule class by clicking on the Ignore Rule button. Grammatik will ignore that particular rule for the rest of your grammar-checking session.

As Grammatik checks your document, you'll have the opportunity to accept or reject its suggested corrections. Depending on your style of writing, you may not have to accept these suggestions. Remember that Grammatik's preset formats are based on broad standards for a given kind of writing, and your needs can vary.

When you're finished, simply close the checking window and save your file (especially if you've made corrections based on Grammatik's suggestions).

If you've turned off any of Grammatik's rules during your session, WordPerfect will ask if you want to save the now-modified checking style as a custom grammar style. Answer Yes and you get a dialog that lets you save the style.

A grammar summary

There isn't a computer available today that will work the way a professional editor does. The rules set down by those two masters of style, Strunk and White, are available digitally, but the program won't *think* for you.

So when you use Grammatik in WordPerfect, accept its suggestions and wisdom, but don't do so uncritically. For example, Grammatik doesn't like sentences that begin with the conjunctions like and or but. Many writers, however, use these words frequently. I'd hate to read a novel by John Updike, Tom Clancy, Anne Rice, or the incredibly vibrant prose of Peggy Noonan or Molly Ivins, after their work has been homogenized by a computer program, which is why I'm glad none of these writers (so far as I know) rely on a grammar checker as the final authority.

If you're writing to be read and understood by people, and if you can possibly work outside of the narrow strictures of a corporation's or university's style, then merely take the changes suggested by Grammatik as just that — suggestions. Use your own mind and your own common sense.

On the other hand — to reuse an overworked cliché — if you are insecure about your writing and want to avoid any number of common usage mistakes, feel free to lean on Grammatik as much as you like. I've run dozens of documents through this "verb-o-matic" and have never been steered wrong when checking against the most formal of styles.

The real bottom line here is that the choice is *yours*. Don't forget that!

QuickCorrect, the Hidden Asset

Remember your first box of Cracker Jack? Did you enjoy the "surprise" packed inside. Well, WordPerfect for Macintosh isn't candy-coated, but there's a nice little surprise packed inside each box: QuickCorrect, a handy-dandy utility that performs several neat functions.

If you've ever typed "teh" instead of "the," only to see it pop up in a spell-check, QuickCorrect is your kind of feature. Built in at the factory is a list of words that are either common misspellings or are abbreviations for larger words or phrases. Type "teh" with QuickCorrect around, and WordPerfect automatically changes it to "the" — faster than any spell checker.

As you run a spell check in any WordPerfect document, you can highlight typos and misspellings for QuickCorrect's attention. When the spell-checker finds a misspelled word, click on QuickCorrect (see Figure 10-17). The error is added to the list of words that WordPerfect for Macintosh will automatically correct when it is typed the "wrong" way.

Figure 10-17:
The Edit
QuickCorrect
List.

I can see some high school teachers pooh-poohing this feature right now: "How is Johnny going to learn to spell if the computer corrects it for him?" Deal with it. While good spelling is everyone's goal, even the best of us can foul up on some words occasionally, sometimes regularly. And some of us are great spellers but can't type to save our skins. Better to have a computer fix simple errors than to send your work out in public and have it reflect poorly upon you.

There's another way to add QuickCorrect words to the list, and that's to choose the QuickCorrect command in the Tools menu. Doing so brings up the QuickCorrect word list, an example of which is shown in Figure 10-18.

You'll see two noteworthy things here:

- ✔ Editing the QuickCorrect list is simply a matter of entering the "incorrect" typing in the Replace field and typing the "correct" item in the With field.

- ✔ WordPerfect is already programmed with the substitution of the copyright symbol, ©, for (c) which many of us have used for years as an alternative, particularly on typewriters.

Figure 10-18:
The
QuickCorrect
word list.

(c)	©
acomodate	accommodate
acsesory	accessory
adn	and
adress	address
allready	already
alot	a lot

Complicated typing made super fast

The real, hidden value of QuickCorrect, friend, is that you can use this nifty little tool to make WordPerfect do the heavy, repetitive lifting of word processing: typing names and phrases you use constantly but would rather not keyboard.

You may not have counted, but "WordPerfect for Macintosh" is made up of 26 characters. That means 26 keystrokes each time I wanted to type it in this book — and in a book all about this program, I use the name dozens of times. But whenever I write "WordPerfect for Macintosh," I don't type all of it; the program does.

Using QuickCorrect, I have made the letters "wpm" stand for the name "WordPerfect for Macintosh," and every time I type those three letters, QuickCorrect does the rest. It's easier and faster than creating a macro, and the possibilities are pretty strong. If you ever forget what you've defined with QuickCorrect, merely bring up the Edit QuickCorrect window and you can check your abbreviations against what they've been defined to mean.

I don't know about you, but I like to be lazy sometimes. Particularly when a computer can do what it does best — save time and repetitive effort. QuickCorrect meets those criteria superbly, and I'd encourage you to make as liberal use of it as you possibly can. You won't be disappointed.

QuickCorrect preferences

Just like the old Ginsu knife commercials, wait . . . there's more to QuickCorrect than typing words in quickly or even correcting spelling errors. You can tell QuickCorrect to do a whole range of tasks that will ensure the uniform appearance of your documents. Check out Figure 10-19.

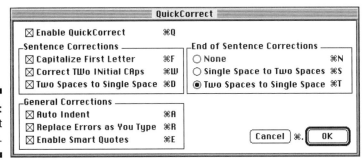

Figure 10-19:
QuickCorrect
preferences.

To get to the dialog box in Figure 10-19, just click on the Options button in the QuickCorrect menu. Then you can enable and disable QuickCorrect and set parameters for various kinds of corrections. Check the check boxes and select the radio buttons next to the options that you wish to use. When the settings are to your liking, click OK to accept them.

Most of these preferences are straightforward: what should the program look for and what should it automatically correct. If you're unsure about a certain parameter either in terms of grammar or company style, check first with the Strunk & White book I mentioned before. And for your firm's writing, ask a manager or colleague or consult the company's style manual, if one exists.

You can also reach this dialog box by choosing the Preferences command in the Edit menu. In the resulting window, click the QuickCorrect icon.

I like having all the sentence corrections on when I write. I rarely forget to capitalize the first word of a sentence, but I sometimes type two letters in an initial word in capitals because I keep a finger on the Shift key a little too long. And in a carryover from typewriter days, many of us insert two spaces after a sentence, despite the fact that most word processors, including WordPerfect, produce better looking results when only one space is placed after a period. Having these corrections made automatically is a tremendous plus.

By now, your spelling, your grammar, and even your punctuation and spacing should be near perfection. The next chapter covers the tools that Apple Computer provides with the Macintosh OS to make computing life easier.

The 5th Wave   By Rich Tennant

"WE NEVER HAD MUCH LUCK BUILDING A DECENT HANDWRITING RECOGNITION SYSTEM, BUT ROY THERE'S DONE REAL GOOD MAKING A FLAT SCREEN NOTEBOOK THAT READS LIPS."

Chapter 11

Using Apple's Tools with WordPerfect

In This Chapter

▶ Apple Guide

▶ AppleScript

▶ Drag and Drop

▶ Apple Events

▶ GX Printing

▶ QuickTime

▶ WorldScript

*O*ne of the nicest things about the Macintosh operating system — in fact, something just being discovered by all those Windows guys — is that Apple Computer has built its operating system with a whole bunch of tools to make your computing life easier. The whole idea is to make using a Mac easy *and* powerful. (After all, the "easiest" word processing device remains a pencil and paper, but its power to manipulate and format text is generally limited to the size of your eraser and the proximity of scissors and paste.)

In this chapter, I take a look at some of these tools and how they can help you enjoy WordPerfect to the fullest.

Apple Guide — Online Help Made Simple

The whole subject of online help is discussed more fully in Chapter 23, but for now, let's take a quick look at how Apple Guide works with your Mac and WordPerfect.

If you have System 7.5 installed on your Mac, you already have Apple Guide. I suggest that you have at least 8 MB of RAM to run both System 7.5 and Apple Guide. Sorry, Cedric, but speed and power and capability do have a price!

So where was I? Oh, yes, Apple Guide. Like Yoda in *Star Wars* or Virgil in Dante's *Divine Comedy,* Apple Guide, which in this incarnation becomes WordPerfect Guide, walks you through common tasks as you try to get things done.

Figure 11-1 shows the initial screen for WordPerfect Guide, which allows you to select from help steps by topic, from an index of topics, or even by key word. If you want to have the WordPerfect Guide lead you through the steps of the mail merge process, you can go through each one right here, as Figure 11-2 illustrates.

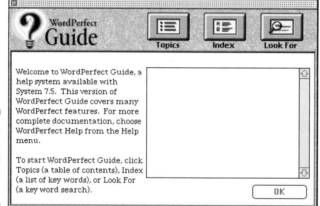

Figure 11-1:
The
WordPerfect
Guide
screen.

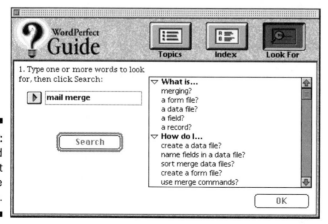

Figure 11-2:
A completed
WordPerfect
Guide
search.

There's more information on doing a mail merge back in Chapter 9. But for now, the thing to remember about WordPerfect Guide is that it's there, it's based on the Apple Guide technology, and it's pretty neat.

Version 2.0 of Apple Guide is now available, and it also works with System 7.0 and 7.1, earlier versions of the Mac operating system. You can download it from Apple's ftp site (ftp.info.apple.com).

AppleScript and Apple Events — Way Beyond Macros

A macro is an awfully nice way to get certain things done. However, there are times when more is needed. You need the power to coordinate the activities of WordPerfect, say, and one or two other programs, or you need the ability to really automate aspects of your business.

Well, Clytemnestra, Apple hasn't forgotten you. There's AppleScript, the magical, mysterious way of getting it all together. Books have been written about it (the best perhaps being *AppleScript For Dummies* by Tom Trinko; the runner-up being Bob LeVitus's discussion of AppleScript in *Macintosh System 7.5 For Dummies*). Songs and poems have praised it. Well, not really, but I wouldn't be surprised if some appear.

What can you do with AppleScript that you can't do with a WordPerfect macro? Plenty. You can set it up to pull data from CompuServe and paste it into a word processing document. You can manage a database for mail merges by selecting a given set of records and creating merge letters. You can even write an AppleScript to take care of assembling a weekly publication using Publish and Subscribe. You can . . .well, I think you get the idea.

AppleScript works hand in hand — or, better, hand in glove — with Apple Events, the command language that the operating system uses to perform its job. Not every Apple Event will do what you need, but used in conjunction with WordPerfect's macro capability, it will get you there.

You need the AppleScript Editor to write a script. You'll find a copy of it in System 7.5, or call Apple at 1-800-SOS-APPL for more information. (WordPerfect's manual suggests that you can use compatible editors, but why bother when you can find the best.)

QuicKeys

Although I've not had direct experience with it, devotees of the QuicKeys program swear that it is much, much better than AppleScript for many repetitive tasks. QuicKeys is a system for automating various tasks using keyboard-driven macros and keystroke combinations. And it has won legions of fans.

Just ask Tim Gallan, my editor, who has this to say: "I think that QuicKeys is ten times better than AppleScript (mostly because all of the QuicKeys I've written actually work, while very few of my AppleScripts ever worked). In addition, a lot of very useful programs aren't easily scriptable — Word, Excel, and PageMaker come to mind."

Well, Tim, "Word" is a dirty word 'round these parts, but your point is well taken. QuicKeys costs around $100 in stores and is well worth exploring if you want to advance your use of WordPerfect and other programs. (Now, if only I could find the macro that writes the book for you!)

It's not our purpose here to teach you how to write an AppleScript script (Bob LeVitus does that very well in his book, and I won't try to top that!). But I can give you a couple of insights that will help.

- ✔ Use a *Tell* statement to issue a command to WordPerfect from an AppleScript. These statements work with *Reference forms* to instruct WordPerfect in what it is you want done. You can refer to *Window 1* for the document screen or use its title (which is its file name). You can also work relationally, saying, "Move paragraph 1 to After paragraph 5," for example. Note the capitalization in this statement. AppleScript, like any programming language, requires precise language.

- ✔ The other insight is to practice, once or twice at least, before you depend on an AppleScript to do your bidding. This kind of shakedown will help you find any problems in your AppleScript and allow you to fix them.

Drag and Drop — Make Your Desktop Work

I really like the Drag and Drop feature of WordPerfect and the Mac, even though it might seem hokey to some of us. It's also a bit embarrassing to write about this feature because I get to show you (gasp!) my Mac desktop. Take a look at Figure 11-3.

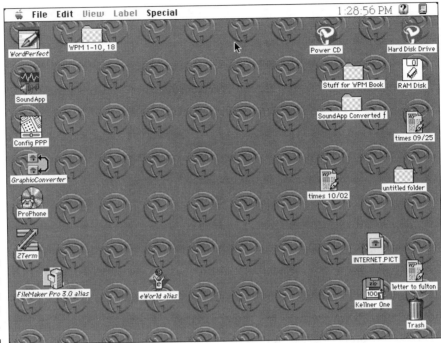

Figure 11-3:
Mark's
messy Mac
desktop.

OK, I'm sorry to admit this, but Figure 11-3 shows what my Mac desktop looks like now, today, as I'm writing this. Now, take a look at the WordPerfect icon in the upper-left corner (see Figure 11-4).

Figure 11-4:
A
WordPerfect
alias icon.

See the icon? (If you can't, please call your eye doctor.) I used the Finder's Make Alias command to create this icon. Here's how you do it:

1. **Locate the WordPerfect application icon on your hard disk.**

2. **Click on the icon to select it.**

3. Choose the Make Alias command from File menu (⌘-M).

The Finder makes a copy of the WordPerfect application icon called *WordPerfect alias.* This alias icon does not represent a copy of the WordPerfect application. In fact, it only takes up about 3K of hard disk space. Think of this icon as merely a button with which you can access WordPerfect, and you can store this button just about anywhere on your Mac's hard disk.

4. Drag the *WordPerfect alias* icon to the desktop and place it wherever you like.

5. You may want to rename the alias to something shorter, like *WordPerfect* or maybe just *WP.*

You can *drag* WordPerfect documents onto this icon in order to open them instantly. This method is faster and easier than (1) starting up WordPerfect, (2) clicking the Open button, (3) finding the file, and (4) telling WordPerfect to open that file. Four steps telescope down to one, and that's gotta be more efficient.

Using aliases is a great way to get down to work, so long as you know your files' locations and so long as you have a WordPerfect icon on your desktop (or wherever you want it to be). Having an alias in an easy-to-reach place is also really handy when you get a file on disk or via e-mail: just drag it to the WordPerfect icon and, presto!, you're in business.

Dragging and dropping on the desktop makes it easy to open more than one document at a time. Select and drag a bunch of documents onto the WordPerfect icon and each will open in its own window, subject to available memory.

Let's say Leo over in London sends you a file in Microsoft Word or one of the other files formats supported by WordPerfect. Open up the floppy Leo sent, drag the file's icon over to your WordPerfect icon and drop it in. Not only will WordPerfect start up, but you also get an automatic conversion — possibly the only one this side of the NFL.

Drag and Drop is a neat feature. You'll see in a moment with GX printing (and a very nice alternative to GX printing) that you can also drag a WordPerfect document onto a desktop printer icon to have WordPerfect launch and initiate the print routine, again saving a bunch of steps.

Now, wasn't it nice, Horatio, that Apple put Drag and Drop into the Mac operating system?

More Drag and Drop Fun: Desktop Clippings

But wait, there's more to Drag and Drop than what I've just discussed. Another Drag and Drop feature is *desktop clippings,* which is available if you are running WordPerfect with System 7.5.

To activate desktop clippings, you simply highlight a block of text for copying and pasting into another program and then drag what you've highlighted to the desktop, and that block of text becomes a "text clipping."

Then, when you open the other Drag-and-Drop compatible program, you can drag the text clipping onto the document window and, presto!, a copy of the text clipping is pasted into the document. When you're done with the clipping, you just drag it to the Trash. Using desktop clippings is a great way to transfer text and graphics from one program to another without having to clutter up the Clipboard.

In fact, this feature is like having an unlimited number of clipboards. The only down side is that some major programs (Word 6 and Excel 5) don't support desktop clippings, but WordPerfect does.

Here's a run-through of how to create and use a desktop clipping:

1. **Highlight a block of text in a WordPerfect document.**

2. **Drag it onto your Mac's desktop and let go of the mouse button.**

3. **An icon with the name text clipping appears on the desktop (see Figure 11-5).**

   You can change the name of the icon to whatever you desire.

4. **Open another Drag-and-Drop-capable application like SimpleText.**

5. **Drag the clipping onto the application's active window.**

   Your clipping is pasted automatically.

Figure 11-5:
A text
clipping
icon.

Don't forget that when you're done dragging clippings into documents, you can then trash them as if they were normal document files.

GX Printing — Easier Output

The name sounds like a cartoon character from the '60s, but QuickDraw GX isn't animation. It's real, and it's a really nice way to work with printing on a Macintosh. If . . .

. . . your printer and application each support GX printing; if you have enough RAM for GX on your Mac; if you don't mind a different Print dialog box than you may be used to seeing; if you can live with some other quirks found in the GX way of doing things.

On the other hand, GX printing can offer speed and convenience, plus, as mentioned before, the capability to drag and drop a document onto a desktop printer icon and start things up quickly.

To make QuickDraw GX printing work, you will need a Mac with a 68020 processor or better, 8MB of RAM, and either System 7.1 or System 7.5. QuickDraw GX ships with System 7.5 (another reason to upgrade, perhaps), and is available from Apple and third parties, such as Peirce Software of San Jose, California.

There's one other downside of GX printing you should know about before you decide to install it. It'll take approximately 1MB of system RAM, which can be tough!

Oh, and you'll also need a GX printer driver for your printer. Now if your printer is an Apple laser printer, a StyleWriter, or, for that matter, any PostScript printer, you can use a GX printer driver. There's one for the Global Village Fax Modem, and other fax modem brands may also support the GX standard.

However, if, like me, you own a nonstandard Mac printer, say the Epson Color Stylus inkjet (a good printer, by the way), you need to get a GX driver from the manufacturer. In Epson's case, good luck: I'm fortunate enough to have working, regular printer drivers, and I know enough not to push my luck!

A chief advantage of GX printing is that it allows you to do some neat things with the Page Setup dialog box. Bob LeVitus explains this all so very well in *Macintosh System 7.5 For Dummies,* and the capability to flip and invert print images is a helpful one in many situations. You will need to get used to some new printing menus, but on the whole, GX printing — when it works — is a good thing.

The bottom line is that if you have the RAM to spare, GX is a help. Otherwise, you can get one of the best GX features — desktop printing — by getting your hands on Aladdin Desktop Tools, a neat package of utilities from Aladdin Systems, Inc., of Watsonville, CA. Among the desktop tools is Desktop Printer, which allows you to have the desktop printing icons GX provides. It also supports fax modems, which allows you to fax from the desktop. The software lists for $89.95, and Aladdin can be reached at 408-761-6200 for more information.

Along with Desktop Tools, which I like, my editor, Tim Gallan, suggests another option for LaserWriter users:

> Apple released the LaserWriter 8.3 driver in mid-1995, and it offers all the conveniences of desktop printer without the quirks of QuickDraw GX. When installed, all you have to do is select and set up a printer in the Chooser, close the Chooser, and lo and behold, a printer icon appears on your desktop. You can repeat this process for as many printers as you want, and you use the Print menu in the Finder to select the default printer (the one to which applications will print).

> LaserWriter 8.3 is available free from Apple's ftp site and probably all the major online services, but it's a very large download. It did not come installed on my new Power Mac 7500, however, so I had to perform the installation myself from the files I downloaded. This driver works with all the LaserWriters and HP Laserjets we have at IDG without requiring the use of new printer drivers. In addition to the LaserWriter 8 driver, the installer places the Desktop Printer Extension, the Desktop Printer Spooler, and the Desktop PrintMonitor in the Extensions folder.

This sounds like a good — and cheap — solution for LaserWriter users, but if you own an inkjet printer (as I do) or a non-PostScript-based laser printer, this solution may not work for you. For these reasons, I still suggest Desktop Tools from Aladdin as something you should at least consider.

QuickTime — Movies Made Easy

As you saw back in Chapter 7, graphics can enhance a WordPerfect document in any one of a number of ways. And those graphics can range from line art to a color photo.

But what about adding a movie to your next annual report? A little film clip for your sales pitch. Hey, you can be the Cecil B. DeMille of newsletters! (I'm ready for my close-up, CB!)

To do add movies to your WordPerfect documents, your Mac needs System 7 and QuickTime, the magic energy food that allows your Mac to play video and sound. (There's a QuickTime for Windows, too.) System 7 and 7.5 each come with QuickTime players, and these are generally installed when you install QuickTime. (If in doubt, see the System 7.x documentation or *Macintosh System 7.5 For Dummies.* Or have I mentioned that book already?)

Inserting a movie into your document is done much the same way you would insert a graphic or other file, but with a twist: Pull down the Tools menu and hold down the mouse button on Movie; from the submenu that appears, choose the Insert command (see Figure 11-6). The Insert dialog box appears.

Using the Insert dialog box shown in Figure 11-7, you maneuver to the folder containing the movie you want to select. When you highlight a movie, you see a preview screen that looks like the box above the Preview drop-down menu in Figure 11-7.

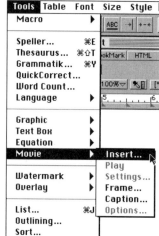

Figure 11-6:
Selecting
the Insert
Movie
command.

The latest on QuickTime

As of August 1995, the latest available version of QuickTime, version 2.1, runs in native (faster) mode on Power Macintosh computers, as does a new version of the Apple MoviePlayer. Both are available online from Apple's ftp site, from eWorld, and elsewhere. They're large files; one user reported a 40-minute download time at 14.4 Kbps.

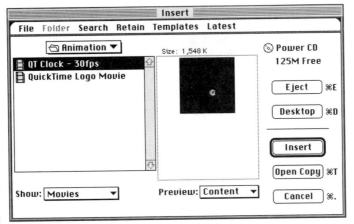

Figure 11-7:
A movie highlighted. Here, you can preview what it looks like.

To make your selection, click the Insert button, and your movie becomes a part of your document.

Inserting a movie is especially useful when you are preparing an *electronic* document, either for a disk or for publishing in another electronic format. The recipients can see the movie in full motion color, assuming they have the proper Mac software.

When your movie appears in a document, it is represented much like what is shown in Figure 11-8.

You'll notice that the graphical representation of the movie includes a little icon that resembles a strip of film. Click on that filmstrip and the QuickTime movie plays. That icon is called a *badge*, by the way, and it distinguishes a QuickTime movie from other graphics in a WordPerfect document.

Subtitles and WorldScript: Better than Berlitz

This is a section that will speak volumes to those of you who speak more than one language. You can work with international languages in your document and then subtitle them in English, if you like, or just about any other language.

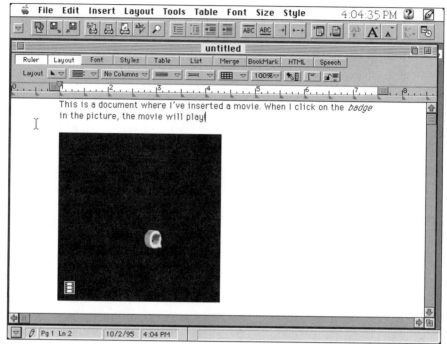

Figure 11-8:
A movie in a
document
window.

These techniques are not for the faint-hearted. You need to be very sure of your command of a language, or have help from those who do, in order to make it all work properly. When in doubt, *find a good professional translator,* preferably one who can give you output in WordPerfect!

That said, you can use WordPerfect to create multilingual documents. In part, that's thanks to WorldScript, which allows the Mac operating system to support multiple languages, including 2-byte character languages such as Kanji, the alphabet system of Japan and China, and Hangul, the Korean alphabet. (You do need to have the language tools required to write in those languages; they are generally available from Apple and third-party sources.)

Creating a subtitle involves highlighting a paragraph and then selecting the Subtitle command from the Language submenu of the Tools menu, as shown in Figure 11-9.

In order to select the Subtitle command, you must have text highlighted in your document. Only then will the option be available from the Tools menu.

After invoking the Subtitle command, you see a window in which you can edit your subtitle. It's shown in Figure 11-10.

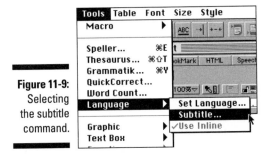

Figure 11-9:
Selecting
the subtitle
command.

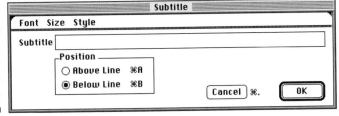

Figure 11-10:
Edit your
subtitle
here.

From the Subtitle dialog box, you can select whether to place the subtitle above or below the main text (and yes, I know, it would be a *surtitle* if it appears above the main text). You can also determine the font, size, and style of the subtitle. Click the OK button and your subtitle appears as you specified.

Part III
How to Wow Friends and Influence Bosses

The 5th Wave   By Rich Tennant

IF BOB DYLAN HAD PURSUED A CAREER IN COMPUTERS.

"PUT HIM IN FRONT OF A TERMINAL AND HE'S A GENIUS, BUT OTHER-
WISE THE GUY IS SUCH A BROODING, GLOOMY GUS HE'LL NEVER
BREAK INTO MANAGEMENT."

In this part . . .

Whether it's a newsletter project, business document, expense report, or scientific research paper, this is the place to turn when you want to scale the loftiest heights of WordPerfect and reach the Everest of word processing. But it's not just the sophisticated stuff you'll learn here, I promise. You'll also find a lot of nifty stuff designed to make your everyday tasks easier. Promise! I'm talking about style sheets, macros, and even, of all things, a Web browser called Netscape.

Chapter 12

All the News That's Fit to Word Process

More Than Letters and Memos

By now, you'll probably agree that WordPerfect is, well, a superior word processor. It does its work efficiently and well, and you can use all sorts of Apple-supplied tools to make your word processing tasks easier.

In this chapter, I move on from simple tasks such as letters and memos and into something a bit more complex, a bit more demanding, and a bit more like the work you can do (and perhaps will do) as you move along with WordPerfect.

By the way, it seems that there's an explosion of newsletter publishing these days. Whether it's for a company, an organization, or even a family event such as the holidays or a family reunion, the newsletter format is super-popular. With a Macintosh and WordPerfect, it's also easy to construct, as you'll see.

Basic Building Blocks of a Newsletter

In its raw form, a newsletter should be a simple thing. Get a name, add some headlines and text, perhaps a graphic or two, and presto!, you're ready to print. In real life, however, this simplicity is hardly the case.

In editing a newsletter, or even preparing one for publication, you quickly learn that the best-laid plans of mice and men often fail. An article is too short, or too long, or there's not enough copy. You've got too many illustrations, or too few. And then there's the fun of putting it all together. It can be as challenging as a good game of chess, where strategy is often as important as skill.

Well, I can't help you select the stories for each issue, but I can move you along on the newsletter-creating trail. In fact, WordPerfect can help you, too, because the program now includes some templates, which makes putting a newsletter together somewhat easier.

Dummies books are supposed to be non-linear volumes where you can jump in on any topic and follow along, but I have to tell you that you will probably get the most out of this chapter — and the newsletter-creating experience — by making sure you understand the concepts contained in the earlier chapters of this book. You will find Chapter 2, which discusses menus, Chapter 6, which covers reports and long documents, and Chapter 7, which covers graphics, all to be very useful here.

The Greyhound Bus Gambit

Before you get creative and try designing our own newsletter, I suggest you start with one of the four templates WordPerfect offers you. I call this method the *Greyhound Bus Gambit* because you're leaving the driving to WordPerfect. (Get it?)

Opening and setting up a template

The newsletter templates WordPerfect supplies are most likely to be found on your hard disk. Go to the File menu and select the Templates command. You'll then see both a list of available templates and the option to open still others, as shown in Figure 12-1.

For now, choose the Open command from the Templates submenu.

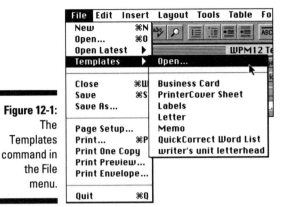

Figure 12-1:
The
Templates
command in
the File
menu.

Your desired file is nestled in a folder within a folder within the More Templates folder. Open the More Templates folder and double-click on the Desktop Publishing folder to open it. Congratulations! You've found the Newsletter templates. For now, pick Newsletter 1 (see Figure 12-2).

Open this template and you'll find something which is common to many WordPerfect templates: fill-in macros, which ask you to supply information, and the program then fits that text to the format you desire. This question-and-answer format (at the beginning of the editing process) makes the early steps in creating a newsletter less taxing (see Figure 12-3).

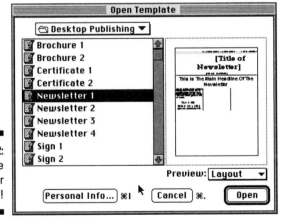

Figure 12-2:
At last! The
Newsletter
1 template!

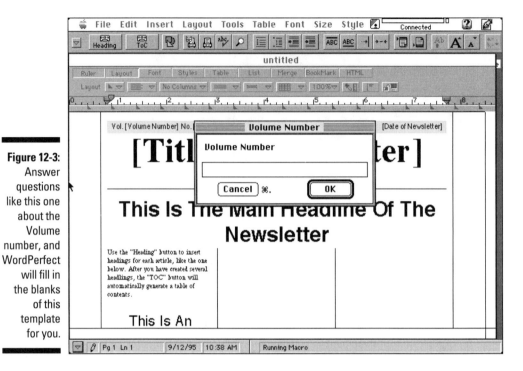

Figure 12-3:
Answer
questions
like this one
about the
Volume
number, and
WordPerfect
will fill in
the blanks
of this
template
for you.

When you open this file, you will be presented with a series of these questions, and when you're done, you'll have a front page that looks rather professional — if a bit empty, as Figure 12-4 displays.

Figure 12-4:
A filled-in
template.

What you get to do now is add headlines and text, as well as build a table of contents (you want people to *find* the articles, right?). Well, putting in the main headline of this newsletter is no problem: just highlight the text and type in what you want to replace the filler copy.

Inserting headings and building a TOC

As you insert your own text, you'll notice two buttons at the top of your screen, which are shown in Figure 12-5. One will tell WordPerfect where to insert an article heading (or headline) in your copy; the other will issue a command to generate a table of contents.

The two buttons work together. Click on the Heading button and WordPerfect will ask you for text which it will then place, in the appropriate type size and style, at your current insertion point. In turn, WordPerfect marks the heading for inclusion in the table of contents on the first page of your newsletter.

Figure 12-5:
Heading and
ToC buttons.

After each heading, be sure to insert some text. You can do this by importing a file or by typing directly into the newsletter. My suggestion: prepare texts as separate files and import them. This method will preserve an original of each article *and* give you something to work with as you prepare your newsletter. (You can also cut and paste text between two open files, but the import method, I believe, is cleaner.)

Eventually, you'll have added all the text you want, as well as headings. When you've done this, position the insertion point in the Contents area on page one, click on the ToC button to generate the Contents listing (shown in Figure 12-6), print out a final copy, and sit back and smile.

Figure 12-6:
Do it right,
and your
TOC will
appear.

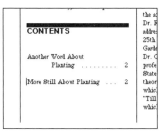

You're not finished yet

Well, almost. Once you see your newsletter in print, you will probably want or need to rearrange some elements of the newsletter. You may need to trim copy — or add some. You might want to place a photo or illustration in the newsletter. You make these changes in the same way as you would in any other WordPerfect document. But be sure that you have completed all macro-based tasks, such as answering the questions for each headline and generating your TOC. The TOC can be changed and regenerated if your page count changes, but doing this once will assure the information is in the right place.

There are three other newsletter templates in the folder where you found this one. Experiment with these designs and make them your own, and you'll be well on your way to creating a newsletter of distinction — without breaking a sweat.

I know, I know, there will be those — perhaps in your office or group — who will gripe and moan about using a "standard" layout that is no different from a hundred other newsletters. If you have elected to use the *Greyhound Bus Gambit,* I suggest two responses. One, if the objectors are strident enough, tell 'em to do the newsletter themselves. On a more productive note, take the suggestion I made in the preceding paragraph (customize the basic layouts you use) and that should quiet most critics. If that suggestion doesn't work, then start with the next section of this chapter.

Multiple Columns and Column Balancing

There are those, however, who relish the challenge of staking their own claim on the digital landscape: of starting with a blank sheet of paper — or in this case a blank screen — and crafting their newsletter in the fashion and style they desire.

They are called pioneers, innovators, and individualists. They are also called fools, usually by themselves, when they see puffy eyes in a mirror after an all-night edit/design session.

For those brave souls — and for you, too — the first element to master in doing a newsletter yourself involves placing multiple columns on a page and then making sure that these columns balance. Figure 12-7 shows a pair of columns.

I'll let you in on a little secret. When you "columnize" text, it is easy to have a "balanced" first page with text moving to a second page, as you see in Figure 12-7. That's because WordPerfect, like any word processor, will make your text fit on a given page. It's when your articles run short, or when you need to put several articles on a page, that column balancing becomes important.

"On Computers" Reports

September 11, 1995   Volume 5, No. 34

Clone Alone: New Power Computing Machine Delivers Real Mac-style Value for Money

By Mark A. Kellner

After years of waiting, moaning, complaining and general griping by Macintosh devotees, the first "clone" of a Mac has arrived, and it works very well. Power Computing's Power 100 machine packs a tremendous amount of power into its machine, and then adds an incredible value in terms of software.

It's about time, Mac fans would say. Walk into any computer store, and you're likely to find more than one brand of IBM-compatible "clone" PCs. But wander over to the Macintosh section and you'll find ... only Apple products. They're great machines, yes and they do great things, but with only one vendor, it's been tough

for any aesthetics questions.

Unlike PCs running Windows, which traditionally have engendered all sorts of tasks while unpacking the machines, the Power 100, like its Apple "cousins," is simplicity itself in terms of set up. In part, that's because the operating system software is pre-loaded, along with a raft of applications programs. The other factor is that, like the Mac, the concept of "plug and play," new to Windows 95, is something the Mac operating system has had for years.

In testing the machine, I've tried to replicate the software/peripherals setup of my Apple Computer-manufactured Power Macintosh

Figure 12-7: The front page of a two-column newsletter with balanced columns.

By the way, *balancing* columns means that when you have a story that runs short, that is, it does not fill a page, you are able to even out the columns so that the copy is balanced.

Creating columns

But before you can balance any columns, you need to create some. In WordPerfect, you can create multiple columns and mix these on a page with regular text. Here's what you do:

1. **Prepare your page as normal.**

   By this I mean type in your copy, or import the text, and lay it out in the order you desire. (Titles and headlines at the top of the page; text beginning at the point you select.)

2. **Highlight the text you want in columns.**

   Doing so will set up WordPerfect to respond to your next task.

3. **Click on the Columns pull-down menu on the Layout ribbon bar and choose the desired number of columns (see Figure 12-8).**

   For this step you *must* have the Layout ribbon bar active.

You can choose up to 24 columns for your document, but there is no way on earth I would recommend that many columns on a page. Two or three columns should suffice — four if you absolutely, positively must. Anything more than four columns across a page does not belong on an 8¹/₂ by 11 inch sheet of paper. It belongs on a standard newspaper page, like *The Wall Street Journal's,* a size known as a broadsheet.

4. Once you've picked the number of columns, release the mouse button and presto!, you get your columns.

Now that wasn't too difficult, was it?

Figure 12-8:
The
Columns
pull-down
menu from
the Layout
ribbon.

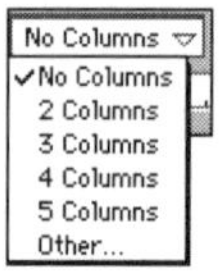

Balancing columns

In balancing columns, the goal is to make then even, of course. The example in Figure 12-9 contains a right column that is one line shorter than the left column, but it is close enough to be generally considered balanced by most people. How to do this? You insert a column break, which WordPerfect uses to shove text over from column A to column B, or from B to C, and so on. (No egg roll cracks, please.)

Before I go into the details of inserting a column break, I think it will help if you and see the columns unbalanced, which is what Figure 12-10 shows.

To balance this bit of text, count the number of lines you find (17 in this case) and divide by 2. That would tell you to place the column break at line 8.5, which doesn't exist. Instead, you place it immediately after line 9, and the remaining 8 lines move over to the right. Place a border below the columns, fiddle with the spacing a bit, and you've got it made.

By the way, you insert a column break by choosing the Column Break command from the Insert menu.

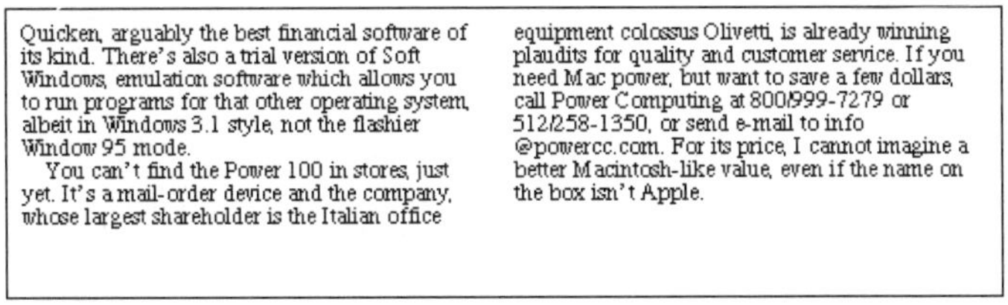

Figure 12-9:
Balanced
columns on
a second
page.

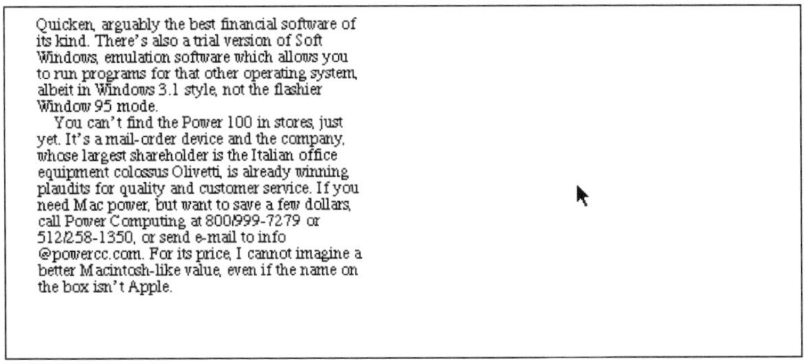

Quicken, arguably the best financial software of its kind. There's also a trial version of Soft Windows, emulation software which allows you to run programs for that other operating system, albeit in Windows 3.1 style, not the flashier Window 95 mode.

You can't find the Power 100 in stores, just yet. It's a mail-order device and the company, whose largest shareholder is the Italian office equipment colossus Olivetti, is already winning plaudits for quality and customer service. If you need Mac power, but want to save a few dollars, call Power Computing at 800/999-7279 or 512/258-1350, or send e-mail to info @powercc.com. For its price, I cannot imagine a better Macintosh-like value, even if the name on the box isn't Apple.

Figure 12-10:
The
unbalanced
text.

Quicken, arguably the best financial software of its kind. There's also a trial version of Soft Windows, emulation software which allows you to run programs for that other operating system, albeit in Windows 3.1 style, not the flashier Window 95 mode.

You can't find the Power 100 in stores, just yet. It's a mail-order device and the company, whose largest shareholder is the Italian office equipment colossus Olivetti, is already winning plaudits for quality and customer service. If you need Mac power, but want to save a few dollars, call Power Computing at 800/999-7279 or 512/258-1350, or send e-mail to info @powercc.com. For its price, I cannot imagine a better Macintosh-like value, even if the name on the box isn't Apple.

Many people who do this sort of thing with WordPerfect do the "big" work of formatting once. They then save that format (as a template perhaps) and call it up every time they need a new document. Because, as you can see, creating new documents from scratch involves a fair amount of work, you might wish to consider the option of reusing the format of old documents.

Drop Caps

There are some people who like the look of a *drop* or initial capital at the beginning of an article. It sets off the copy surrounding it and it can look rather distinguished. The tradition began with the hand-lettered books produced in Europe before and after Gutenberg, and it continues today in many publications. And there's no doubt that a drop cap draws your eye to the page and to the text.

Creating a drop cap (the hard way)

At least two ways exist for you to create a drop cap. One involves working with WordPerfect to do the formatting; the other is a neat little macro. I'll show you how to do the hard stuff first because I'm a slave to the notion that learning the more difficult way is better. If you don't share that belief, or if you are time challenged, skip ahead to the section called "Creating a drop cap (the easy way)."

1. **In the Tools menu, choose the Text Box option and then choose New from the submenu that appears to the right.**

2. **After the text box appears, type the letter you desire for the drop cap.**

3. **Highlight the letter.**

4. **Size the text so that it looks the way you want it to (by choosing a font size from the Font ribbon).**

   My recommendation is at least double the size of body text, and perhaps triple.

5. **Click somewhere off of the text box.**

6. **Click back on the letter.**

   You should now be able to see the sizing handles of the text box.

7. **Using the sizing handles, resize the text box to fit the text.**

   I suggest sizing the text box so that it fits snugly around the letter.

8. **If you want to format the frame of the text box, choose the Frame command from the Text Box submenu of the Tools menu.**

   The Text Box Frame dialog box appears (see Figure 12-11).

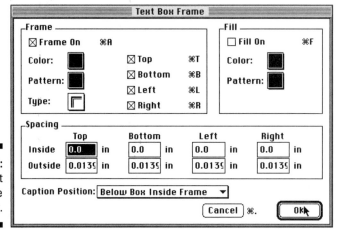

Figure 12-11:
The Text Box Frame dialog box.

9. **Configure the spacing, colors, and patterns of the text box using the options in the Text Box Frame dialog box.**

   If you don't want a box around your drop cap, simply uncheck the Frame On check box in the upper-left corner of the dialog box.

10. **When you are finished, click OK.**

Positioning a drop cap

You will want to position a drop cap in the proper spot — below the first line of text so that the rest of the paragraph wraps around your character. Here's what you do:

1. **Highlight the text box you want to position.**

2. **Go to the Text Box submenu of the Tools menu and choose the Options command.**

   The Text Box Options dialog box appears.

3. **Select the Paragraph option in the Anchor To drop-down menu (see Figure 12-12).**

4. **Check the Wrap Text Around Box option (as shown in Figure 12-12).**

5. **Click OK to exit the dialog box.**

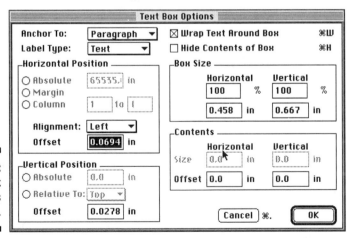

Figure 12-12:
Text Box
Options
dialog box.

Creating a drop cap (the easy way)

You can take advantage of the Drop Cap macro which is supplied with the WordPerfect disk and CD-ROM. Install the Macro using the Librarian dialog box, which you access by clicking the Librarian button in the Preferences dialog box, which pops-up after you select the Preferences command from the Edit menu. Working with macros is covered in more detail in Chapter 18. Fiddling with WordPerfect's preferences is the subject of Chapter 19.

All you have to do is highlight a letter and run the Drop Cap macro. WordPerfect does the rest, creating the box and sizing the drop cap to the proper size. You can then edit the newly-created text box to fit your needs or leave it as is.

Me? I'm glad to know the hard way to create drop caps, but I'm also glad there's a macro to do the work when I need it in a hurry!

Footers and Headers, Borders and Boxes

By now, you might be wondering how to add some of the fancy touches you see in other newsletters. Things such as a line at the top (or bottom) of a page which indicates the name of the publication and the issue, or a border around an article, or maybe a separate box for a piece of text.

WordPerfect has the tools for each of these tasks, and while I've explained these in other chapters, here's a quick review of how to tackle each of these tasks.

Adding a folio line

The line at the bottom of the page of a newsletter, or the top of the page of this book, is called a *folio,* and it indicates what the readers are reading and where they are in the document.

The simplest way to add this line is to begin a header or footer on the desired page (either page one or page two, depending on your publication's style) and type in the desired copy. All subsequent pages will have the same folio line, updated for page numbers.

To do this, select the Header/Footer command from the Layout menu and then choose Header A or B (or the same for footer) and up pops a window in which you can edit the folio line. (A complete discussion of headers and footers is found in Chapter 6.)

Once you've edited the appropriate header (or footer), click on the Close Window button to, well, close that editing window and apply the desired item to your document.

Putting a box or border around a story

As you layout a page, you might want to place a box around a given item. The easy way to do this is to create a text box and place the desired copy within that box.

As you saw in the section on drop caps, text boxes are flexible and offer a variety of options. You can choose from a variety of borders for the text box, or you can use the default border, which is a double-rule box. You can also select a fill pattern to add shading to the text, so it really is set off from the rest of the page. You'll find the tools to do all of these things in the Text Box Frame dialog box.

Select the New command from the Text Box submenu of the Tools menu (as highlighted in Figure 12-13) and a box appears on your screen at your current insertion point. You can type text into this box, and it will expand to fit the amount of text you insert. Once finished, you can go back to the Text Box submenu to select from several options.

The Edit command choice brings up a dialog box that lets you select which text box option you wish to edit: the text, the caption, or the options associated with a text box. Among the options worth noting in this dialog box is the way

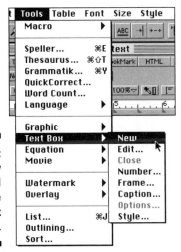

Figure 12-13:
The New command on the Text Box submenu.

you choose to anchor the text box. If you want copy to reflow around the box, you might want to anchor it to the page. If you want the box to stay relative in position to a given paragraph or character, you can select from these options as well.

Editing the text in a text box is straightforward: you use the same commands you'd use in editing any other text.

A *caption* in a text box might be a footnote or other descriptive text that is subsidiary to the main text in a box. When you create a caption, WordPerfect will number it, but you can delete that number and the program will keep track of its number.

The Number command brings up a dialog box that lets you decide how WordPerfect will number your text boxes (see Figure 12-14). You can select from several varieties including the Arabic numerals we use every day (1, 2, 3, and so forth) or Roman numerals (I, II, III, and the like).

Once you've figured out the numbering convention you like — or if you decide you want to forgo numbering — a trip to the Frame command will allow you to decide on whether you want your text box to have a frame and what kind (see Figure 12-15).

As you can see in Figure 12-15, there are plenty of ways you can select just the look you want for a text box frame. First is the Frame section itself; you can turn framing on and off, as well as select the color and pattern of each frame. The pattern options are the same as those found in the graphics tools palette; the color options are the full range of colors you get for fonts in WordPerfect. In this section, you can also decide whether you want the border, or frame, on each side of the text box or on specific side.

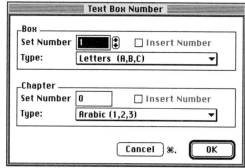

Figure 12-14:
Numbering
options for
your text
box.

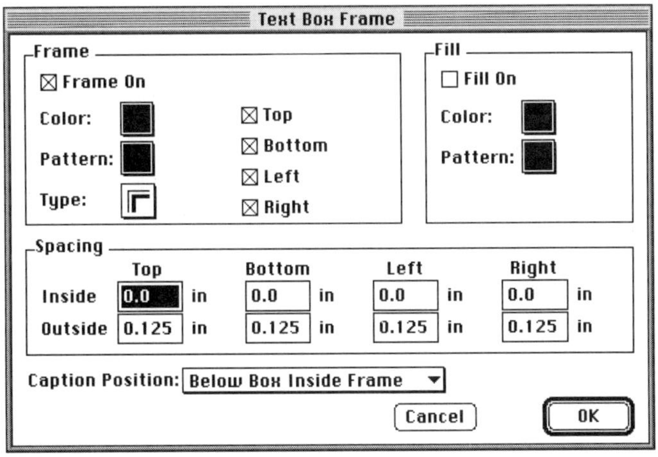

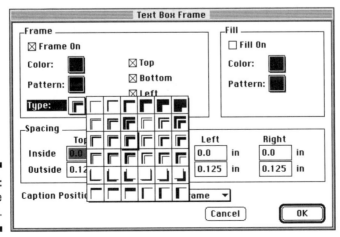

Text Box Frame

Figure 12-15:
Text Box
Frame
options.

Another nice feature of WordPerfect is that you can select from a good variety of text frame styles, as you can see in Figure 12-16. If you can't find the kind of frame you want, you'll want to try the graphics tools and, failing that, go out and hire a graphic artist.

My point is not to be sarcastic, but rather to suggest that WordPerfect offers a good variety of ways to design your border.

The Text Box Frame dialog box also offers you several ways in which you can change the spacing of the frame both from the text within the box and the border outside the box. I have tended to use the default settings, but you can modify these to get a closer "wrap" of text around the box.

Figure 12-16:
Text Frame
types.

At the same time, you can also select the desired position for your text box's caption.

Graphics

We've all heard the saying about the value of a picture: it's easily worth a thousand words. And using graphics and pictures to enhance a newsletter is very much worthwhile — who wants to read just a block of text, anyway?

The mechanics of placing graphics in a document is explained, fully, in Chapter 7. Here, though, is a quick review of what is involved in inserting a graphic in a document:

1. **Place the insertion point where you would like to insert your graphic file.**

2. **Pull down the Insert pull-down menu and select File.**

3. **Highlight the desired graphic if it is in the current directory, or maneuver to where the graphic file is located.**

4. **Select the file and click the Open button.**

   You can also double-click on the file name to open it.

   The graphic appears, full size, at the point where you had your cursor.

When you click on the graphic, sizing handles will appear, and you can use them to resize the image. Or use the graphics screen (accessible from the button bar) to edit and size the graphic.

You can drag the graphic anywhere on the page, and your text will wrap around it.

The above is a very brief discussion of graphics and it assumes two things: you know the Mac's file system and how it works, and you have a greater understanding of using graphics in WordPerfect than is presented here (because, perhaps, you've read Chapter 7).

Text Rotation

One of the things you can do to make a newsletter more attractive is to change the way some of your text looks. Most often, people use different fonts and sizes, as well as effects such as boldface and italics.

Now, it's time to take a different slant on text effects. Try rotating text.

As you can see from Figure 12-17, it's possible to use graphics tools in WordPerfect to rotate the text and give it a different appearance.

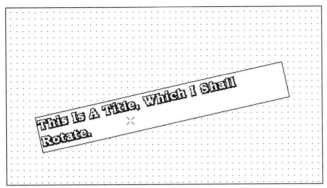

Figure 12-17:
Rotated
text gives
headlines a
new slant.

Rotating text involves the Graphics tools, which are highlighted in Chapter 7. Meanwhile, here's a quick guide to rotating text with WordPerfect:

1. **Highlight the text you wish to rotate and then copy it using the ⌘-C key combination or the Copy command from the Edit menu.**

2. **Click on the Graphics button in the button bar.**

3. **After the Graphics screen appears, create a text box using the Text Box tool (the letter A on the Tool palette).**

4. **Paste the copied text in the text box using ⌘-V or the Paste command in the Edit menu.**

5. **Click on the Rotation Tool and use it to grab a corner of the text box. Click on that corner and hold the mouse button down.**

   As you move that corner in the direction you choose, the text box will move. Stop the movement and the text will appear in the slant you want.

6. **You'll see the text in this new position in the actual document when you click on the Text button (the fountain pen nib) in the button bar.**

   To rotate the box again, you need to go back to the graphics screen.

As you might suspect, you can use various text effects such as outline and shadow to make this text more striking in appearance. Experiment and see what you can accomplish!

Made in the Shade: Put a Screen on a Text Block

Another useful technique for pull quotes and other text items to which you want to call attention is to put a *screen* on a block of text. The screen, which some people would call shading, separates text, as you've seen in the sidebars in this book.

To shade a block of text, you'll need to put it in a text box — using steps that will be familiar from the "Rotating Text" section of this chapter — and then follow some additional steps. Let's see how it's done:

1. **Highlight the text you wish to rotate and then copy it using the ⌘-C key combination or the Copy command from the Edit menu.**

2. **Click on the Graphics button in the button bar**

3. **When you're in the graphics screen, create a text box by using on the Text Box tool (the letter A on the Tool palette).**

4. **Paste the copied text in the text box.**

   Make sure that the text box is remains selected (that is, you can see it's sizing handles) when you perform Step 5.

5. **Click on the Fill tool so that it's button looks like a tipping paint bucket, as shown in Figure 12-18.**

   Clicking on the Fill tool toggles it so that this feature is either on or off. In this set of steps, it needs to be on.

Figure 12-18:
Click on the
Fill tool so
that it looks
like this.

6. **Click on and hold the mouse button down on the Pattern tool immediately below the Fill tool from Step 5. Figure 12-19 shows what I mean.**

7. **With the mouse button still pressed, drag your mouse pointer to black, which is the option in the upper-left corner of the Pattern palette; then let go of the mouse button.**

You can choose a different pattern if you'd like, but I recommend a solid pattern when you're working with text. Often, text becomes to hard to read when placed above some sort of pattern.

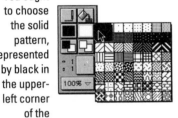

Figure 12-19:
You ought to choose the solid pattern, represented by black in the upper-left corner of the palette.

8. **Click on and hold the mouse button down on the Background Color tool.**

   Be sure to click on the square that appears to be above a second square within the button. Figure 12-20 shows exactly where you need to click.

   A palette of colors will appear and remain as long as you hold the mouse button down. Figure 12-21 shows this Color palette.

9. **With the mouse button still pressed, drag your mouse pointer to the color or shade of gray you'd like as a background for your text box; then let go of the mouse button.**

   WordPerfect fills in the text box with your desired color.

Figure 12-20:
You need to click where the cursor is pointing.

Figure 12-21:
The Color palette appears when you hold the mouse button down.

You have a range of shading choices within WordPerfect, but they don't exactly equal the variations that can be produced by a full-blown desktop publishing program such as QuarkXPress. If your work needs that kind of flexibility, you'll want to get that kind of program.

Captions and Pull Quotes

To add a little spice to your newsletter, you can add illustrations and photographs. But how do you place a caption under the picture? One easy way that I've found is to add a text box below (or alongside) the illustration in question.

Here's a step-by-step approach:

1. **Click on the Graphics button in the button bar.**

2. **After the graphics screen appears, create a text box using the text box tool (the letter A on the Tool palette).**

3. **Type the text you desire in the box.**

4. **Click on the Text button (the fountain pen nib) to return to your document.**

5. **Position the caption where you desire.**

Here's an extra thought about captions in newsletters: You might want to use a *sans serif* typeface (such as Geneva or Helvetica or Ariel) for the caption and set the caption in a size of 8 or 9 points, which should still be legible and will provide a good contrast to your text, particularly if the text is in a serifed font such as Times.

What's a *pull quote?* Some people call it an embedded quote or a blow quote. You see them in magazines and newsletters all the time: a few words from an article in large type, usually set off by a rule above and below the text. Like the headline, this device calls attention to the story and can also make for a brighter layout. Figure 12-22 shows an example.

Creating a pull quote is similar to the steps used for creating a caption: Go into the graphics screen and create a text box using the earlier steps. You'll notice that your text box has, well, a box around it. To remove this box, go back into the graphics screen and select the Pen tool. With this tool, you can erase the border around the text. Then, to put a line above and below the text, use the Line tool.

It sounds more difficult than it is, Freddie, trust me. Take the time to try these steps once or twice. With just a little practice, you'll be embedding quotes with the greatest of ease, I promise.

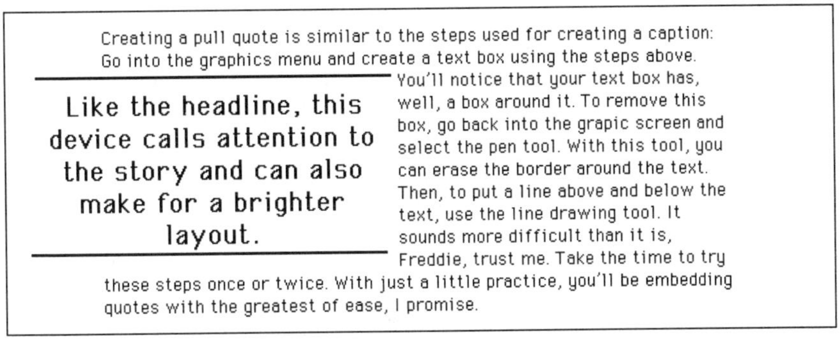

Creating a pull quote is similar to the steps used for creating a caption: Go into the graphics menu and create a text box using the steps above.

> Like the headline, this device calls attention to the story and can also make for a brighter layout.

You'll notice that your text box has, well, a box around it. To remove this box, go back into the grapic screen and select the pen tool. With this tool, you can erase the border around the text. Then, to put a line above and below the text, use the line drawing tool. It sounds more difficult than it is, Freddie, trust me. Take the time to try these steps once or twice. With just a little practice, you'll be embedding quotes with the greatest of ease, I promise.

Figure 12-22: A pull quote.

Printing a Master Copy

Depending on the kind of printer you have, printing can be a simple task. If you are using a laser printer with a resolution of 300 dots-per-inch (dpi) or greater, simply click on the Print button (or choose the Print command in the File menu) and WordPerfect will present you with the Print dialog box. Click on the Print button there, and your Mac will do the rest.

If you are using an inkjet printer, you might have to select a higher resolution than you normally use, and this may require special paper. See your printer's manual for details.

What can you do if you need or desire a sharper resolution than 300 dpi, or if your inkjet just can't cut it. Try your local quick-print shop or service bureau, and you will likely find a copy of WordPerfect and can print at a higher resolution. This topic is discussed in greater detail in Chapter 17.

The beauty of WordPerfect and the Mac is that you can use the same document to get differing degrees of output depending on the printer you select. You can get super-sharp resolution from a document if you want; just find the right printer.

Remember that when you take your file away from your Mac to be printed, other computers may not have the same fonts you do. To make sure your document prints the way you want, carry the fonts you need with you on a separate disk or cartridge. You'll need to install these fonts in the remote computer's System Folder, but you'll also be sure to get what you need in print.

Have an Envoy Deliver Your Newsletter

There's another, novel way to get your newsletter (or booklet, poem, romance novel, and so on) into the hands of your readers, and it doesn't involve paper at all. Instead, let an Envoy do the delivery for you.

 Envoy, which is supplied free on the CD-ROM (or "deluxe") version of WordPerfect, is an electronic publishing program allowing users to create, annotate, and distribute files quickly and easily. Envoy Viewer files can be exchanged easily between Windows and Macintosh platforms, which means documents you create with WordPerfect for Macintosh can be read on systems running Windows 95 — even if they don't have WordPerfect. Envoy's opening screen is shown in Figure 12-23.

Figure 12-23:
The Envoy
opening
screen.

This transportability is becoming increasingly popular among computer users in general. Adobe's Acrobat is a very popular way of creating and distributing electronic files; *The New York Times* uses it every day to distribute an eight-page electronic edition of that venerable daily newspaper.

Envoy, which WordPerfect and Novell created, is a similar distribution method. What's interesting here is that you can publish an Envoy document in a way that readers can highlight and annotate sections of that document. You can then collect the annotated copies you've circulated among, say, a work group at the office, and then print these out or view them and incorporate the changes.

And Envoy works not only with WordPerfect but with a host of other applications including CorelDRAW, FrameMaker, Microsoft Excel, Adobe PageMaker, Microsoft Word, and QuarkXPress. In fact, you can create an Envoy file from just about any Mac application.

What recipients need in order to see your handiwork is the Envoy Distributable Viewer, which also is supplied on the CD-ROM version of WordPerfect for Macintosh. The Viewer lets users view and annotate files created using the full Envoy product.

If you don't want a reader to be able to annotate a document, you can create an Envoy runtime file, which is a self-opening document with its own viewer. This is particularly useful when you're publishing something that you *don't* want to see modified, such as a corporate brochure or news release.

Unlike the HTML features of WordPerfect, however, you can't access Envoy from within the program, except when creating an Envoy file, as you'll see in a moment. Instead, you need to install and launch Envoy separately in order to take full advantage of its features.

Installing Envoy

To install Envoy, place the WordPerfect CD-ROM in your computer's CD-ROM drive and click on the Install Word Perfect icon. Wait for the main installation screen, which is shown in Figure 12-24.

Click on the Install Envoy Viewer button at the bottom of the screen to begin the install. You will first see a document containing the latest information on Envoy and how to use it with various applications, and you can read this stuff on-screen. Another useful option is to print this document for future reference. Once you have either read or printed the document, you can then click the Continue button to install Envoy. The program will ask if you want to restart the computer after installation, and your answer should be Yes. Click that button and Envoy will be installed for you.

Figure 12-24:
The main
installation
screen.

Unlike most other installers, Envoy's install program will put both the basic Macintosh and Power Macintosh versions of itself on your hard disk when you are installing to a Power Mac. Don't ask why, but it happens.

Using Envoy

When you want to create an Envoy document from a WordPerfect file, it's almost as easy as printing a file. You go to the Mac's Chooser and select Envoy as the "printer." Figure 12-25 shows the Envoy option in the Chooser. Once selected, just invoke the Print command in WordPerfect to print your file as an Envoy document.

Another way to create an Envoy document is to drag that document's icon on top of the Envoy program icon. This action launches both Envoy *and* the application which created the file. You will then be guided through the "print to Envoy" process by the two programs.

Your "printed" document will actually be an Envoy file with its own special icon (see Figure 12-26). Click on that icon and you'll launch Envoy's viewer.

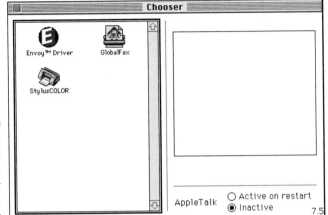

Figure 12-25:
The Envoy
driver is a
Chooser
option.

Figure 12-26:
An Envoy
document's
icon.

When you click on that icon, you will launch the Envoy viewer (see Figure 12-27). At the top of the screen is a button bar representing Envoy's functions. Figure 12-28 shows this button bar.

Many of the functions in the Envoy button bar should be familiar to WordPerfect users. These functions include creating a new document, opening an existing file, saving a file to disk, and printing a file (on a printer, this time). The next four, heading right, involve the kind of cursor which appears on the screen: one that selects text, one that positions the page, and two that zoom in to or out of the text. Continuing right are buttons to add a note to a document, one to invoke a highlighter, one to create hyperlinks to other documents, and one to place bookmarks in a file. The latter function is especially useful when preparing a large file such as a training manual.

The remaining icons on the bar control your movement through the document. You can jump to the first page or the last, and you can page forward and backward one page at a time using these buttons.

Figure 12-27:
An open
Envoy
document.

Figure 12-28:
The Envoy
button bar.

One of the features of Envoy that I most like is the ability to add little sticky notes to documents, which looks very much like those little notes you attach to paper documents (see Figure 12-29). These can travel with an Envoy file, as mentioned, and it's a great way to share comments about a given item.

To create a note, click on the Sticky Note button in the button bar (see Figure 12-30), which brings up a note you can fill in from the keyboard.

In this example, my note features centered text, not flush left, and it's in 14-point Geneva, not 12-point Times Roman. These variations — and others — are possible with the Properties command found under Tools menu in Envoy. Choosing this command opens the Note Properties dialog box shown in Figure 12-31.

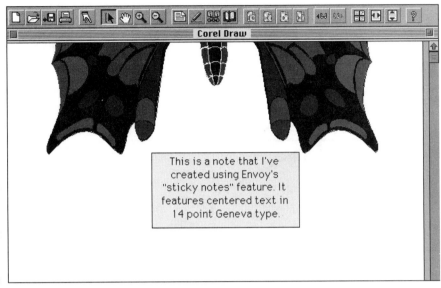

Figure 12-29:
An Envoy
document
with a
sticky note.

Figure 12-30:
The Sticky
Note button.

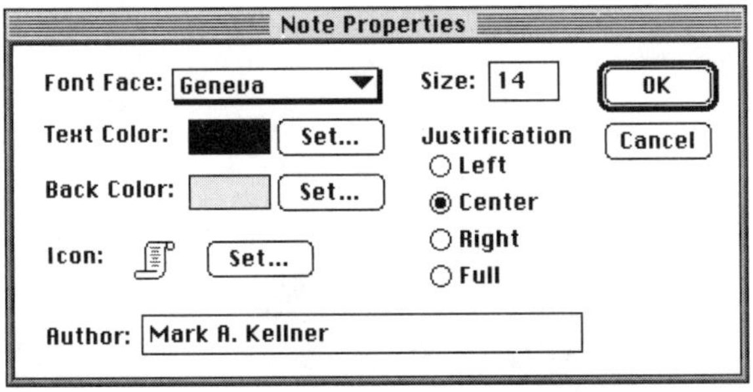

Figure 12-31:
Note
Properties.

You can select any typeface that is installed on your Mac for use in notes, and you can choose a variety of style options. Add an Author name and people will know who wrote which note.

One last thing

Of necessity, this discussion of Envoy has hit only the highlights of its use. The program includes an extensive online help file, which can guide you through preparation and publication of an Envoy document.

"It says,' Seth - Please see us about your idea to wrap newsletter text around company logo. Production!'"

Chapter 13

Takin' Care of Business

- -

- -

*I*f you are in business, you've got enough on your plate to worry about. Bosses and customers (who are sometimes one and the same), fellow employees (or "team members," as the *au courant* phrasing goes), and others who are part of your daily routine — all of these people expect something from you, or want you to expect something from them. WordPerfect can't make them all go away or even make sure you never have problems in the office, but this program *can* help you make your working life easier.

One key to success in business, or so the experts say, is to be organized and precise. Legendary steel magnate Andrew Carnegie (you might have heard of the concert hall he built in New York City) once paid an efficiency expert $25,000 for a simple suggestion: List the tasks you need to do in a day by order of priority and then work down your list until it is completed. As business advanced from the corner store to global corporations, other requirements arose: The accounting department needs an expense report; the personnel office needs to fax material to a headhunter; and marketing wants to keep a mailing list of key contacts at the ready for that new announcement.

All these tasks can be done by hand, but why bother? WordPerfect is here to *free* you from this drudgery, to make life easier for you and to allow you to concentrate on the important things you have to do. But then, you've figured *that* out already because WordPerfect's capabilities let you concentrate on what you're writing and not on the mechanics of doing word processing.

Go Figure — WordPerfect in Business Math

Back in school, I did so good a job at math that I became . . . a writer, and thereby hangs a moral: For those of us who are lousy at math — er, make that, "numerically challenged" — it's good to know that WordPerfect offers some great math features to make life easier for us all.

You use the math features in connection with tables, where you can set up a column that WordPerfect will add up for you. Figure 13-1 shows the kind of table you can put in a management report. It lists the names of three sales representatives, the territories they cover, and what each one sells every month. What's missing? Totals, both for each representative by year and for the group as a whole.

Now, it's certainly possible to whip out the old calculator (or use the Calculator desk accessory provided by the Macintosh operating system) and do the math; one could also utilize pencil and paper. But you're smarter than that, aren't you, Addie? Of course you are!

That's where the special math features of WordPerfect's Table bar come into the picture (see Figure 13-2). They will help you master the math and keep on top of what is happening, number-wise.

The math features appear in a drop-down menu in the Table bar, and they essentially bring a spreadsheet into your WordPerfect table. You can enter simple formulas and have these become a part of your table. Change the numbers and the table will update itself automatically, just like a spreadsheet!

The advantages of this feature should be obvious; the applications might not be. Beyond the idea of using the math features to make your reports a bit snappier, I'll show you how using these features can enable you to make other tasks such as expense reporting a snap.

Figure 13-1:
A table to
sum up.

Name	Region	Monthly Sales	Yearly Sales
Jones, Fred	Mid-Atlantic	$12000.00	
Smith, Martha	South-Central	$15000.00	
Zygmut, George	Pacific Northwest	$13500.00	

Figure 13-2:
The math features in the Table bar.

Yes, Julius, I know: You can work in a spreadsheet, such as Microsoft Excel, and subscribe to a published document you've created from the spreadsheet. But why bother when WordPerfect provides a good substitute, particularly for quick and dirty tasks, or ones that are often repetitive?

Even though a WordPerfect table is *not* a spreadsheet, and even though you are having WordPerfect do most of the work for you, it's good to know some of the basics involved in addition, subtraction, multiplication and division. Another good thing to know is that in computer-speak, * is the preferred multiplication symbol and / is what's used to indicate division. Yes, the symbols are different from what we learned in school, Oscar, but it's not the first time that's happened, is it?

In Figure 13-2, you see that the Table bar has a small field into which you can enter a formula. It's straight math here, spreadsheet style: the value in one cell, plus or times or divided or minus a given number (or the value contained in another cell) equals thus-and-such. Alternatively, you can highlight a group of cells, click on the Sigma button (that's the Greek letter Σ for us non-fraternity types) and it'll do a Sum function for you and insert the formula in an adjacent cell, either to the right or at the bottom of a table.

Be sure that you have room in an adjoining cell for the results the Sigma button comes up with. Otherwise, WordPerfect will tell you that it can't do this job for you.

By using either of these methods — entering the formula yourself or using an automatic function such as the Sigma key — you can speed through some basic math in setting your table. That's one way to keep on top of your work while WordPerfect does the thinking for you.

But wait, there's more. Just like a spreadsheet, you can highlight your numbers and select a *numerical format* for them. The number format can be straight text, numbers with decimal places, or a representation as currency. WordPerfect offers this option in the Math bar (see Figure 13-3): just click on the word Text and your formatting options appear before your eyes. Then select the one you want, and presto!, it's done for you.

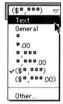

Figure 13-3:
Number
formats
in the
Math bar.

Even though the Currency formatting options have parentheses around them (which in accounting-speak usually indicates a negative number), these are the right choices for representing a number in dollars and cents.

Now take a look at this table after WordPerfect has done its math magic (see Figure 13-4). I've taken the monthly figures and the program calculated them to come up with annual sales per representative as well as total monthly and annual sales for the three people as a group. I then highlighted the group totals and formatted them with bold. As for the titles above each column, I highlighted them and used the Layout bar to center them above each column.

Figure 13-4:
The finished
table!

Name	Region	Monthly Sales	Yearly Sales
Jones, Fred	Mid-Atlantic	$12,475	$149,700
Smith, Martha	South-Central	$15,000	$180,000
Zygmut, George	Pacific Northwest	$13,500	$162,000
TOTAL		**$40,975**	**$491,700**

That's right! You can use all of the formatting tools that can be applied to a paragraph or word or character in each cell of a table! Just highlight the contents of that cell, select the attribute, and click away on the ribbon bars. Now *that's* setting a table!

Now, that I've shown you a simple table, it's time to see what else you can do with the math features.

Expense Reports Made Easier

I hate doing expense reports. Period. Partly it's my fear of math, partly my disdain for organization, and partly because there's rarely been an *easy* way to do them. WordPerfect comes perilously close to changing that viewpoint.

No, the software won't save your receipts for you, but you can move further alone the expense-capture trail by setting up a report that meets your needs — or those of your accounting department.

The easiest method is to jump over to the File menu and open a template. Yes, Agamemnon, WordPerfect has included an expense report template for you and your accounting department to love (see Figure 13-5).

When you first call up this template, you're asked to provide some personal information — your name, title, department, building or mail stop, your extension, supervisor's name, and the purpose of your trip. Then, as with other macro-based templates, WordPerfect fills in the blanks with this information.

The main section of this report is — surprise! — a table. Fill in each blank and, when you're done, click first on the Table ribbon and then the Math button. You'll see the Math bar with the Calculator icon appear. Click the calculator and your calculating chore is done.

You say you need more space to describe something? You can type a fair amount in the description window, but WordPerfect will expand a given cell when more copy is typed in. If you do expand cells, you will want to make sure that the report still fits on one page. Select Print Preview from the File menu and look on your screen before printing out the document.

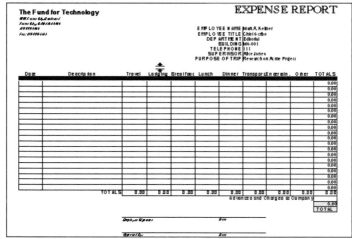

Figure 13-5: The Expense Report template.

You can, within limits, use the new Make It Fit feature of WordPerfect to place that expense report on one page. In the Layout menu, choose the Make It Fit command and adjust the desired page count down to 1. After you've done this, be sure to do a Print Preview in order to avoid a printing disaster!

The other obvious strategy with a template such as the Expense Report is to use it as the baseline, or starting point, for your own design efforts. You can see from this Expense Report template that it's possible to build a complex, table-based form that you can use on a constant basis. Just remember, when you've done your creating for the first time, save the form as a *template*.

Fax Cover Sheets and Faxes

Sending a fax isn't as complicated as doing an expense report — there's usually a lot less math involved — but for some of us, it can present a challenge. There's a cover sheet to be filled in, the pages to be collated, and then the ever-popular trip to the fax machine!

Use WordPerfect, your Mac, and especially a fax modem, and you can do just about everything from your desktop.

If you don't have a fax modem, you need one. Period. End of story. You can buy one that works with a Macintosh for as little as $25 if you're willing to settle for a fax speed of 4800 bits per second, half that of most fax modems. You would be wiser to budget around $200 or so for a 28.8-Kbps data/fax modem, but whatever you buy, make sure it can send and receive faxes with your Mac. My personal favorite is the Global Village fax modem. (Global Village also makes fax modem servers, which function beautifully on Mac networks.)

Let's say you've created a report and want to fax it to your colleague in Phoenix. Fair enough. Here are some steps to use in creating the necessary cover sheet and combining it with the main document to send a fax, either with a fax modem or from a stand-alone fax machine.

1. **Make sure the main document is saved on your hard disk.**

2. **Open the Fax Cover Sheet template from the File menu.**

3. **Answer the personalization questions.**

4. **When you're finished filling out the cover sheet, save it as a separate file (using the Save As command in the File menu) and close that file (using the Close command in the File menu or ⌘-W).**

5. **Go back to your main document.**

   If it is currently open, click on its window to make it the active document. If it's not open, you can probably find it using the Open Latest submenu in the File menu.

6. **Insert a page break at the beginning of your document by choosing the Page Break command from the Insert menu.**

7. **Pull down the Insert menu and select the File command.**

8. **Using the Insert dialog box, maneuver to your cover sheet and click the Insert button.**

   You're almost there!

9. **Now print all the pages together if you plan to manually send your fax, or use your fax software program to send the fax from your Mac.**

Again, consider this road map a starting point for your faxing adventure. As you become more experienced with WordPerfect and its capability to manipulate graphics and text, be creative and see how far you can go.

Mailing Labels Made Easier

To this point, I've covered a few tedious business tasks and how WordPerfect can help you work through them. Here, I deal with one more repetitive task — the mailing list — and how you can make short work of a big job.

The short course is to use the table-filling techniques I discussed previously in this chapter and apply them to creating labels. All you have to do is create a form that fits the label format you use.

To begin, go to the Template submenu on the File menu and choose the Labels template (see Figure 13-6).

What you get is — ta-da! — another table. In this one, you enter names and addresses one-by-one to complete a sheet of labels. You can also add mail merge fields to create a template that you can use with a database or mailing list. Look at Chapter 9 for a discussion of mail merges and how to do this sort of thing.

Either way, WordPerfect can help you make short work of mailing labels. To adjust the size of each label, click on the margin between each cell and move it to the desired position. You may need to experiment a bit in order to create your ideal layout, but WordPerfect gives you the basics with which to start.

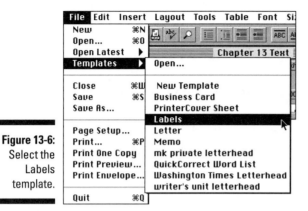

Figure 13-6:
Select the
Labels
template.

Keeping Business Forms and Formulas

From the examples I've shown in this chapter, it's possible to create a small library of business forms and formats for you to use every day. That's the beauty of word processing and computers in general and the specific beauty of WordPerfect. You have the creative tools to not only succeed, but to excel by making short work of repetitive, daily tasks.

One thing to consider is keeping your files organized in folders and subfolders. Whenever you save a document for the first time or save a document as another file (see Chapter 5), you have the option of creating a new folder.

By structuring these folders in an intelligent fashion, you can keep these forms at the ready in order to use them when you have to. You might start with a "master" folder labeled "Business Forms" and then subfolders for specific types of forms or for specific projects.

However you organize files, try to keep your forms in one place on your hard disk. It'll make retrieving them much easier when you need them!

Chapter 14

Lux et Veritas: WordPerfect in Science and Academia

*W*hat good is a word processor if you can't do advanced work with it? Writing letters and memos is one thing, but what about a term paper? Some might quibble, but since few of us know with dead-on certainty just what each of our lives will contain, it's quite possible that you or I might have to write a thesis, use scientific equations, or create a bibliography.

Of course, you might really *need* to do this stuff right now. In either case, this chapter helps you find out how to do the things that make scientific types sing and professors smile.

Make It So: WordPerfect's Equation Editor

OK, OK, so you're not Jean-Luc Picard and you can't command your computer — or your first officer — to make something happen. But when you want to create an equation to demonstrate *how* you make things happen, WordPerfect has something special for you.

It's the Equation Editor (that figures), and using it can save time and add precision to expressing your mathematical or scientific side.

To open the Equation Editor, first pull down the Tools menu and move down to the Equation command. You'll see a submenu of options much like those in Figure 14-1. You can create a new equation, edit an existing one, or select a frame for an equation. (When your document contains an equation, the Options command is also available.) For now, let's select the New command to create an equation. An untitled window and the Equation Editor's tools will appear, as shown in Figure 14-2.

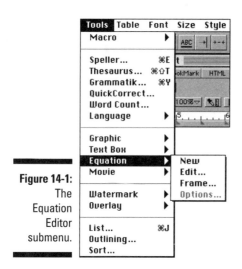

Figure 14-1:
The
Equation
Editor
submenu.

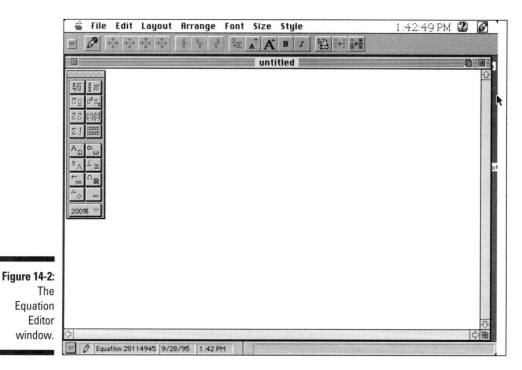

Figure 14-2:
The
Equation
Editor
window.

This Equation Editor screen will remind many of the Graphics Editor screen, and with good reason. You get a blank screen, a tool palette, and buttons, many of which are different from your main document. You use these tools to "sketch" your equation, if you will, just as you might sketch a graphic with the graphics tools, but there are some differences.

For one, the tools with which you work are primarily text-editing and formula-rendering tools. For another, you'll start off with a view at twice the actual size of your equation. This view makes it easier to see what you're doing.

The Equation Tool Palette (shown in Figure 14-3) lets you select from 16 pop-up palettes that let you define functions and insert symbols and characters, such as Greek letters, into your equations. These symbols range from regular and *nth* square roots to diacritical marks, delimiters, operators, and relational operators. If you're writing equations, you know which symbols you need — and it's very likely you'll find them here.

Figure 14-3:
A close-up
of the
Equation
tool palette.

One of the things I always used to wonder about when looking at equations is . . . what does all that stuff mean? OK, the *other* thing I wondered about was . . . how do they line up and position all that stuff on a page. With WordPerfect, the short answer is using the tools on the Equation button bar, shown in Figure 14-4.

Figure 14-4:
The
Equation
button bar.

The longer answer is that you can use each of the tools in the Equation bar to move selected parts of the equation one point up or down from the baseline of the entire equation or one point to the left or right. You can also center and align characters in a given field, and you can increase or reduce the type size of a character by a point, and you can add bold and italic if you like.

Moving components of equations are exacting movements which would have to have been done manually through trial and error were it not for these features. You can experiment, too, but on screen and with Print Preview (accessed via the third button from the right on the Equation bar), thus saving paper!

Editing an equation gives birth to something new and different. What you're creating, therefore, will be part of your document, but it will also be separate from that document. You will need to save the equation on its own, just as you would with a graphic you create using the graphics screen. (This requirement is a good thing, by the way, because it allows you to use an equation in more than one document.) Be sure, therefore, to save your equations when you are finished editing them!

Understand that the Equation Editor is designed to let you *type in and display an equation,* not to solve one. Unlike the math features available in WordPerfect tables, the Equation Editor has *no* computational power.

To, ahem, sum up, the Equation Editor could well be your best friend if you're given to such scientific tasks. But it also illustrates the great capabilities of WordPerfect that let you create exacting, precise presentations of what you want, just as you want it.

More Detailed Footnotes

Back in Chapter 6, I talk about creating footnotes and show the neat editing window you can use to create them.

Adding greater detail to such footnotes is very much a matter of "more of the same," if you will. One of the great secrets of the WordPerfect footnote window is that you can create a footnote that is as long as you would like. It will still appear in the main document in the place where it normally would.

You can also paste graphics — and, by extension, equations — in a footnote. These elements, too, will appear in their usual place in the footnote and main document.

How large can a footnote be? In testing, I cheated: I created a footnote, copied a block of text, and merely kept pasting the block several times. By the time I stopped, my footnote was 1,800 words long — or roughly eight pages of this book.

Is that detailed enough for you? I would hope so.

Just because you *can* have a footnote with 1,800 words doesn't mean you necessarily *should*. As you shall see in the section on "Formatting your thesis," it's important to make sure that your entire document is formatted within the guidelines of what your audience expects, whether that's a professor or a scientific association.

Tables of Authorities

You've got your coffee table, your dining table, your tray table (the one on which you have a TV dinner while watching *Cybill*). So what's a table of authorities and why do you need one?

If you deal in legal matters — or if your boss does — you will probably need to add a table of authorities to a document such as a brief or pleading. This table lists citations of other legal cases or statutes. WordPerfect, long popular in legal offices, recognizes the need to produce such documents and provides an easy way to make it happen. In essence, WordPerfect takes the concept of the table of contents (or TOC) and refines it for legal use.

Just as with the TOC, you'll want to insert your table of authorities at a specific point in your document, either just after the TOC or perhaps at the back of your document, before the index. Where you put it will probably depend on the style used by your organization or the organization that is receiving your document. How you place it is simple:

1. **Find the place in your document for the Table of Authorities and put the insertion point (cursor) there (by clicking, of course).**

2. **Pull down the Tools menu and choose List (see Figure 14-5). Or from the List bar, click the Other button (see Figure 14-6).**

   The List dialog box appears (see Figure 14-7).

Figure 14-5:
The Tools
pull-down
menu.

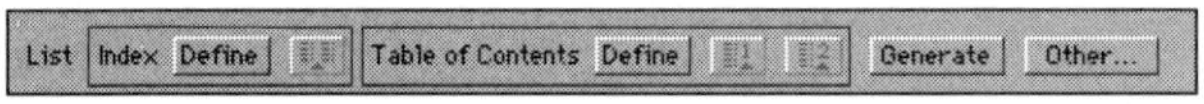

Tools | Table | Font
Macro ▶

Speller... ⌘E
Thesaurus... ⌘⇧T
Grammatik... ⌘Y
QuickCorrect...
Word Count...
Language ▶

Graphic ▶
Text Box ▶
Equation ▶
Movie ▶

Watermark ▶
Overlay ▶

List... ⌘J
Outlining...
Sort...

Figure 14-6:
The List
ribbon bar.

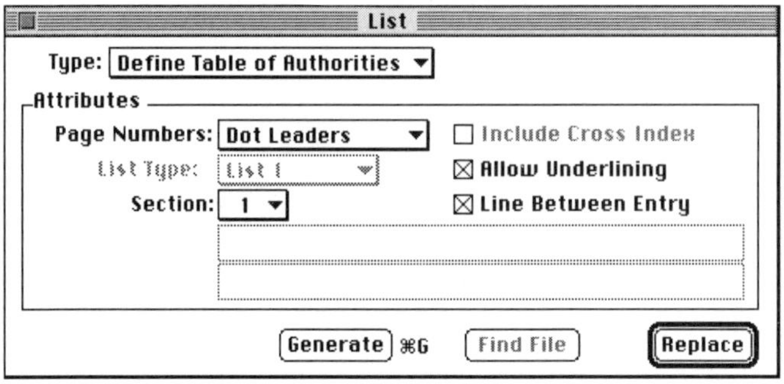

List | Index | Define | | Table of Contents | Define | | | Generate | Other...

Figure 14-7:
The List
dialog box.

List

Type: Define Table of Authorities ▼

Attributes

Page Numbers: Dot Leaders ▼   ☐ Include Cross Index

List Type: List 1 ▼   ☒ Allow Underlining

Section: 1 ▼   ☒ Line Between Entry

Generate ⌘G   Find File   Replace

3. Select the desired attributes for your table.

A dot leader produces listings that look like a table of contents, with a series of dots between the citation and the page number. You can also have the page numbers appear flush right without dots or follow the entry with or without parentheses. You can also tell WordPerfect to produce the table without numbers at all. Other options include allowing the underlining within the table or placing a line of space between each citation.

A table of authorities can cite cases, statutes, and other references, each organized under a different section. As you define your Table, you can also define each section and have as many as 16 sections.

After you've designed your table of authorities, you can start marking citations. For the first time you cite a given authority, you will want to use the Mark Full Form version; subsequent references will require the Mark Short Form command.

To reach each of these commands, follow these steps:

1. **Choose the List command in the Tools menu or click the Other button on the List ribbon bar.**

   The List dialog box appears.

2. **Click on the Type drop-down menu and select the Mark Full Form option, as shown in Figure 14-8.**

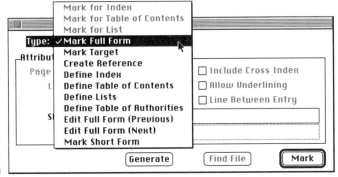

Figure 14-8:
Select the
Mark
Full Form
option.

3. **Type the short form of this citation in the appropriate field of this dialog box.**

4. **Click the Mark button when finished.**

For subsequent references to the same authority, click on the Mark Short Form option, and WordPerfect will link the references together in the final table.

Repeat these steps for each reference (choosing the appropriate Full or Short form marking as needed), and you will be well on your way to getting your table of authorities set.

To generate this table, go back to the List dialog box (you should know how to get there by now) and click on the Generate button. Within seconds (or minutes if you're setting up a very long table) you will have your table of authorities in a way that would make Oliver Wendell Holmes envious.

Defining the Table of Authorities isn't just for lawyer-types, you know. You can use the same method to define a list of figures in a report or a list of tables. Just follow the same steps and revise the "Table of Authorities" title to say what you want. In short, Gladys, be creative and you can do a lot with these formatting tools. Neat, huh?

Bibliographies for Everyone

OK, so you're not Perry Mason and you don't prepare legal briefs every day. But you *are* writing a term paper, report, thesis, or the next Pulitzer Prize winner for history. You need a bibliography, and you want it to look right.

Well, Molly, you've got a friend. Me. Well, actually, your friend is WordPerfect, but I'm here to show you just how helpful the software can be when it comes to bibliography-making. (By the way, this book is an original — more or less — so don't expect a bibliography. Sorry.)

You normally want to place a bibliography at the end of a report, and you will want it to reflect the kind of format that your report reflects. To do this effectively, you can use the List features to create a list, linking bibliographical references in your document and footnotes, and then generating a bibliography (with a cross reference, no less) at the end of your document.

The limits here are only those of your imagination and the conventions of the readership of your report. In other words, if your school uses Chicago style, then stick to it, Leo. But as you've seen with the table of authorities and other generated lists, a little creativity can go a long way.

You will want to pay particular attention to being creative when you are preparing a document to be published in electronic form, on disk, on a CD-ROM, or the Internet. Making additional information easily available to your (electronic) reader will win you plaudits from that reader — I promise!

Formatting Your Thesis

By now, you're probably thinking that I am going to suggest that you somehow use the List features of WordPerfect to format a doctoral thesis. After all, I've made mention of these features in the last two sections.

Sorry, list generating won't help you much here.

However, WordPerfect won't leave you alone when it comes time to prepare a thesis. You can chose from American Psychological Association format, Modern Language Association format, or Turabanian format, a hybrid format for term papers.

These templates promise perfectly formatted term papers that will include page numbers, a running head, and footnotes. The major divisions of the paper are already in the template: title page, abstract, report body, reference page, and footnote page.

When you open one of the term paper templates and answer the fill-in macro questions to determine the name and details of the term paper, you will see the Term Paper button bar at the top of the editing screen like the one in Figure 14-9.

Figure 14-9:
The Term
Paper
button bar.

← add to these

Among the useful buttons here, the Heading buttons allow users to quickly create logical divisions in a report. The Quote button formats the paper for block quotations, and the Note button automates the creation and numbering of footnotes. Click on any of these buttons and you will get instant results.

Creating a term paper represents a lot of research and hard work. When it comes time to assemble the final product, however, these templates can make the final steps less taxing, freeing you up to worry about more important things — like final exams.

The 5th Wave

By Rich Tennant

"A BRIEF ANNOUNCEMENT CLASS — AN OPEN FACED PEANUT BUTTER SANDWICH IS NOT AN APPROPRIATE REPLACEMENT FOR A MISSING MOUSEPAD."

Chapter 15

This Is a Long Distance Call

*I*f you think of WordPerfect as merely a word processor, this chapter will, I hope, help change your thinking. Lurking beneath the surface of this program are powerful communications tools that you can use to be more productive and efficient, and you may even pull ahead of your competition.

With the proper computer connections, you can send and receive e-mail from within WordPerfect, share files with your coworkers, and work smarter, not harder. No, it isn't too much effort to send files with a network program such as QuickMail or cc:Mail, stand-alone programs such as Claris Emailer, or the client software from CompuServe and America Online. But why not make it as easy as possible whenever you can use the tools WordPerfect provides?

The most explosive feature of the new release of this program is WordPerfect's ability to create *and translate* documents for the Internet's World Wide Web using the *Hypertext Markup Language,* or HTML. As of this writing, no other word processor offers *both* abilities, and I don't know of any better way to do it than with WordPerfect. It's so easy, as you'll see, that you might well leave others in the dust with your speed at doing what a couple of years ago was virtually unknown and what in 1994 was considered by many to be a mysterious science.

To give unfamiliar readers some insight into why you should care about the growth of e-mail and the use of WordPerfect for electronic communications, here's a quick and painless survey of how important these forms of communications have become.

The Explosive Growth of E-Mail, Groupware, and the Internet

There's no doubt that our lives today have changed because of e-mail. Whether you work for a major corporation (Hewlett-Packard, for example, has all 85,000 of its employees on e-mail) or are running a small business from home, the digital postman likely rings more than once, and you're glad for that.

Unlike the telephone, and for less cost and trouble than a fax, you can e-mail anyone at anytime and they'll receive the message at their convenience. There's no fax paper to jam (or run out), no long-distance charges to run up (in most cases), and because it's in writing, the chance for a miscommunication is substantially lower than with other means.

Groupware offers a similar opportunity. Using your office network — and external e-mail — you can share files of work-in-progress and get comments from others involved. If Thomas Jefferson and the Continental Congress had these features, the Declaration of Independence might have been produced in one day, instead of several weeks. (We would have lost some great history and a wonderful play, *1776*, but I digress.)

Going beyond e-mail, which excels at one-to-one communications, and groupware, the one-to-many way of sharing files, we reach the Internet. There, it's you (and me) against the world, or more precisely, the World Wide Web. If Andy Warhol saw the future as giving everyone 15 minutes of fame; WordPerfect allows everyone to easily create documents which can be stored for access by millions of people — perhaps 30 million or more worldwide as of this writing, and literally thousands more joining every day.

Whatever your interest, the Internet probably contains a resource that can help you. In turn, you can reach millions with *your* message. But to do that, you need to be able to prepare that message in the proper format, and here, WordPerfect is uniquely qualified to help you.

It's likely that there is nowhere for these trends to go but up. The Internet is increasing in popularity, as noted, and the need for group-oriented work and telecommuting is growing. In the United States, federal statutes will require big cities such as New York, Washington, D.C., Los Angeles, and San Francisco to reduce traffic. That means a growth in telecommuting and a growth in electronic communications. Other nations may well jump on the telecommuting option, particularly as American companies export their work policies overseas.

Let's begin to get some understanding of how WordPerfect works for you in the digital age.

Send and Receive E-Mail with WordPerfect

As noted, you can send and receive e-mail from within WordPerfect. Why do this? For one, it's easier than starting and stopping your work to handle mail. For another, sending a document on the fly becomes easier when all it takes to do this is the click of a button.

Face it, Heathcliffe: if you snooze on the work-sharing front, you lose. Both with e-mail and groupware, your career could turn on how well you share work with others. Share work and ideas, the current wisdom goes, and you'll keep everyone informed and build a better team spirit. The best way to do this is, I believe, is to take advantage of technology to keep your colleagues apprised of your progress, to share ideas, and to get feedback. Easier than looking for a new job, Heath old boy, isn't it?

To send e-mail from within WordPerfect, you need power. More specifically, you need PowerTalk, the Apple utility that uses your AppleTalk network to set up a messaging system. If PowerTalk is installed on your system, you'll see a Mailer button on the WordPerfect ribbon (see Figure 15-1).

Figure 15-1:
The Mailer
button.

When you click on this button, a window opens allowing you to send a document from WordPerfect over the PowerTalk system. You need to either create a new document or have an existing document in mind before starting the Mailer process.

If you know what you're planning to send, you'll see the options in Figure 15-2 on the Mailer window.

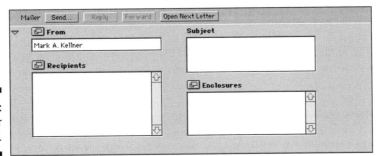

Figure 15-2:
The Mailer
window.

From this bar, select the Subject command and type a subject for your message. Then click on the Recipients icon. This will open the Catalog Browser dialog box (see Figure 15-3), from which you can select who will receive your message.

Figure 15-3:
The Catalog Browser dialog box.

When you send a message, you can select more than one recipient. You can make all of these the *To,* or primary recipient, or you can send a *carbon copy,* or CC, to others, and a *blind carbon copy,* to still others. A blind copy, by the way, is what you send when you want John to see a copy of what you're sending Anne, but you don't want Anne to know that John is seeing this. And *carbon,* for those too young to remember, is what people used to use with typewriters to make more than one copy at a time. It sounds Jurassic, but it worked, way back when!

To finish the addressing of your message, click Done. Then you can click on Enclosures to add more documents to send along with this message, up to 50 documents.

After you've done all this, you're ready to "send" your message. Click on the Send button, and the Send dialog box presents itself. Here, you'll have three choices, as Figure 15-4 illustrates.

Figure 15-4:
The Send dialog box.

If you are sending a file to people who are using WordPerfect, then you'd want to use that format. If it's a mixed environment, you might want to use AppleMail, which preserves the text but not the formatting. If you want your recipients to just see what you're working on, select the Snapshot option. Doing so will preserve a PICT image of the file, which recipients can view, cut, and paste into another document.

What to do if you can't decide on which format to use? Check the Multiple Formats button and then select one or two formats to use. This feature gives your recipients the choice of which format they want to use to view the file.

After you've figured all these steps out, you need to decide on two more things before you can click the all-important Send button. One is whether or not to assign a digital signature to the mail, which is similar to adding a password and adds security to your file. The other is to decide the priority of the message — High, Normal, or Low.

Did you do all that, Jamie? Then you can click Send, lean back in your chair, put your feet up, and dream about that corner office for about 30 seconds. OK, that's enough! Now get back to work!

Sharing Files in Group Settings

Today, the concept of groupware on the Mac is something of a paradox. Groupware includes programs such as GroupWise by Novell and Notes from Lotus Development Corp., which was slated to become part of IBM as of this writing.

The good news is that these programs allow users who are connected to networks (and even the Internet) to share files across the company, or around the world. Using client software for GroupWise or Notes, you can become part of the "group," sending and receiving files via e-mail. Yes, you can do the same thing, locally, with PowerTalk, but GroupWise, for example, works across networks and across platforms and adds some other nifty features. For one, it can keep your schedule in sync with your colleagues, providing a way to set up a departmental meeting (or a company-wide one) without spending an eternity in phone-tag limbo (or voice-mail jail).

The "bad" news — and I use this word with some trepidation — is that while both GroupWise and Lotus Notes have client software for the Mac, you need to be connected, via a local area network or a dial-up telephone link, to a server running Microsoft Windows or IBM's OS/2. Obviously, in most enterprise computing environments, this won't be a problem. But you'll have to look elsewhere for a groupware solution if your organization is standardized on Macs and Macs alone.

Sending a WordPerfect file using these programs is easy: in each case, the document attaches to an e-mail file. Then others can call up or download the file and import it into their programs (Lotus Notes, for example, supports several types of Mac file translation filters).

Using groupware beats plain old e-mail because it can be collaborative and collegial. What's more, with a document being stored in a central location, everyone can access the same information easily, and everyone sees any updates that are made.

If your company is connected to a groupware system, check with your system administrator or IT department to find out how you can get in sync with everyone else, electronically.

Publish and Subscribe

Publish and Subscribe are features that WordPerfect uses to communicate with other applications and are, in fact, part of the beauty of Macintosh's System 7.*x* operating software. For a full discussion, check out *Macworld Mac and Power Mac Secrets,* an excellent book written by David Pogue and Joseph Schorr, and which, oddly enough, is published by IDG Books. *Quelle coincidence!*

If that's the case, why discuss Publish and Subscribe here? In part, because it seemed appropriate, and in part, because they work over networked connections, making it a good choice for this section.

The *Publish* and *Subscribe* terms refer to being able to do two kinds of things to a file. When you publish a document on the Macintosh, you make the file, or a selected portion thereof, available to others for inclusion in files of their own. The info you publish can be a portion of a word processing document, a table from a spreadsheet, or a graphic created with another program. (Not every Mac application supports Publish and Subscribe, but most of the major ones do.)

Similarly, when you subscribe to a document or a portion of one, you sign up for those contents, both *as it is now* and *as it might become.* If you select numbers in a spreadsheet, for example, you will get those numbers as they appear. But if someone changes the numbers in that spreadsheet, for example, your document will change as well. That's because the Publish and Subscribe process is intelligent; if it can access the Publisher file, it will see that something has been changed and pull in the new data.

As you can see, this feature can be rather nifty. If, for example, you prepare a weekly status report, you can set the format once, subscribe to a document (or several) that contain the relevant data, and as the information changes each week, your report will change to reflect the updates. That makes short work of some repetitive tasks, as you can see.

When you subscribe to a given document, make sure that you (a) really want to do this and (b) save a separate copy (on your computer or in print) of each version of that document. Having a changing data set for the weekly report is OK, but you'll want to save each report, most likely, if you ever have to go back and review things.

A Quick Publish and Subscribe Exercise

Mac mavens Pogue and Schorr, whose book is mentioned a few paragraphs back, succinctly explain why Publish and Subscribe hasn't become all the rage in Mac-land: "It's just too darned hard." Yes, Publish and Subscribe is not easy, but I hope a quick exercise will show you the basics. To learn more, get *Macworld Mac and Power Mac Secrets*.

Select something to publish

You start the publishing process by selecting a block of text to publish. For this example, I created a simple table (see Figure 15-5).

Name of Account	Sales Per Month Goal	Actual Sales Per Month	Percent Achieved
Jones Hardware	$500	$450	85 percent
Smith Appliance	$1000	$750	75 percent
Acme Dry Goods	$1500	$1290	86 percent
Reliance Tools	$2500	$1687.5	67.5 percent

Figure 15-5:
The table
is set.

The table in Figure 15-5 is the kind of table you might find in a report, and it's one where the data might change. Now, let's select the table and publish it. The following illustration, Figure 15-6, shows the pull-down menu you use to select the Create Publisher command, which in turn reveals the Publish dialog box. Note that you must select some text before you can publish it.

Figure 15-7 shows the Publish dialog box suggesting how you can publish the item. In this dialog box, I can merely click on the Publish button if I want to publish it in the location specified. Otherwise, I use this dialog box to select the location on my hard disk, desktop, or network where I want to place the file.

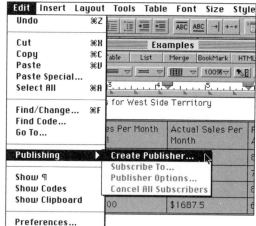

Figure 15-6:
The Create
Publisher
command.

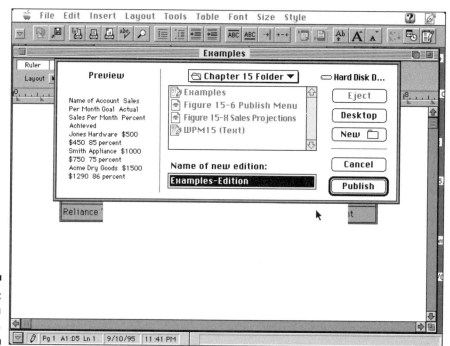

Figure 15-7:
The Publish
dialog box.

Place the published document in a subscriber file

Figure 15-8 shows the table as published in another document, in this case a memorandum. By publishing the table here, I always have it available, and any updates can be reflected instantly.

For our widget sales force, the big news is that sales are up. In the next version of this report, you see the difference. To enter the changes, though, you need to call up the publisher using the Subscribe To command in the Publisher submenu of the Edit menu (see Figure 15-9).

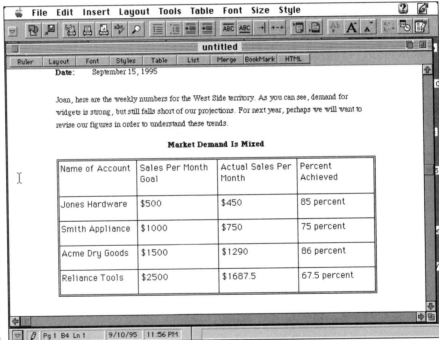

Figure 15-8: The published file.

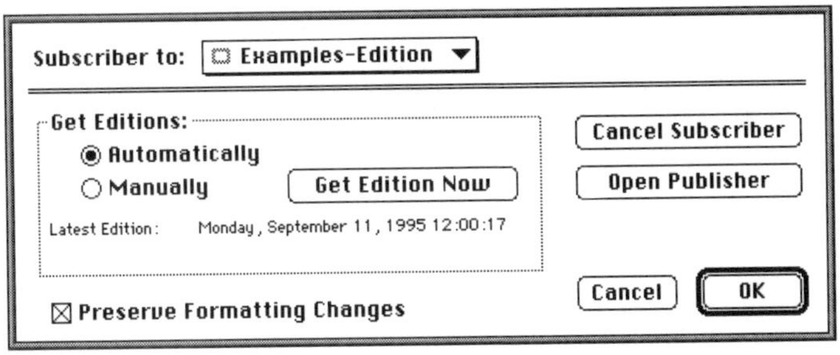

Figure 15-9: Open the publisher with this dialog box.

See the results

After the changes are noted in the publisher file, you can see them reflected in the subscriber file, as Figure 15-10 shows.

Because this is a static book — and because I don't have an animator/illustrator handy to show you the magic, there's no view of the process by which updates are published in subscriber files. But believe me, please, that this happens when you follow the steps. Try it.

In case you're an absolute beginner (and don't worry, we *all*, with the possible exception of Kim Komando, started that way), don't try Publish and Subscribe for the first time on live or important or mission-critical stuff for your job/school/home/organization without a little bit of practice. Even 15 minutes of trying might help you avoid a mistake.

This concludes our quick-and-dirty tour of Publish and Subscribe. We hit just the highlights, friends, but it's not that hard to master.

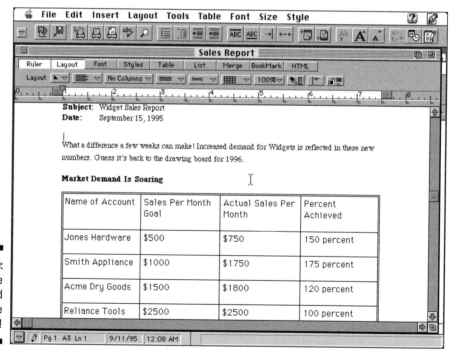

Figure 15-10: Voila! The updated results are here!

HTML for Everyone! (Including You)

At the beginning of this chapter, I mentioned that other word processors can create documents for the World Wide Web, some can also edit such documents without having to resort to add-in software. All this, as mentioned, involves being able to take a plain word processing document and turn it into something with the Hypertext Markup Language, or HTML.

As of this writing — and probably for some time to follow — no other word processor for the Mac can do everything with HTML, the building block of World Wide Web pages, that WordPerfect can. Period. End of discussion.

With WordPerfect, you can master just about everything you'd need to be an Internet publishing genius. You can create an HTML page; you can edit an existing one; and you can *import* a page from the Web, edit it, preview how it will look with the Netscape web browser, and then save it in HTML format.

You get all these features when you buy WordPerfect, plus the Netscape Navigator, which, in my view, is the best Web browser of them all. Using these two programs, especially as integrated by WordPerfect, makes the whole Web-authoring job easier. What others have to master in weeks, you can learn in minutes and put to use almost instantly.

Creating Web documents from WordPerfect

Creating a Web document with WordPerfect is, as you'll see, easy. While you don't need to know as much about the HTML system as you might have to otherwise, it will pay to get some understanding of the Internet and how the Web and HTML work.

I know, I know. All it seems I do is plug books from IDG. Well, they happen to be rather good, including the ever-popular *Internet For Macs For Dummies* and *HTML For Dummies*. But you can also check out Adam Engst's *Internet Starter Kit,* the Mac version, and Daniel P. Dern's *Internet Guide for New Users.* Dan has noodled around this stuff for ages, and few people know more of the Net lore and wisdom.

And even if you don't read another book on the Net, do spend *some* time there looking at Web pages before you start trying to create one. This exploration will help you understand the layout and give you a feel for what happens in a design.

Having done any or all of the above, you're in a good position to understand how WordPerfect deals with the Web. For now, I'll take a basic look at the HTML features in WordPerfect. It is beyond the scope of this book to go into Web page design per se, which is another good reason for scoping out the other books I mentioned.

You'll notice, now, that the WordPerfect ribbon menu includes an option called HTML. Click on it, and you'll see a range of HTML options (see Figure 15-11).

Here, you can set a variety of styles for your HTML document (see Figure 15-12). You can give your page a *head,* or title, that will be seen whenever it is open. You can apply one of six different heading formats and apply any of a number of HTML styles to a selected portion of text.

Figure 15-11:
The HTML bar.

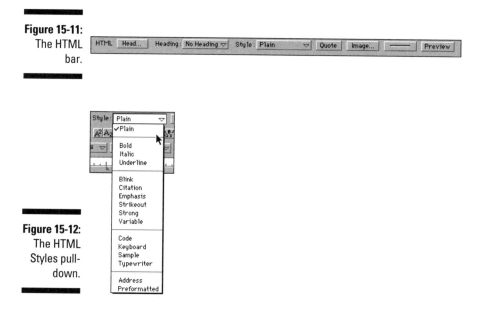

Figure 15-12:
The HTML Styles pull-down.

You'll notice that the styles here are different from those found in the WordPerfect Styles bar. Each of these is designed to create a certain effect that a user sees online. Some are obvious (bold, italic, and so forth); others, such as Address, are designed to spur certain actions. Click on an Address style in a Web page, for example, and most browsers will open up a form with which you can send an e-mail message.

To the right are three more buttons indicating the placement of a quotation (offset from the left and right margins), the insertion of an image, and the addition of a rule (to mark off a section). There's also a Preview button. This one is exciting. As I'm writing this chapter, for example, I could click on the Preview button and see an HTML version of it appear.

Just click on the Preview button and you will launch Netscape (provided you have enough memory) and see an image of your document as it would appear on the Web (see Figure 15-13). This is a great feature for previewing a document, and because it's not connected to an Internet service, there's no online time to pay for.

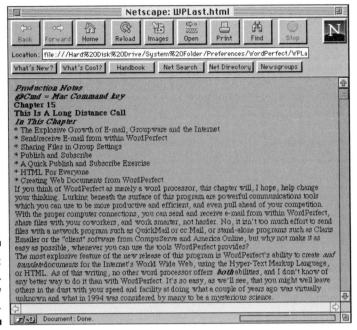

Figure 15-13:
The HTML
Preview
view.

The beauty of this system, in a nutshell, is that you can edit a Web page in much the way you prepare an WordPerfect document. You can then add or use the necessary HTML codes to link people to other pages at your site or other Web sites. And you can preview all this as often as you need until you get it right.

Neat, huh?

Importing Web pages for fun and profit

Along with creating Web pages, WordPerfect allows you to import and edit existing ones. The best way to do this is as follows:

1. **Use your Web browser to find the desired page.**

2. **Save the page as HTML source code on your disk. Remember the file name.**

3. **Quit the browser and launch WordPerfect.**

4. **Open the HTML file (see, I told you to remember the name).**

5. **Edit as usual.**

Now that's not too much of an oversimplification. Just as you can use WordPerfect's editing tools to create a Web page, you can apply them to the editing process, which by now, should be rather familiar. If not, take a gander at some of the earlier chapters.

WordPerfect's Web page importing feature is a great way to capture some of the knowledge that's out there on the Web and put it to practical use — within legal limits, of course.

Just because something is on the World Wide Web does not mean it's free for the picking. If an item is copyrighted, you *must* get the permission of the copyright owner before republishing or recirculating it; particularly if money is to be involved. Even if it is not copyrighted, the polite thing is to ask permission — e-mail might suffice — to reprint something. Using copyrighted material for your *personal* edification is OK as far as the law goes.

Chapter 16

A Matter of Style(s)

• •

• •

The Wonderful World of WordPerfect Styles

We each have a style of our own. For some of us, it can be *GQ* or *Glamour.* For others, it's Sears or Penney's. And for techno-dweebs like me, maybe Goodwill.

In fact, we each have *styles* of our own. We dress one way for work and another way when we go to a major public event. We can be casual on Sunday and button-down on Monday. (I'm wearing a doctor's scrub suit as I write; it's cheap, comfortable and casual. Besides, I can pretend I'm on *Chicago Hope* and can sing like Mandy Patinkin. Yeah, right.)

In the same way, most of the documents you will create with WordPerfect will each have a style of its own — or more than one style, just like you and me during the course of a week.

But changing styles in WordPerfect does not mean going through a clothes closet or down to the local thrift shop. Being stylish in WordPerfect involves using some rather powerful tools to create just the look you want, and you then use that look again and again.

You can even be super-creative here, linking styles to keystrokes and, with keystrokes, linking styles to each other. Styles can also be contained in template documents, making sure WordPerfect sets up a template in a given way but then uses your preferred style when the actual "new" typing begins.

In short, style-conscious WordPerfect users can exploit some pretty powerful tools to make their work easier, while the output is consistent in its appearance.

If you work in an office where there are plenty of repetitive typing tasks — a law office, real estate firm, or bank, to name but three — these styles can really help make your life easier. And if you're planning to use WordPerfect to write the next multi-million-dollar Hollywood screen play, styles can help you there, too, by linking various formatting tools to create your document more quickly and easily.

It can't be stressed strongly enough: The whole point of WordPerfect styles is to make your work simpler. In so doing, you can automate your work to the point where it moves much more quickly than you thought possible. That alone should be motivation enough to learn — and use — styles.

Let's begin with the Styles ribbon bar. You may have seen it in Chapter 3. It deserves a more detailed examination here.

Meet the Styles Ribbon

If some of the following sounds familiar to you, it's because I discussed it briefly back in Chapter 3.

Click on the Styles button at the top of the WordPerfect window to bring up the Styles ribbon, which lists all of the styles available to you in either WordPerfect or the current document (see Figure 16-1).

Figure 16-1:
The Styles
ribbon.

Click on the button immediately to the right of the word "Styles" and you'll see a list of styles for your document. In my case, as you can see in Figure 16-2, the number of styles I can select is rather large because there are many different elements in a book manuscript. If you work in a large organization, or for several individuals, or on many different types of documents, you could end up with a list that is as long as this one, if not longer.

None

Bullet
Bullet 2
Bullet 2 Last
Bullet Last
caption
Chap #
Chap Title
Code
Code Last
Document
Footer
Footer1
Header
Heading 1
Heading 2
Heading 3
Heading 4
Intro Head
Intro Last
Intro Text
M1
M2
✓Normal
Note
Num 2 Last
Num Last
Num List
Num List 2
Production
SB body
SB Code
SB head
SB indent
Step body
Step Head
▼

Figure 16-2:
My styles
list for this
book.

The next four buttons on the Styles ribbon, moving from left to right, tell WordPerfect to Update a style, create a New style, Edit an existing style, and set Options for a style. I'll explore these options as I move through the process of using styles.

Styles and document translation

All of the styles I used in formatting this book were provided to me by my editor at IDG books, who happens to use Microsoft Word 6 for the Mac (poor fella). If you find yourself transferring files back and worth with users of Word 6, rest assured that your documents will retain their styles.

For example, if I save a WordPerfect 3.5 file as a Word 6 document (using the Save As dialog box), that Word document will have all of the styles I created in WordPerfect. Along the same lines, if I open a Word document in WordPerfect, my WordPerfect version of that document will have all of its styles.

How to Create a Style of Your Own . . .
or Modify an Existing One

Me? I always like to go to Brooks Brothers or a Ralph Lauren store, maybe Rick Pallack's in Sherman Oaks . . . sorry, I got sidetracked. Here, I'm going to get into the nuts and bolts of working with WordPerfect's styles, and I'm going to help you create your own styles.

(Then again, considering I'm still in that hospital scrub suit, maybe I'm *not* the best person to go to for fashion advice.)

A small digression: why *would* you want to create a style? As mentioned in the first section of this chapter, a style lets you apply various formatting features — and even text — consistently throughout a document. That's a great time-saver, and it makes for consistency in documents, something readers — and picky clients and bosses — always appreciate.

OK, that said, let's create a style.

You don't have to have any text selected before you create a new style.

You begin by clicking the New button in the Styles bar, which brings, you guessed it, the New Style dialog box, which happens to be shown in Figure 16-3.

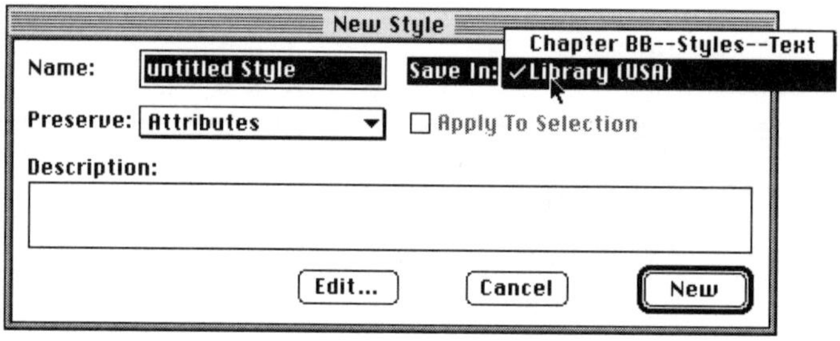

Figure 16-3:
The New
Styles dialog
box with a
Save In
location
selected.

New Style

Chapter BB--Styles--Text

Name: untitled Style   Save In: ✓Library (USA)

Preserve: Attributes   ☐ Apply To Selection

Description:

[Edit...]   [Cancel]   [New]

The first thing you'll notice about the new style option, is that you have the chance to *name* the style. You can name your new style anything you like, of course, but it's best to pick a *functional* name like "Chapter Heading."

The next decision you'll need to make is whether you want to save the Style with your document or in the Styles library, shown here as **Library (USA)**, a WordPerfect default. Again, the choice is yours.

Here's some help in making that decision: if you save the style with your document, the style will go along for the ride when you send that document to others. If you save it in the Library, it will not travel with your document except as specific attributes to a given item (subhead, chapter title, what have you). In this latter case, the recipient of a document can save the style by highlighting the desired section, creating a style from that text, and saving it.

Your next decision is to determine which attributes you wish to preserve in your new style (see Figure 16-4). It can be a case of all or nothing at all here: You can preserve the attributes and formatting in your style, the attributes or the formatting, or none of the above. The default is to save the attributes of the current style into the new style.

Figure 16-4:
The
Preserve
pop-up
menu
presents
you with
some
cryptic
choices.

What do I mean by attributes and formatting? I wish WordPerfect had chosen more descriptive terms. Anyway, here's the rundown:

- ✔ **Attributes** refers to the character formatting of the style — its font, font size, color, and type style (bold, italic, underline).

- ✔ **Formatting** refers to things like tab settings, margins, line spacing, and other non-character related formatting.

For most styles, I recommend that you choose to preserve *both* attributes and formatting. For example, let's say you want to create a style for indented text, like the following paragraph:

> *This is a paragraph of indented text. Its attributes (character formatting) are black, italic text in 9.5-point Cheltenham. Its formatting includes line spacing of 11 points and about a half inch of left indent.*

If I want the indented text style to look like the preceding paragraph every time I use the style, I need to retain both formatting and attributes. If I want to create a style for a centered, 18-point heading, I also need to preserve both formatting and attributes. If, however, I want to create a style that simply produces blue text, I really only need to preserve the attributes and not the formatting.

Also in the New Style dialog box is a field for you to add a description to the style. This description can be particularly useful if you have many similar styles to juggle. For example, you're working for three lawyers and need to create different styles for each lawyer's contracts. You can name the styles "Contract/Bill," "Contract/Nancy," and "Contract/Sue," while in the description you clarify what each style contains. This way, if someone else needs to use these styles (or if you forget just which style contains what), you'll have a ready reference. Of course, you don't *have* to insert a description, but it can help if you do.

You have one other choice to make before you can leave the New Style dialog box. You can choose to save the style as new by clicking on the New button. Or you can Edit your style. (Your third choice is to scrap everything and cancel the operation, but let's assume you don't want to do that.)

Click on the New button and the style is saved and you're returned to your document.

Click the Edit button, however, and up pops a window like the one shown in Figure 16-5.

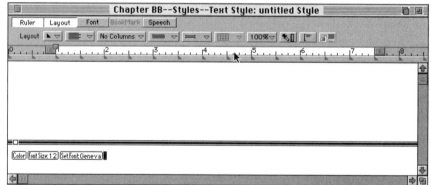

Figure 16-5:
A window
for editing
styles.

The Edit Styles window is at first glance similar to a regular document editing screen, but there are some crucial differences. First, you'll notice that here, the Reveal Codes feature is turned on. You *see* every code, every formatting feature, and every space, which allows you to *edit* these attributes easily and with certainty: once you change an attribute, it is applied to every appearance of the style in your document.

So in this Edit Style window, you apply all of the formatting you'd like your style to contain. You can specify line spacing, tabs, text color, font size, font style, and a whole lot of other stuff. If you want your table headings to be 12-point bold Times, then create a Table Heading style with those features. If you want your body text to be green and right-aligned, you can do that, too.

The other thing to notice is that you can enter some type in the Edit Style window, and that text will appear every time you invoke the style. An example: by now, you've probably noticed that every illustration in this book is accompanied by a caption that includes the word "Figure" along with a colon. I can type "Figure:" at every turn, which, frankly I did for a good chunk of this book, or I can type the word once in the style and presto!, the word appears as if by magic.

Well, Ezra, it's not really magic, but when you use the Styles menu to create your style, then you're in control.

Please remember that there is virtually no limit to what you can include in a Style in terms of formatting — but remember that whatever you include will appear *every* time you use that style.

When you have finished editing your Style, click on the close box in the upper-left corner of the window, and you'll return to the New Styles dialog box. Click on the New button and your style is saved!

Repeat this process for each style you wish to create and you'll soon have a library of styles to use in a variety of situations and documents.

Linking Styles, Why You Should, and Other Options

How do you link one style to another, and, Lavinia, why should you?

Let's take the second part of that question first. You can use styles to establish the layout of a document. You can have one style for a heading, one for introductory information, one for subheads, and one for text. As you move from item to item in creating your document, you need to select each separate style each time you want to use it.

This process becomes more cumbersome in documents in which you use certain styles over and over, particularly in a given order. Remember that mention of a multi-million-dollar screenplay? Well, Hollywood types like their screenplays in a given format, and you can use the styles to create that format. Repeating the selection of each style, each time, however, can become tedious.

That's where linking comes in. If you want to go from one style to another to another, *automatically* within a document, you can. Here's an example: This book has a Chapter Number and a Chapter Title style. With linking, after I type a chapter number, apply the Chapter Number style, and press the Enter key (*not* the Return key — more on this detail in a sec), the next line automatically has the Chapter Title style. With linking, you can alternate between styles within a document, if you prefer. And you can change horses in midstream — as you'll learn about in just a moment.

Creating a link

How to link? It's a simple, step-by-step process:

1. **From the Styles ribbon, click the Options button.**

   The Style Options dialog box appears, as shown in Figure 16-6. Your current style will be highlighted.

Style Options	
Style:	**Location:**
Normal	Library (USA)
Note	Library (USA)
Num 2 Last	Library (USA)
Num Last	Library (USA)

Based On: Normal ▾

Link To: Heading 1 ▾

☒ Show Style in Menu ⌘S

Keystrokes:
⌃⇧N [Assign...] ⌘A [Remove]

Description:

[Done]

Figure 16-6:
The Style
Options
dialog box.

2. **If the currently highlighted style is not the one to which you'd like to link a second style, then scroll through the list of styles to find the one you want.**

3. **In the Link To pop-up menu, find the style that you want to link to the first style.**

4. **Click on the Done button and WordPerfect will establish your link.**

Activating your link

It's easy. You apply your first style to the text you want. When you press the Enter key — *not* the Return key — you will activate your link to the next style. In other words, the next line will be coded with the second style in the link. For more details, see "The hidden secret of the Enter key" sidebar.

TIP

The hidden secret of the Enter key

If you're using an AppleDesign or Extended Keyboard with your Mac, then you will notice, on the far right, the numeric keypad and its Enter key. This key can be very useful with WordPerfect styles.

Use the Enter key and you can transition from one style to the next. It's really neat if you're moving sequentially through styles from one to

the other. It'll speed up your work and improve your consistency.

But remember, I'm talking about the Enter key here, *not* the Return key. Keep that in mind and your life will be happier.

(Special thanks to Marsha Terry of Novell, Inc.'s WordPerfect unit for this tip and its explanation.)

Assigning Keystrokes to Styles

If you look carefully at Figure 16-6, you see that a combination of keystrokes — in this case, Ctrl-Shift-N — has been assigned to my Normal style. If I highlight a piece of text and press this combination, the style is instantly changed to Normal.

Assigning a keystroke combination to a style may seem to go against the Macintosh way of relying on the mouse and pull-down menus and the like. But it's a very good way of working productively, especially if you're a touch typist who likes to keep your hands on the keys.

To assign a keystroke to a style, just follow these steps:

1. **Click the Options button on the Styles ribbon.**

   The Style Options dialog box appears.

2. **In the Styles list at the top of the dialog box, highlight the style to which you want to add a keystroke combination.**

3. **Click the Assign button in the Keystrokes area of the dialog box (see Figure 16-7).**

Figure 16-7:
Click the
Assign
button here.

Keystrokes:

⌃⇧N   Assign... ⌘A

Remove

The Assign Keystroke dialog box appears, as shown in Figure 16-8.

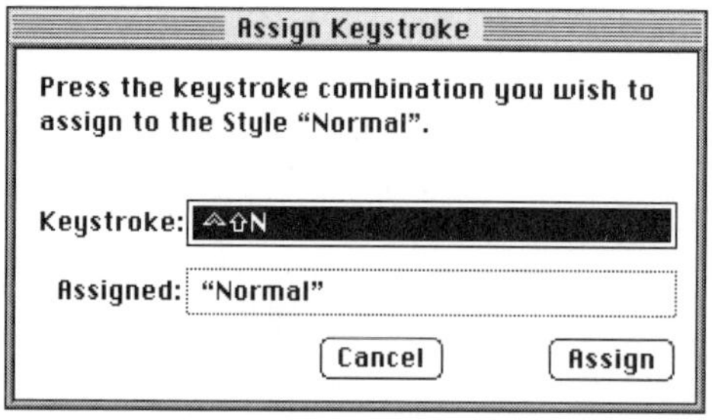

Figure 16-8:
You press
your desired
key
combination
in the
Keystroke
field.

Assign Keystroke

Press the keystroke combination you wish to
assign to the Style "Normal".

Keystroke: ⌃⇧N

Assigned: "Normal"

[Cancel]   [Assign]

4. **Press the keystrokes you want to assign to the style you chose.**

   WordPerfect will show you whether the combination you desire has been
   assigned to another function, such as Option-F3, which is used by
   WordPerfect to count words.

5. **When satisfied, click the Assign button.**

   Your keystroke combination will be listed in the Style Options dialog box
   when you highlight the style it's assigned to in the list of styles.

To remove a keystroke assignment from a style, go to the Style Options dialog
box, select the style from the list, highlight the combination in the Keystroke
area, and then click on the Remove button. That style will no longer have the
keystroke combination.

Chapter 17

More Than You Ever Wanted to Know about Printing

*1*n other chapters, I've looked at the quick and dirty way to print (Chapter 1), and I've examined other related subjects such as GX Printing (Chapter 11) and printing a final copy of a document such as a news-letter (Chapter 12). Here, I'll try to answer just about every other question you might have about printing and maybe some you hadn't thought about asking.

I said it before and I'll repeat: There's little good in creating a great-looking document if you can't print it out. Even if your ultimate goal is electronic publishing — creating electronic books, let's say, or pages for the World Wide Web (see Chapter 15) — you will want to see a hard copy at some point, or perhaps your boss or investors will.

On the Apple Macintosh more than with any other computer system I've used, it's easy to sit back, relax, and let the computer handle the hard work of printing for you. Most of what needs to be configured is handled by the operating software, which for most of us is System 7.x or System 7.5.

But you're braver and smarter than the rest of the crowd, aren't you, Gerty? You want to do more. You want to really make things happen. Well, you can. Using the information in this chapter, WordPerfect and you will turn out sparkling documents, presentations, and other fun things. And they'll come out the way you want because you took the time to read this chapter. Let's begin.

Some Basics of Printing

The chief basic, I suppose, is to really get to know your printer. Whether it's laser or inkjet, you should take the time to familiarize yourself with every aspect of the printer's operations. That means remembering the three most important initials in computing. No, they're not IBM, Stephen. They're RTM, which stands for "Read the Manual."

In the dark recesses of these volumes, you'll find all sorts of nifty details, like the fact that each and every computer printer ever made has to be connected and turned on in order to work properly. But you'll also find out how to best operate that printer so that you get the results you desire.

However, it's just as important to read *between* the lines of a printer manual as it is to read what's on the lines. Manufacturers always present the *best case* scenario of how their product will perform. Unfortunately, we sometimes run up against less-optimal situations in our work — not enough RAM, conflicting software, whatever. Reading the manual is often best augmented by getting in touch with other users, both in user group meetings and online. For information on both of these options, see Chapter 23. And when you're ready to use your printer — especially if you're installing a new printer — be sure to test it out *before* a critical deadline approaches.

It may seem obvious, but other things to be certain of before printing, particularly a mail merge (see Chapter 9) or other project, are that you've got sufficient paper and ink or toner in the printer, and that, if you're using preprinted letterhead, you've got it properly inserted in the printer so that the print appears where you want it. Sounds dumb, I know, but I've seen it happen on more than one occasion in an office — and never at the right time.

Color Printing

One of the great revolutions in computing during the last few years has been the availability of color printers, both inkjet and laser, for Macintosh users. Apple Computer has led the way on both fronts, with its Color StyleWriters and Color LaserWriter, but companies such as Hewlett Packard, Tektronix, and Epson aren't far behind with machines in their lines that are designed for Mac users. Both Epson and HP now offer color inkjet printers that work with both Macintosh and Windows-compatible systems.

Because WordPerfect lends itself to producing so many different kinds of documents — and even documents that aren't really "documents," such as presentations — you can expect to have the occasional need to print in color.

The next three subsections provide some tips for color printing.

Use color sparingly in text documents

If you do a main headline or logo in red, use red in spots throughout the text, but don't switch from red to blue to green to yellow to mauve — at least not without some scheme for color use in mind. Without planning, it'll look like something an over-anxious five-year-old might do. Of course, if you're printing something for five-year-olds, be as wild as you like.

You can go way beyond the primary colors in WordPerfect

The color palette offers a wide variety of choices, and these should be faithfully reproduced by your output device. Among the best in this regard, in my experience, are the Apple Color LaserWriter (which can be found in every Kinko's in the U.S.), the Apple Color StyleWriter, and the Epson Stylus Color.

You may need special paper

When printing in color, remember that your printer may require special paper for the higher-resolution printing that shows off your text and graphics to best advantage. Inkjet printers from Hewlett-Packard and Epson, for example, require special paper when printing at ultra-high resolutions, such as Epson's 720 dots per inch. This paper isn't cheap — between 8 and 10 cents per sheet; the process uses a fair amount of ink; and the printing itself can take minutes, not seconds. But the results can be nothing short of spectacular, and once printed on the special paper, the ever-popular color photocopier can take over and generate either duplicates or transparencies, if desired, in multiple copies.

Black-and-white concerns

Black-and-white printing is pretty straightforward; after all, it's what most of us do on a computer every day. It is worth remembering, though, that Apple's more recent laser printers incorporate PhotoGrade, a technology that reproduces photos and some other art at up to 105 lines per inch, which is much sharper than some other laser printers. Still other lasers, from Apple and others, print text at 600 dots-per-inch, which is twice as dense as a 300 dpi printer, resulting in nicer-looking print. These features can be especially useful when printing a newsletter.

Confused about lines-per-inch and dots-per-inch? Read a good book on desktop publishing (yes, Dolores, one such as Roger C. Parker's excellent *Desktop Publishing and Design For Dummies*) or ask your local printer. Either way, you'll get a good explanation of these technicalities, and along the way, you'll pick up some knowledge of how printing works, and you'll develop strategies for making your printed work look better.

Printing to a Postscript File

There may come a time when you will want or need to print to a PostScript file. It could be you need to transport the document to another system (such as the one at a service bureau).

The most common motive, as noted by David Pogue and Joseph Schorr in their book *Macworld Mac and Power Mac Secrets* (yes, another IDG title!) is to create a file that can be sent to a PostScript printer using the LaserWriter font utility. Because all the PostScript codes have already been generated in creating the PostScript file, the printing is much faster than if you wait for the printer to do it all at once.

That's good to know when you've got a big file to print and if you have the disk space to contain the PostScript file. Given those two situations, you're a candidate.

To print to a PostScript file, you must have a PostScript-compatible laser printer driver installed on your Macintosh. Issue the Print command from either the File menu or use the ⌘-P combination. Where you see Destination in the Print dialog box, choose the PostScript File option and then click on the Save button (see Figure 17-1). You'll be prompted for a destination for the file. By default, "PostScript" is appended to the file name, but you can change it if needed.

Figure 17-1:
Select
PostScript
File as the
destination.

```
LaserWriter "LaserWriter 4/600 PS"          7.1.2    [ Save ]
Copies:[1]        Pages: ◉ All  ○ From:[   ]  To:[   ] [Cancel]
Cover Page:   ◉ No ○ First Page ○ Last Page
Paper Source: ◉ Paper Cassette  ○ Manual Feed
Print:        ◉ Black & White   ○ Color/Grayscale
Destination:  ○ Printer         ◉ PostScript® File
☐ Every Other Page ⌘E   ☐ Print Backwards   ⌘B
☐ Print Selection       ☒ Print Overlay Layer ⌘L
```

Once you print a document to a PostScript file, that PostScript file can be used *only* for printing. You cannot open the PostScript file to edit the document's text or formatting. Therefore, be sure to save your work in a WordPerfect-compatible file format *before* printing a PostScript file!

Page Setup

The Page Setup dialog box, which you can access by choosing Page Setup from the File menu, is a way to tell WordPerfect what kind of paper you'll print on, which in turn determines the amount of text and graphics you can put on a given page. It's all a part of making your document fit the available space and giving you a layout that is easy on the eyes. Figure 17-2 shows the Page Setup dialog box for my printer.

Please note that different printers have different Page Setup dialog boxes with different kinds of available options.

Figure 17-2:
The Page
Setup dialog
box for my
Epson
printer.

```
EPSON                                              [ OK ]
© Seiko Epson Corporation 1994    StylusCOLOR v1.20A
                                                  [ Cancel ]
Paper Sizes: [ Letter        ▼ ]                  [ Options ]
                                                  [ Paper ]
Orientation: [👤][👤]    Reduce or [100]%        [ Help ]
                          Enlarge:

Binding Width [0.0]  inches
☐ Fractional Character Widths  ⌘F  ☐ Save As Default⌘S
```

I discuss the paper size and page orientation features in the next section, but it's also useful to note that you can select a percentage by which WordPerfect will enlarge or reduce the image printed on the page.

You can set other print options by clicking on the Options button. These options vary by printer, so, again, be sure to RTM before plunging into parts unknown.

Page Orientation and Paper Size

No, I'm not talking about orienting yourself on a page, or even when you're out in the country on a hike. More simply, it's useful to know that you can print pages in one of two orientations: portrait or landscape.

Portrait orientation puts the narrow edge of the paper at the top, very much like a photographic portrait. It's the layout preferred for letters, reports, memos, manuscripts, and the like. Why? Because the Portrait layout limits the length of a line across the page, so a reader's eyes won't easily tire when reading your document.

Landscape, on the other hand, puts the longer edge of a sheet of paper at the top, making it the ideal format for large tables and presentation-style documents. You can put text in a landscape format and still keep it legible if you break it down into multiple columns.

Figure 17-3 shows the part of the Page Setup dialog box where you determine your document's orientation.

Figure 17-3:
Portrait and
landscape
orientations.

When trying to decide on a page orientation, you ought to be aware of the *print area* that your particular printer supports because almost every printer requires a certain built-in margin into which it cannot print. (Some more expensive 600- and 1200-dpi printers can print to the edge of the paper, but most printers don't have that feature.)

Related to paper orientation is, of course, the *size* of the paper on which you are printing. Some printers allow you to print on all sorts of paper sizes, as you can see in Figure 17-4. Along with the traditional 8½-by-11-inch letter size and the 8½-by-14-inch legal size, you can print on a variety of other sizes that have been configured by the printer manufacturer, along with various envelope sizes. Check your printer manual for the specifications of these sizes; what looks like a "Statement" to you might not be a statement to them!

Figure 17-4:
Paper size
options for
the Epson
Stylus Color
printer.

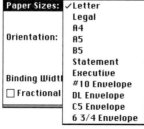

Page Ranges

After you finish tweaking the options in the Page Setup dialog box, return to your document, and finally hit ⌘-P to get the Print dialog box, it might be worth noticing that you can select a range of pages in a document to print. I use this feature all the time to print just the first page of a long document to see how it will look, or to print a page that might be missing or damaged. Figure 17-5 shows the Print dialog box of my Epson printer.

Figure 17-5:
I've
selected a
page range
so that only
the first half
of my
upcoming
epic poem
gets printed.

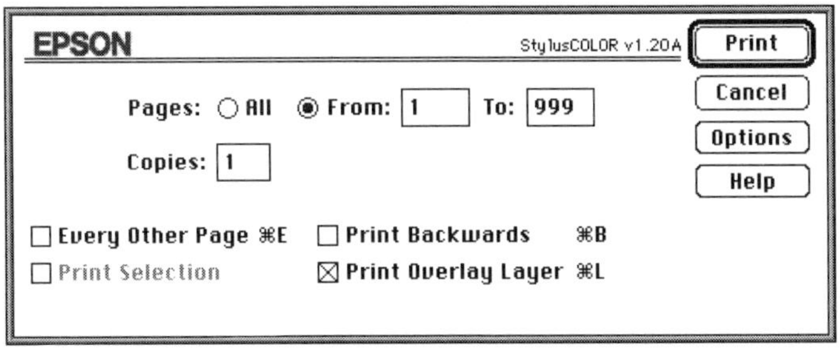

EPSON	StylusCOLOR v1.20A	**Print**

Pages: ○ All   ● From: `1`   To: `999`

Copies: `1`

Cancel
Options
Help

☐ Every Other Page ⌘E   ☐ Print Backwards   ⌘B
☐ Print Selection   ☒ Print Overlay Layer ⌘L

Specifying a page range is simple. In the Print dialog box, click on the From field and enter your beginning page number. Then press the Tab key. Your cursor will jump to the To field automatically. Now enter the ending page number in the box. Click on the Print button and that range prints.

Simple and effective. Just what you were looking for, right?

Chapter 18

All Things Macro...Plus Bookmarks and Hyperlinks!

• •

In This Chapter

▶ Getting the big picture

▶ Using WordPerfect's supplied macros

▶ Writing your own macros

▶ Editing macros

▶ Using bookmarks and hyperlinks

• •

Getting the Big Picture

Like it's Macro — get it? OK, we'll save the yuks for later. After all, a *macro* in WordPerfect is not something that's necessarily large, but rather a way of combining keystrokes and functions to make your life easier.

Let's say you're a secretary to someone who dictates letters. Lots of letters. A whole pile of letters. (I know of one secretary who literally *cringes* when her boss goes *away* from the office! Said boss returns with a pile of those little micro-cassette tapes just stuffed with dictation.) You get the idea.

Let's say that every single letter — or virtually every single one — that your boss dictates ends the same way:

> Cordially,
> Jane Jones,
> President-for-Life

It's just six words, but try typing it 20 or 30 times in a day and your brain will ache. Mine does just thinking about it.

So what if . . . what if you could type those five words just once and have WordPerfect do the job every other time today, and every other time you type a letter after today? How much time — and how many brain cells — would you save?

Time and little gray cells aside, Hercule, you *will* save effort when you reduce that closing block into a macro. Other functions can be macro-ized, too, as you shall see.

The uses for macros are almost as varied as your imagination. All it requires is the knowledge of some simple steps, a little patience, and perhaps some shameless thievery will automate just about everything you need to do.

Then you'll have some free time for more important things. Like shopping.

The Macro Is Your Friend

Think of the macro as one of your invisible friends. I know you gave all that up at around age five or six. (OK, OK, it did take me a little longer. What's it to ya?) But unlike your imaginary playmates, and unlike that rabbit Harvey, made famous by Jimmy Stewart, your friend the macro can do some really useful things.

First, let's figure out where to find macros.

WordPerfect ships with several macros preinstalled; others can be added. Right now, I've got 12 different macros permanently installed on my system, ranging from the relatively simple to the sublime (see Figure 18-1). The Arrow macro, for example, draws an arrow in the length you want, and puts the arrowhead on either the left or right end of the arrow — or both. The Clean Text macro takes a piece of text imported from an Internet newsgroup or online service, which usually comes with a hard return at the end of each line as well as additional spaces, and cleans the text so you can use it in other documents.

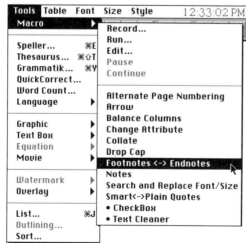

Figure 18-1:
Macros are
found here
on the
Tools menu.

It goes without saying that anything you pull down from the Internet or any online service may be subject to copyright and therefore you cannot reprint or republish it commercially or for general circulation without permission. When in doubt, check a reference book on the subject of copyright, or ask a lawyer who is knowledgeable in such matters.

The point is that a WordPerfect macro can do all sorts of wonderful things to make your life easier and more productive. The macros that come with the program — and others that are available online (see Chapter 23 on where to find them) — will help you achieve your productivity goals.

Using WordPerfect's Supplied Macros

Using an existing macro — either one supplied with the program or one downloaded — is easy. Just go to the Tools menu, choose the Macro command, and from the submenu that appears to the right, select your desired operation from those that appear in the bottom portion of the submenu.

Macros will generally operate at the place your insertion point is located when you initiate the operation. If you're in the middle of a page, the macro will start there. The main exception to this rule is when you're running a macro that involves working on a preselected block of text, such as the Clean Text macro discussed earlier. For a macro like this, you need to first highlight the text on which you want the operation performed.

Unlike other word processors I've known, the beauty of WordPerfect's macros is that they don't involve keystrokes to invoke. It's point-and-click easy, which takes a lot of the effort out of the process. (You can, however, *assign* a keystroke combination to a macro should you desire.)

Writing Your Own Macros

The easiest way to create a macro is to let WordPerfect do it for you. How? By letting the program record your keystrokes, saving the recording as a macro, and then playing it back.

Here's what you do:

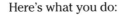

1. **From the Tools menu, choose the Macro command and then choose Record from the Macro submenu, as shown in Figure 18-2.**

   The New Macro dialog box appears, as shown in Figure 18-3.

Figure 18-2:
Selecting
the Record
Macro
command.

Figure 18-3:
The New
Macro
dialog box.

2. **Name the macro by typing a name in the Name box.**

   As you might guess, it's most helpful to name the macro with something easy to understand, such as "Signature Block" for the letter-ending lines I talked about before. You might want to abbreviate the name, however, if you need to create similar macros for different people in your work group.

3. **Use the Save In pop-up menu to select a place to save the macro (see Figure 18-4).**

   Save the macro in the Library and you'll be able to use it in all your documents. Save the macro with your document and it is only available when you use that particular document. The choice depends on your needs. If you're creating a form for your sales force to complete, adding macros could help everyone speed their work. If you're working on your own, then you will probably want to save your macros in the Library for future use in other files.

4. **Check the Show Macro in Menu option if you would like your macro to appear in the Macro submenu of the Tools menu.**

   The choice again depends on your needs and on how much you want to wade through in a pull-down menu. My advice? Put the macros you use most often in the menu and leave the rest on the side.

Figure 18-4:
The "Save In"
selection.

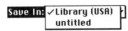

5. **To begin recording your macro, click on the New button, which closes the dialog box.**

   You are returned to your document window. WordPerfect opens a second window in the background with the name of the macro in the title bar. In this window, all of the commands you use and text you type are recorded.

6. **On your document screen, type the text and initiate the commands you want to include.**

   Everything you type and select will be recorded until you tell WordPerfect to stop recording.

   WordPerfect will record all of the keystrokes you care to enter in a macro, both in terms of text and keyboard-issued commands. It will *not* record mouse clicks, and you'll get a warning message to that effect any time you try to move your mouse. Don't worry: You can use the mouse in some limited fashions, but you'll need to use ⌘-A, for example, to select the entire contents of your document.

   Don't worry if your macro contains too much — or too little. You can edit it after you've recorded the macro.

7. **When you have finished with your macro, select the Stop Recording command from the Macro submenu of the Tools menu (see Figure 18-5).**

8. **In the resulting dialog box (see Figure 18-6), click the Save button to save your macro for posterity, at least until you edit it.**

Figure 18-5:
Selecting
the Stop
Recording
command.

Figure 18-6:
The Save
Changes
dialog box.

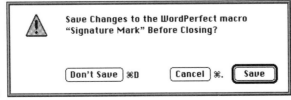

Editing Macros

OK, so you've recorded your macro. But you're not quite happy with what you've recorded. You want to change it around. Here's how:

1. **Select Edit from the Macro submenu on the Tools menu.**

   The Edit Macro dialog box appears (see Figure 18-7).

2. **From the list of macros in the Edit Macro dialog box, choose the macro you wish to edit.**

3. **Click the Edit Content button.**

   The selected macro appears in a document window with its name in the title bar. You can now edit the macro as if it were a normal text document.

```
┌──────────────────────── Edit Macro ────────────────────────┐
│                                                             │
│  Macro:                        Location:                    │
│  ┌──────────────────────────────────────────────────────┐  │
│  │ AutoFill             ▶       Library (USA)          ▲ │  │
│  │ Alternate Page Numbering     Library (USA)           │  │
│  │ Arrow                        Library (USA)           │  │
│  │ Balance Columns              Library (USA)           │  │
│  │ Change Attribute             Library (USA)          ▼ │  │
│  └──────────────────────────────────────────────────────┘  │
│                              ┌─ Keystrokes ──────────────┐  │
│                              │            ▲  ( Assign... )│  │
│  ☐ Show Macro In Menu        │            ▼  ( Remove )   │  │
│                              └───────────────────────────┘  │
│  Description:                                               │
│  ┌───────────────────────────────────────────────────┐    │
│  │                                                     │    │
│  └───────────────────────────────────────────────────┘    │
│                    ( Done ) ⌘.      ( Edit Content )        │
└─────────────────────────────────────────────────────────────┘
```

Figure 18-7: The Edit Macro dialog box.

Here, you need to be somewhat careful if you are planning to edit one of the supplied macros. Figure 18-8 shows the contents of Drop Cap macro.

Here's a rundown of the buttons at the top of the macro window:

✔ **Save:** You use this button to save the changes you made to the current macro.

✔ **Save As:** After making changes to a macro, you can use this button to save the edited macro with a new name. This button is helpful when you want to use the basic elements of a current macro to create a new macro.

✔ **Save Text:** Pressing this button saves the macro as a text document.

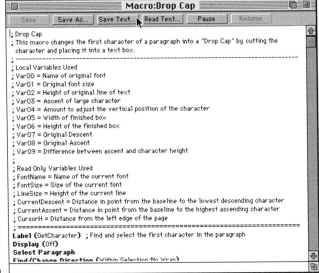

Figure 18-8:
What the
Drop Cap
Macro looks
like.

✔ **Read Text:** You use this button to import text (text that you may have saved from another document or macro) into the current macro.

✔ **Pause:** If you are in the process of recording a macro, you can press this button to temporarily pause the recording.

✔ **Resume:** After pausing, click this button to continue recording a macro.

As Figure 18-8 demonstrates, WordPerfect uses a rather sophisticated language for creating macros, and you'll find full details of this language not in the WordPerfect documentation, but online in the Help files (see Chapter 23).

For your own macros, editing is much easier, since it is very likely that you won't use as many of the fancier commands that the WordPerfect folks use.

When you are finished editing a macro, click the Save button and the macro will be stored in the place where it was originally housed. To save the edited macro under another name or in another place, click the Save As button.

Using Bookmarks and Hyperlinks

Two other automated features of WordPerfect allow you to mark places in a document and to both collect those place markers and link them together.

These features are bookmarks and hyperlinks, and I think they're pretty neat.

A bookmark in WordPerfect is very much like a regular bookmark in a regular book, and yet it's not. It can indicate a place marker for where you've left off in a document. But it can also serve as a souped-up table of contents that not only indicates certain sections of a document but also takes you there.

To create a bookmark

1. **Highlight the text where you want to place the bookmark.**

2. **Click on the BookMark button to reveal the BookMark/Hyperlink ribbon.**

   The BookMark ribbon is shown in Figure 18-9.

Figure 18-9:
The BookMark/ Hyperlink ribbon.

3. **Click the Mark button to create a bookmark.**

   A dialog box appears asking you to name the bookmark.

4. **Give the bookmark a name and click OK.**

   The bookmark will appear in the BookMark drop-down list, as shown in Figure 18-10.

Figure 18-10:
The BookMark drop-down list shows available bookmarks.

To access a bookmark, select it from the BookMark drop-down list in the BookMark ribbon. When you select a bookmark, WordPerfect immediately takes you to that point in the document.

You can also arrange bookmarks in alphabetical order from that drop-down menu, and you can issue an UnMark command as well. When you select the UnMark command, the UnMark dialog box appears (see Figure 18-11).

Select the bookmark you want to remove from the Remove Mark drop-down list and then click OK. It's history.

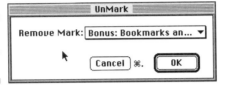

Figure 18-11:
The UnMark
dialog box.

To create a hyperlink

Hyperlinks are similar to bookmarks — but much more powerful. You can create a hyperlink to a bookmark, yes, but not only to a bookmark within a document. You can link to bookmarks in another document, an Internet Web page, or a macro, which in turn runs the macro.

Here are the steps to follow in creating a hyperlink:

1. **You should first create the bookmark, document, Web page, or macro you want to link to, although you *can* create your hyperlink first and then create the linked item later.**

2. **Open the WordPerfect document in which you want to create the hyperlink.**

3. **Click the BookMark button to reveal the BookMark/Hyperlink ribbon.**

4. **Highlight the elements in your document that you want to use as the hyperlink.**

5. **Click the Create button in the Hyperlink section of the BookMark/Hyperlink ribbon.**

   The Create Hyperlink dialog box appears, as shown in Figure 18-12.

Figure 18-12:
The Create
Hyperlink
dialog box.

6. **Using the Link To drop-down list, select the type of link you want to create and fill in any required information.**

The list of linking options is shown in Figure 18-13.

Figure 18-13:
Link To
selections.

Link To:	Current Document
	Other Document...
	Internet Address
	Macro...

7. **Click the Create button to finish the job.**

The hyperlinked area of your document will be underlined and in blue (on color displays, of course).

Now, whenever you or someone else is in a document, you can use the hyperlink to jump just about anywhere. This feature is a great way to take compound elements of a large document, break them down into smaller files, and view them either individually or dynamically using links.

You can edit a hyperlink by positioning your cursor on the link in question, going to the BookMark/Hyperlink ribbon, clicking on the Disable Links button (to stop WordPerfect from jumping at your command), and then clicking on the Edit button. You'll return to the Create Hyperlink dialog box, from which you can select other places to link to or make any other changes you desire.

To delete a hyperlink, disable links once again and click on the Remove button. Your link will be history, and you can enable links to reactivate the other ones.

Hyperlinks are new in this release of WordPerfect. Experiment with them, and you will probably end up discovering a raft of uses that will help you in your work.

Chapter 19
A Matter of Personal Preference

*O*ne of the words we sometimes forget is that the machines we use, by and large, are *personal* computers. Apart from the bad old mainframe and minicomputer days, the box sitting before you is largely yours — even if it's on a network. As you work with your Mac, you'll know that you can customize its appearance in a dozen different ways to make the computer more like you, reflective of your own style.

Well, Humbert, the same applies to WordPerfect. Yes, I know, I know, it's a big program created by a big corporation and it adheres to certain standards. That's true. And a lot of that standards-toting is necessary; it allows you and me to do things like exchange files with each other, or with people running WordPerfect or another word processor (is there another brand?) over on a PC running Windows or Windows 95.

But the way you look at the world is different from the way I look at the world. For one, I'm sitting in Reston, Virginia, right now, and you might be in, oh, Fairbanks, Alaska. For another, I might like to type on a screen where black letters appear on a white background, while you might prefer white lettering on a blue background.

WordPerfect can't help you with your geographic location (unless you use it to prepare a résumé that takes you from Fairbanks to Florida), but you can change the way that you see your computer screen — at least a little — if you know what to do.

That knowledge comes from understanding the Preferences customization tools WordPerfect offers. By the way, that is just what I'll be showing you in these next few pages. (Some of the topics discussed in this chapter were touched on in Chapter 2; others are mentioned elsewhere. This chapter is designed for those who want to *really* customize WordPerfect.)

A Little Background

A long, long time ago — many years ago — OK, back in the mid-1980s — those of us who hadn't yet had the epiphany that the Macintosh was a better computing platform struggled along with MS-DOS. To use a word processor there, you had to configure it and tailor it and mold it to your will, or thereabouts.

James Fallows, who earlier had fame as a speech writer for Jimmy Carter, and who later achieved still more fame writing about the Pacific Rim for *The Atlantic Monthly*, got his 15 minutes of computer-industry fame for writing an article — in *The Atlantic,* no less — helping people debug the DOS (and CP/M) versions of WordStar, an ancient and venerated word processing program. By showing people how to customize a piece of software, Fallows came close to being worshipped as a god by tens of thousands of users.

Now, I'm not expecting veneration for showing you how to customize WordPerfect on your Mac, but then, it's much easier now than it was in the '80s — and you can't say that about everything, can you? (If you don't *remember* the '80s, then you were either too young or too stoned. In the case of the former, *you* will have your own decade to look back on, I promise. If, however, you *were* there in the '80s and don't remember it, there are several clinics you might want to investigate, starting with Betty Ford's.)

Working with Some of the Preferences

Where was I? Oh, yes, it's easier to customize the Mac version of WordPerfect than it ever was to customize the DOS version of WordStar because WordPerfect puts the choices right in front of you.

Once you select the Preferences command from the Edit menu (see Figure 19-1), you get to designate the preference you want to change via the window shown in Figure 19-2.

On this screen, you see a dozen different preference categories, from something called Environment (which has nothing to do with tree hugging) to Word Services (is that when your words need fixing?) to HTML, which, if you are not familiar with those letters, is explained in Chapters 15 and 20.

As you might suspect, the purpose of these categories is to allow you to make choices for each of these features. Let's examine these in some detail.

WordPerfect 3.5 For Macs® For Dummies®

Cheat Sheet

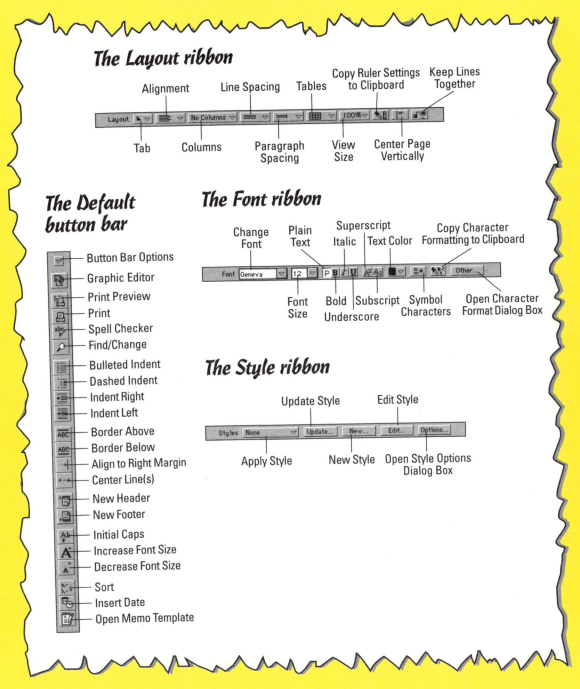

The Layout ribbon

- Alignment
- Line Spacing
- Tables
- Copy Ruler Settings to Clipboard
- Keep Lines Together
- Tab
- Columns
- Paragraph Spacing
- View Size
- Center Page Vertically

The Default button bar

- Button Bar Options
- Graphic Editor
- Print Preview
- Print
- Spell Checker
- Find/Change
- Bulleted Indent
- Dashed Indent
- Indent Right
- Indent Left
- Border Above
- Border Below
- Align to Right Margin
- Center Line(s)
- New Header
- New Footer
- Initial Caps
- Increase Font Size
- Decrease Font Size
- Sort
- Insert Date
- Open Memo Template

The Font ribbon

- Change Font
- Plain Text
- Superscript
- Italic
- Text Color
- Copy Character Formatting to Clipboard
- Font Size
- Bold
- Underscore
- Subscript
- Symbol Characters
- Open Character Format Dialog Box

The Style ribbon

- Update Style
- Edit Style
- Apply Style
- New Style
- Open Style Options Dialog Box

. . . For Dummies: #1 Computer Book Series for Beginners

COMPUTER
BOOK SERIES
FROM IDG

WordPerfect 3.5 For Macs® For Dummies®

Cheat Sheet

Styles and keystroke combinations

Chapter 16 tells you what a wonderful feature styles are, and they're even better when you can apply them with keystroke combinations. Here's how you assign key combinations to styles:

1. Click the Options button on the Styles ribbon.

   The Style Options dialog box appears.

2. In the Styles list at the top of the dialog box, highlight the style to which you want to attach a keystroke combination.

3. Click the Assign button in the Keystrokes area of the Style Options dialog box.

   The Assign Keystroke dialog box appears.

4. Press the keystrokes you want to assign to the style you chose.

   WordPerfect will show you whether the combination you desire has been assigned to another function.

5. When satisfied, click the Assign button.

Text selection shortcuts in WordPerfect

To Select This	Do This
Word	Double-click on word
Paragraph	Triple-click within paragraph
Whole document	Press ⌘-A

Drag and Drop tricks

WordPerfect allows you to use the Mac's great Desktop Clippings feature (something Microsoft didn't bother with in Word 6, mind you). The following steps demonstrate what a timesaver desktop clippings can be when moving a graphics file from an application like Photoshop and into WordPerfect.

1. Select the graphic in Photoshop (or some other graphics program).

   ⌘-A is the usual key combination for selecting an entire graphic, if that's what you need to do.

2. Drag the selected graphic onto your Mac's desktop and let go of the mouse button.

3. An icon with the name "picture clipping" appears on the desktop.

   This picture clipping is a *copy* of the graphic you selected.

4. Open the WordPerfect document in which you would like to place the graphic.

5. Drag the picture clipping onto the WordPerfect document's window and let go of the mouse button.

The picture pastes itself into the document at the cursor's location when you let go of the mouse button. If you want to relocate the picture, simply click on it (it's sizing handles will appear) and drag it wherever you please within the document.

IDG BOOKS WORLDWIDE

Copyright © 1995 IDG Books Worldwide, Inc. All rights reserved.

Cheat Sheet $2.95 value. Item 913-3.

For more information about IDG Books, call 1-800-762-2974.

. . . For Dummies: #1 Computer Book Series for Beginners

Figure 19-1:
The
Preferences
command
on the Edit
menu.

Figure 19-2:
The main
Preferences
window.

Environment preferences

These preferences determine the way WordPerfect looks to you when you operate it and how it measures the size of a page, among other things. Clicking on the Environment button in the Preferences window brings up the dialog box shown in Figure 19-3.

The first thing you'll notice is that you get to set two basic — and important — items. One is the frequency and type of backups. The default is to create a backup file every 15 minutes (which is also the minimum I'd suggest) and whether or not you want to make an "Original File Backup" along with your newly-saved copy.

If you *don't* select the Original File Backup option, the WordPerfect will only make a copy of your current work, save it in a temporary file, and recover that file if your system crashes or is otherwise rebooted. Check the Original File

Environment

Format Options Windows Graphics Units Language

Backup
☒ Backup Every [15] ⬍ Minutes   ☐ Original File Backup

Screen Colors
Foreground: ■   Background: ☐   Highlight: ▨

[Cancel]   [OK]

Figure 19-3: The Environment dialog box.

Backup option and WordPerfect will save both a copy of your working file *and* keep a reserve copy of the file as you first opened it. Yes, this option takes up more disk space, Quilty, but, yes, it's a more certain way of saving your original work.

You can adjust the backup time down to as little as once a minute, but doing so can slow down your machine. If, like me, you tend towards paranoia about data files, may I suggest you check out the discussion of Last Resort, a software program, in Chapter 21. It's a great utility which will record your every key- stroke and save it in a file. Should you crash, you can recover the essence of your work, although it will take some editing to resurrect the file in a readable form.

The other chief options in the Environment dialog box involve the foreground, background, and highlight colors. If you have a monochrome screen, my apologies. For the rest of us, these options gives you the chance to create a look for WordPerfect that is extremely eye-friendly, or, if you want to give your neighbor in the next cubicle a headache, something that would make Andy Warhol blanche. (Which, by the way, might not be that difficult. I met Warhol once, and he seemed to be extremely shy, which was odd for a man who almost single-handedly defined the concept of media exposure for a generation.)

Anyway, in each of these selections, you have the full palette of colors that you can select for type and graphics in WordPerfect. The default is black and white, as noted before, but others prefer white on blue. For me, the highlight color is most important because I want to be able to *see* the text I've highlighted. For my purposes, a light green fits the bill.

The Format menu

From the menu bar of the Environments dialog box, you can select several other options. Under the Format pull-down menu (shown in Figure 19-4), clicking on the Paragraph option (which is a WordPerfect default) will cause WordPerfect to format the current paragraph *and subsequent ones* in the same fashion, until you change the format. If you choose to format using the Single Paragraph option, each paragraph is formatted individually.

Figure 19-4:
The Format
pull-down
menu.

The Dormant Return option will pass over a Return on a single line at the top of a page, so as to avoid inserting a blank line at the top of a new page following a soft page break. Japanese Hyphenation is used with a Japanese language tool, and applies only if you're writing in Kanji.

Font Mapping, another option under the Format menu, is more important if you import a lot of documents from other programs on other systems. Since Fred might have Bookman on his Mac and you have Century Schoolbook, you might be disappointed opening files from Fred. Select the Font Mapping option and WordPerfect will try to match Bookman and show you a special character when there's not a match. If Font Mapping is off, WordPerfect just uses whatever character is equal to the same value of the incoming font, which means you can lose important items from incoming files. (Having font mapping on is a WordPerfect default, by the way.)

The Options menu

In the Options pull down menu (see Figure 19-5), you can select a variety of display and operations formats that will make your life with WordPerfect easier. The Graphic Font Menu option, for example displays each of your fonts as they appear in the Font menu, instead of as a straight list. This what-you-see-is-what-you-get approach can be very helpful as you lay out a document.

If you are a real keyboard junkie, select the Extra Menu Keys option. This feature will show extra command key combinations in the pull-down menus. Use these and you'll save some time.

Figure 19-5:
The Options
pull-down
menu.

I wouldn't even *think* about turning off the Drag and Drop feature, the utility that lets you, well, drag selected text or graphics across a document, or between windows.

Keeping the Num Lock option checked makes it easy to use the numeric keypad to enter numbers. Otherwise, you'd have to turn the keypad on at each turn.

Choosing a Wrap Around search means that during a Find/Change operation, searches that begin in the middle on a document will go to the end of the document and then continue at the beginning.

The three ruler items — Snap to Grid, Show Ruler Guides, and Preselect Items In Ruler — each determine how ruler actions are to take place. Snap to Grid makes ruler actions snap, or line up, with preselected points on the ruler — in English measure, every $\frac{1}{16}$th of an inch. When moving tab markers and the like on the ruler, the Show Ruler Guides will show you where the mark is moving. (Personally, I like this feature.) Preselect Items In Ruler turns on and off the highlighting of the buttons on the ribbon bars and the button bar. Anytime your cursor is over a button, such as the No Columns button in the Layout ribbon, a little outline appears, highlighting the button. If you don't like that look, uncheck this option to turn it off.

(By the way, you won't read anything about this feature in the documentation for WordPerfect, either the printed volume or online. You find this explanation here courtesy of yours truly and Marsha Terry of Novell. Thanks, Marsha!)

The Windows menu

Next over from the Options menu is one for Windows (see Figure 19-6). Here, you can determine how WordPerfect displays windows and their contents.

The Remember Window Locations option tells WordPerfect to remember where you have placed a given document window on screen. It's on by default, and it's very useful when you're working with a bunch of documents and want to arrange them in a certain way for viewing or cut-and-paste editing.

If you select Remember Cursor Location, you will return to the last location of your cursor in a document when you open it again. Not to be confused with Bookmarks (see Chapter 18), this little feature is really neat. I use it — you might want to as well.

Figure 19-6:
The
Windows
menu.

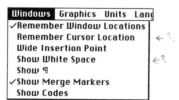

The standard WordPerfect insertion point is a narrow strip which some might find difficult to see. Choose the Wide Insertion Point feature and you'll get a better one.

Want to be sure you see your margins as you edit your document? Click on the Show White Space option and you will.

I like to see the spaces in a document and the marks — ¶ — at the end of each paragraph. Select Show ¶ from this menu, and you'll see them, too.

Mail merging is tricky enough without being able to track the codes used (see Chapter 10). That's why Show Merge Marks is on by default in WordPerfect. Trust me, you'll appreciate it!

Last on the options parade in the Windows menu is the option to Show Codes. This option will keep the codes window open constantly. If you are doing very technical document publishing with WordPerfect — which you can do, by the way — you might want to keep the codes window open to make sure everything is coded the way you want. Me, I leave it off.

The Graphics menu

How do you place your graphics on a page? Are they linked to the adjacent character? The page itself? A given paragraph? The Graphics menu (see Figure 19-7) gives you each of these options, with the Character option being the default. Look at Chapter 7 for more details on graphics.

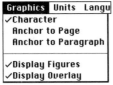

Figure 19-7:
The
Graphics
menu.

If you have a lot of graphics in a document and don't need to see them time and time again, turn off the Display Figures and Display Overlay options. Your scrolling will be much faster, and your graphics will print regardless.

The Unit menu

The Unit menu (see Figure 19-8) is one of the simplest in the Environment pull-downs. You use it to select the units of measure for the ruler, and by extension, the page on which you're working. The default in the U.S. is inches, and for most of us, it'll never change.

Figure 19-8:
The Unit
menu.

The Language menu

Last menu in the Environment dialog box up is the Language menu, which is shown in Figure 19-9. The Show Unknown Alphabets feature is on by default so that you can see unknown character symbols when you open an imported file. Again, this helps when assembling documents from a bunch of contributors into a single product — such as a newsletter.

Figure 19-9:
The
Language
menu.

Search Mixed Alphabets is useful if your document blends English with, say Cyrillic or Hebrew letters.

When you have a language kit installed, such as Japanese or Chinese, you can switch between the languages by pressing ⌘-spacebar. The Synchronize Font and Keyboard option makes the language-changing process easier by automatically switching the active font and keyboard to one that matches the language you are using, which makes editing multilingual documents easier.

For the linguistically adventurous among us, the Use Inline option can be switched on and off to accommodate front-end processors for different languages and character sets. If you're using something truly esoteric, the documentation for that font, and not WordPerfect's instructions, will tell you what you need to do.

Date/Time preferences

From the Preferences window, a click on the Date/Time button brings up the Date and Time dialog box (see Figure 19-10) with which you can set several options to represent the date and time in documents.

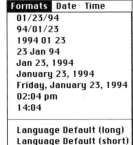

Figure 19-10:
The Date/
Time dialog
box.

When you open this dialog box, the date is displayed as it is currently formatted for inclusion in WordPerfect. In Figure 19-10, it's a standard, American date usage.

The Formats menu

Most of the choices in this menu are self-evident (see Figure 19-11). The Language Default option refers to using WordPerfect's standard default for a given language/region. In U.S. English, the long default would be October 27, 1995. The short default: 10/27/95.

Figure 19-11:
The Formats
menu.

The Date menu

Most of the options in the Date menu (see Figure 19-12) allow you to create your own kind of date. By specifying Day Number, Month Name, and 4 Digit Year, for example, you end up with 27 October 1995, which is the date format preferred by many U.S. Government agencies. The other selections are pretty apparent, including options on using a Leading Zero (as in 04 May, 1995) or a different kind of Date Separator, such as 10-23-96, instead of the slashes.

If you're working in a country such as Japan, where the official calendar changes with each new emperor's reign, the Relative Year feature will help you there. And if you want to be truly proper, you can add st/nd/rd/th to the numbers in your dates, as in 27th October, 1995.

Figure 19-12:
The Date
menu.

The Time menu

Time is on my side, yes it is. Well, maybe not, but with the Time menu (see Figure 19-13), you can select the kind of time you enter automatically in documents. This feature is particularly useful, again, in military and government situations, where you may need to time-stamp a document and meet a certain format. The choices are self-explanatory.

Figure 19-13:
The Time
menu.

Folders preferences

Setting a course for your documents — filing them in various folders and paths — is the goal of the Folders preferences, which you access with a click on its icon in the Preferences window. When the Folders dialog box opens, you see the *current path* of documents, as shown in Figure 19-14.

Your chief option is to select a path for each of seven folder types in the program, as shown in Figure 19-15. This feature is especially useful when you're working on a network and want to share files with colleagues. You can automatically route documents to a public folder on a network.

Figure 19-14:
The Folders
dialog box.

Folders
Type: Documents ▼
Current Path:
Undefined
Set Path...   Clear   Cancel   OK

Figure 19-15:
Folder
types.

Keyboard preferences

Click on the Keyboard icon in the Preferences window and you'll get the ability
to customize and map the WordPerfect keyboard in a variety of fashions (see
Figure 19-16).

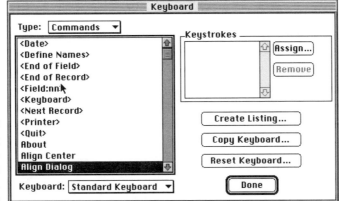

Figure 19-16:
The
Keyboard
dialog box.

You can select the various keyboard options you wish to customize with the
drop-down menu shown in Figure 19-17.

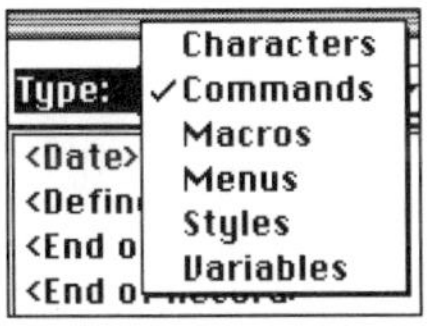

Figure 19-17:
The various
commands
and
functions
you can
customize.

For example, let's say you want to change the mapping of the Enter key, which normally switches you from one style to another. Marsha Terry of Novell's WordPerfect group offers the following system for altering this function:

1. **Select Commands from the Types drop-down menu.**

2. **Scroll through the list until you find Enter.**

3. **Click on Enter to select it and then click the Assign button.**

   The Assign Keystroke dialog box appears.

4. **Enter the keystroke you would like to assign to the Enter key.**

   Remember, if you assign a keystroke, it will replace the current assignment. The Assign Keystroke dialog box will show you the keystroke you will be replacing. WordPerfect suggests you use a modifier key such as the Command, Option, or Control keys so that you don't change something you may need, such as the letter A.)

5. **Click the Assign button to return to the Keyboard dialog box.**

6. **If you are finished assigning keystrokes, click the Done button.**

Your new keystroke assignments become active when you close the Preferences window.

Other Preferences

Several of the preferences you find in this menu — Word Services, Fonts, Show Bars, and QuickCorrect — have been discussed in other chapters relative to those items. In order to keep this chapter to a reasonable length, I'll discuss one of the preferences not mentioned elsewhere, and that's HTML.

In Chapter 15, I delve into editing and creating documents using HTML. In order to make this feature work most effectively with WordPerfect, you can set certain options by clicking the HTML icon in the Preferences window, which brings up the dialog box shown in Figure 19-18.

The top part of this dialog box lets you specify various elements of how tag is represented on screen. The bottom lets you choose a browser with which you can work.

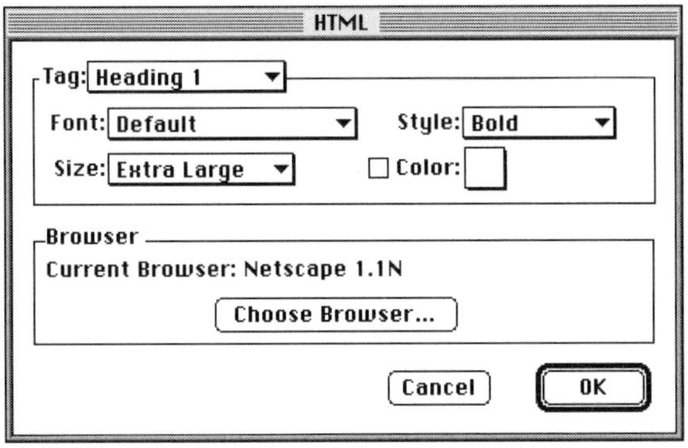

Figure 19-18: The HTML preferences dialog box.

Chapter 20

The Joys of Netscape

*F*or those of you installing WordPerfect 3.5, you'll find something which, I believe, no other word processing program bundles in: a copy of Netscape, the top-drawer *Web browser* that lets you view the content of World Wide Web sites on the Internet.

Back in Chapter 15, I explored the Internet and Web sites a little bit; here, I take a closer look at Netscape, which I (and many others) feel is a first-class Web browser.

What a Browser!

For that matter, what *is* a browser? Let's answer that question first. In order to utilize the graphical features of one part of the Internet known as the World Wide Web, you need software that translates all the data into its proper form. What's more, this software needs to be able to activate *links* to other World Wide Web pages — known as *sites* — so that this service is a truly dynamic part of the Internet and not just a static collection of information.

And what, you ask, is the Internet? Well, originally the brainchild of defense and research scientists, the Internet has grown from a mere forum for techno-dweebs into a massive "town square" which operates on a 24-hour, seven-day-per-week basis. The Internet is a collection of computer networks that have been designed to interconnect with each other using standardized communications protocols. These protocols allow the computers attached to these networks to exchange data with each other. The most common protocol is TCP/IP (Transport Connection Protocol/Internet Protocol), which evolved out of the UNIX software community.

With this common data language, Internet-linked computers can then share graphics, text, and audio and video clips in, you guessed it, common formats. In 1991, all this came into sharper focus with the introduction of the World Wide Web (a.k.a. "the Web" or "WWW"). The Web is the brainchild of Tim Berners-Lee and a programming team at CERN, the European Particle Physics Laboratory in Switzerland. The standards created there allowed physicists to organize, access, and display research data.

These Web standards comprise a text coding system — or markup language — where, with special codes, a text document such as this can be displayed on a Web browser such as Netscape and searched for using hotlinks, which are cross-references to other Web sites.

Now do you see why you need Netscape, Chauncey? It's the key to unlocking all of the stuff on the Web. Yes, you can use other browsers (Mosaic is a popular choice), but why bother when you get Netscape "free" inside each box of WordPerfect, with no added sugar or salt!

What's so good about Netscape? In brief, it allows you to view Web pages with ease and flexibility. And as you shall see, many sites are designed to work best — or even only — with Netscape. (For example, if you're a customer of Wells Fargo Bank and want to look up your account information, you can do this on the Internet, but *only* with the Netscape browser.) If you try to view a page designed for Netscape with a Brand X browser, it may or may not display properly. Graphics may crash into each other and text may be difficult to read — those are two of the problems you might encounter trying to read some Netscape-formatted pages without Netscape.

Perhaps more quickly than with any other "standard" in the computer industry, Netscape has emerged as a *de facto* standard for Net surfing, and it seems likely that more of us, rather than fewer of us, will use it to probe the Internet in the months and years to come.

Therefore, it's probably a good idea to get to know — and use — Netscape before too long. It may soon be one of the only games in town.

The preceding message was a *prediction* — and I've been wrong before! Despite my firm belief that Netscape will do well, it's quite possible that something else will, someday, eclipse this fast-rising star in the Internet firmament. But it doesn't seem likely, and you might as well be prepared.

Also, as you'll see in further discussions of Netscape here and in Chapter 15, you can use the HTML features in WordPerfect to design Web pages that can be read by both Netscape *and* other browsers. The key in this instance is to keep your designs *simple* and thus easy for all Internet browser software to read; eschew some of the fancier tricks of the Web page trade and you can still create an interesting Web page that will communicate with others.

But enough about Internet theology — an apt term when discussing Web browsers and people's preferences about them since partisans can get rather dogmatic about the whole thing. Besides, I'm right, so why quibble!

Installing and Firing Up Netscape

Let's dispense with the easy part: Installing Netscape. That is done for you when you install WordPerfect, provided you did not do a custom installation and chose to skip installing Netscape. (If you did exclude Netscape, you can add it by going back to the Install procedure, selecting the Custom option, and installing only Netscape.)

Most of us, however, choose the Easy Install option, which puts everything, including Netscape, in its proper place.

How to start up the Netscape browser, then? If you are working in WordPerfect and you merely want to view an HTML file as it would appear on the Web (without graphics unless said graphics are on your system and their locations are cross-linked to your document), then go to the HTML ribbon bar and click on the Preview button to start up Netscape (see Figure 20-1).

Figure 20-1:
The Preview button in the HTML ribbon.

From this point, you'll quickly see the Netscape browser appear. If all you want to do is preview a document, that document will show up on-screen, as demonstrated in Figure 20-2.

Note again here that the file can be viewed as it will appear on-screen without the attendant graphics, unless the links to those graphics are available to Netscape. However, you'll get a good idea of how the basic page layout will work because the "missing" graphics will appear as boxes of the appropriate size for the actual graphic.

If you are live on a direct Internet connection from your Mac, or if you have a modem and software configured for Internet connections, Netscape will attempt to open an Internet link and then take you to the Netscape home page. Otherwise, you may need to invoke the helper program that connects your Mac to the Internet separately. This can be a utility such as MacPPP and/or MacTCP; your Internet provider will be able to help you.

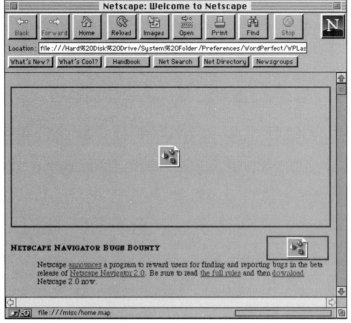

Figure 20-2:
The
Netscape
Home Page
viewed from
a file saved
to a Mac.

Afraid of getting your feet wet?

If you're a little scared of giving the Internet a try, don't worry because a lot of us have felt the same way. The Internet is a world of its own with rules of its own. The good news is that in the last year or so, using the Internet (and especially the World Wide Web) has gotten much friendlier and more Mac-like. UNIX may be the backbone of the Internet, but enough software companies and service providers out there realized that they can make lots of money by making the Internet more readily accessible for ordinary, non-programmer-type folks. You're much more likely to spend hours browsing Web sites (and paying your service provider for those hours) if your Internet connection is easy to use.

A year or two ago, you had to know cryptic UNIX commands just to send e-mail or download files. Today, many services provide a point-and-click interface. If you haven't ever used the Net (to download files, join newsgroups, or simply chat with folks around the world), and if you've never seen a Web site, getting started isn't nearly as painful as you might think. National service providers such as America Online, eWorld, and CompuServe have tried to make things as easy as possible for Mac users as well as Internet newbies (folks who are new to the Internet). If you decide to go with a direct Internet connection through a local service provider, rest assured that the software you use to access FTP, Gopher, e-mail, and newsgroups is getting easier to use all the time. As for surfing the Web, you can't do much better than Netscape, which you already own.

The upshot: the Internet is getting easier to use every day. Sure, it's a little chaotic, but that's part of its charm. Becoming a proficient Internet user is no more difficult than learning to use a couple of Mac applications and little jargon. If twelve-year-old kids who can't identify all seven continents can surf the Net, so can you.

Some readers, particularly those new to the Macintosh and computing, may be mystified by the inner working of Macintosh-to-Internet connectivity. Unfortunately, covering Internet connections and online service providers is beyond the scope of this book. *The Internet For Macs For Dummies, 2nd Edition* (yes, another shameless plug for an IDG Book!) really will help you understand it all; I know because the first edition of this work helped me!

Viewing HTML Documents with Netscape

As mentioned earlier, it's easy to view an HTML document being created with WordPerfect or edited with WordPerfect using Netscape: That Preview button will do all the work for you.

You can also drag an HTML file from the WordPerfect folder (or any other spot on your Mac) onto the Netscape icon to launch Netscape and view your file. But it's easier to start things off from WordPerfect, and you can switch back and forth from browser to WordPerfect editor. Wouldn't you agree?

In fact, frankly, you will need to switch between the two programs if you want to edit a Web document effectively. The Netscape browser is a good *viewer* of Web pages and the like, but in this incarnation (Netscape version 1.1N is supplied with WordPerfect 3.5), it isn't really an *editor* of such pages.

While using Netscape, your options are limited to saving and printing a page and reloading the graphics if links to them have been established. To do anything else, you really need to switch over to WordPerfect.

I don't think it's a bad thing to have to edit in WordPerfect and view with Netscape; indeed, it's quite the opposite. Since most of us are struggling to make the most of our word processors, learning the HTML coding as used with WordPerfect makes sense (see Chapter 15). This way, your editing of HTML documents is a part of your word processing, and you don't have to leave the familiar confines of WordPerfect to do it!

Going Online with Netscape

As mentioned before, Netscape is a great way to look at real, live Internet Web pages. You do need to have an Internet connection in order to use Netscape (or any other browser) to surf the Net, of course.

While a full discussion of Internet connectivity is beyond the scope of this book, it should be noted that along with a wide variety of local Internet service providers, or ISPs, CompuServe encourages its Macintosh customers to use

Netscape to get on the Internet via CompuServe. If you have a CompuServe account, you can get Netscape to work with it easily and quickly. (In the USA, you can call 800-848-8990 for information on CompuServe.)

For the moment, I'll use CompuServe rather than a local ISP to illustrate how you can use WordPerfect and Netscape to connect to the World Wide Web through a dial-up connection. Which, Albert, is what you want to do after all, right? Right!

Along with Netscape, you will need to install the two bits of system software extensions and control panels mentioned before, specifically MacTCP and MacPPP.

MacTCP is a control panel created by Apple Computer and is available as a stand-alone piece of software in the Apple System 7.5 operating software. Bottom line is that you *must* have MacTCP to run Netscape in a dial-up mode.

That's because MacPPP, which I heartily recommend, requires MacTCP to run. Go figure. More important, you need to download MacPPP from an online service such as CompuServe or AOL and configure both programs to fit the needs of your ISP, whether local or an online service. (You'll need to call that ISP for information, I'm afraid.)

Once these bits of software are installed and properly working (it took just 10 minutes on the phone with a CompuServe tech support person, in my case, to accomplish this), you can get to the Net this way:

1. **With WordPerfect running, pull down the Apple menu and choose the Control Panels folder.**

2. **Open the ConfigPPP icon in the Control Panels window.**

   Note that if you have hierarchical submenus in your Apple menu, you can select the ConfigPPP control panel simply by maneuvering through the Control Panels submenu of the Apple menu.

   Either way, the ConfigPPP control panel opens, as shown in Figure 20-3.

3. **Click on the Open button to invoke the dial-up routine.**

   ConfigPPP (which is MacPPP) will dial up your ISP and connect, finding and establishing your link to the Web. As the connection process progresses, you'll see a connection monitor as displayed in Figure 20-4

4. **Go back to Netscape and start browsing.**

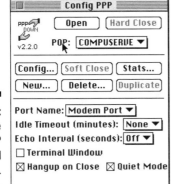

Figure 20-3:
The
ConfigPPP
control
panel.

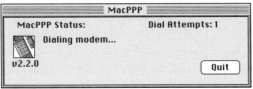

Figure 20-4:
The
MacPPP
status box.

The preceding steps will only work if you have set up an account with a service provider *and* your service provider has told you how to properly configure MacTCP and MacPPP. I can't tell you myself because every service provider requires different settings. What I've tried to do here is show you the basic way in which one gets up and running with Netscape.

Seeing a Site or Two

As you use the Netscape browser to surf the Net, as the saying goes, you will find no shortage of Web sites to view. I'd like to suggest a couple, although the first one will require no searching on your part.

That first one is the Netscape Home Page, which tells you all about activities at Netscape (see Figure 20-5). As versions of the Netscape browser advance, you will be able to download beta copies (at your own risk, of course) and purchase supported versions. This is also a great jumping-off place to find resources about Netscape and the Internet in general.

By the way, if you're new to Web page design and feel intimidated by what you see on the Netscape page, don't be. Remember, these folks have tons of money and loads of staff to help design the spiffy graphics you see here. All you might need to do is create a simple page for your needs. And that's OK.

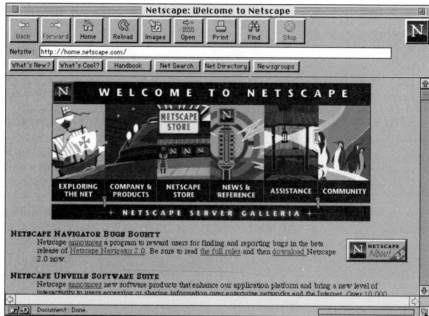

Figure 20-5:
The
Netscape
home page.

The second site I'd like to call your attention to might be a little uncommon for a computer book. It's the home page of The Salvation Army (see Figure 20-6), best-known for its charitable work but less-known as an evangelical Christian denomination which serves the needs of millions of people worldwide. Starting with their home page (http://www.winkcomm.com/SAweb/home.htm), you can jump to information about the Army's activities in close to 200 nations and territories around the globe.

As an example of good Web page design and content, I particularly like the "Why Salvation Army" page illustrated here in Figure 20-7. It shows a piece of line art and regular and boldfaced text, yet it does not overpower a reader. That's my opinion, of course, but you might want to visit it both to see an example of Web design and learn something you might not be aware of!

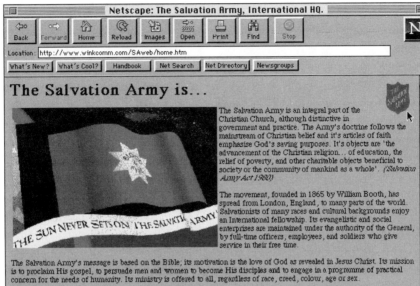

Figure 20-6:
The Salvation Army home page.

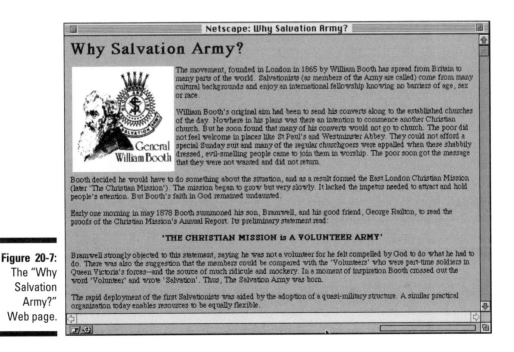

Figure 20-7:
The "Why Salvation Army?" Web page.

Part IV
The Part of Tens

"HOW'S THAT FOR FAST SCROLLING?"

In this part . . .

After you've finished with the nitty-gritty material in previous parts, this is where you come to relax. The chapters in this part are sort of optional lists of info. Read them at your leisure. I take the opportunity to offer the distilled wisdom I've gained in 15 years of working with computers, and I even spout off a bit. It's good, light reading, and more important, you may actually find some helpful advice.

Chapter 21

Ten (or More) Options You Should Consider

No Program Is an Island, Entire unto Itself

By now, you've seen that WordPerfect is a rather comprehensive piece of software. It's not just a word processor, but your gateway to the Internet, a great way to do merge letters, and more. It offers enough desktop publishing capabilities to allow you to create newsletters, business cards, and letterhead. And it can help you manage your documents in an orderly fashion.

For all this, however, WordPerfect is not an island, as John Donne might have written were he a binary kind of guy. Obviously, you need an operating system with which to run your Mac, and, yes, a printer comes in handy when a hard copy is required. But beyond these basics, there are other add-on products you might want to consider as you become more proficient with WordPerfect and as your needs evolve.

The recommendations in this chapter are highly personal — and they may be somewhat transitory. Companies and products come and go all the time in the Macintosh community, and even though every effort is made to assure that the items listed here are catalogued accurately and are still available, unforseeable things might happen.

Also, while I write about computers for a living — and have published, literally, several hundred product reviews in the last 11 years — I'm neither omniscient nor infallible. My preferences are mine, based on a lot of work, a lot of reading and research, and a lot of experience. You might, however, have a greater or lesser amount of satisfaction with a given product, or you might find something else that is better for you and your needs. (If you do, please e-mail me with that info [to MarkKel@aol.com] so that it might be included in any future editions of this book.)

That said, here are some hard-nosed suggestions you will want to consider. I hope they're helpful to you in your work.

The Single Most Important Software Add-On That I Know Of

It's called Last Resort, and it may just save your . . . neck. That's because this typing recovery program will let you recover text that was typed and deleted and text that was typed but never saved.

In short, if you accidentally reboot your machine, if it freezes, if there's a power glitch, whatever, you're covered. The program, which works as a control panel, records every keystroke and automatically saves them to the hard disk. When you need to recover text, you can use WordPerfect or any other word processor to open and edit the text in a Last Resort file.

The downside of this program is that in saving every keystroke, there's a lot of garbage in these files that you might have to clean up with either a spell checker or a macro. The tremendous upside is that Last Resort can really be a digital lifesaver when you have lost a key file. It's far better than having a day's work disappear into the cybervapor because you made a mistake. I know. It's happened to me!

Yes, I know WordPerfect makes backup files, and you can open these files when you restart the program after a crash or other foul-up. But just as airbags in a car make seatbelts more effective, my view is that Last Resort can be extra insurance — as when your WordPerfect backup files are corrupted or accidentally trashed!

Last Resort sells for around $50 in stores and from the publisher. It might be the third-best money you've spent (after buying WordPerfect and this book, of course).

Working Software, Inc., the publisher of Last Resort, can be reached at P.O. Box 1844, Santa Cruz, CA 95061; or by calling 800-229-9675 or 408-423-5696; or by sending a fax message to 408-423-5699.

Additional Spelling/Grammar Tools for Lawyers, Doctors, and Others (Maybe You)

WordPerfect's Speller and Grammatik are excellent tools with which you can check your spelling and grammar (see Chapter 10). By now, you know this, and perhaps by now you've had some experience with how helpful these tools can be when you want to look your best in print.

But what if you're an attorney and you get to use fancy words which the rest of us pay $175 per hour to hear? Nathan Bergerbest, my best friend and a superlative lawyer, uses that kind of language when he files appeals petitions.

Well, Nate uses a Window-based PC, so he can't yet take advantage of the Mac-related specialized dictionaries that serve lawyers, doctors, and others in specialized fields. But you're using WordPerfect and a Macintosh, and you're in the professions, so you might be able to use some extra help. Here are the details of several products which can assist the spelling-challenged.

You might not need as much help as these items provide. WordPerfect's spelling list is rather comprehensive. For example, it found that great Latin word *certiorari* — one of those big words Nate uses on a regular basis. My feeling, however, is that it is better to be safe than sorry, and that by having extra resources at hand, you've got extra insurance.

SciWords

SciWords offers help to those writing about scientific and medical-related topics. Each of the three different add-in SciWords modules, which its publishers claim integrates with WordPerfect, contains more than 75,000 technical words used in chemistry, physics, and biology, with special emphasis on pharmaceuticals, agrochemicals, pesticides, and biochemical materials.

SciWords for Agriculture contains more than 72,000 words, including thousands of systematic and trivial chemical names, while emphasizing the names of pesticides, agrochemicals, and genetic engineering. This module includes many names of plants, species, and microorganisms. SciWords for Environment is supplied with over 60,000 words found in environment-related writing, including pesticide, chemical, and trade names, the names of many flora, fauna, and microorganisms, and the names of cities, states, countries, and rivers from all over the world, as well as environment-related acronyms.

The modules sell for between $50 and $70 each. More information can be obtained from publishers Pool, Heller and Milne, Inc., 9520 Linden Ave., Bethesda, MD 20814; phone 301-493-6595 or fax 301-897-3487.

MilSpell

I could tell you all about the words in MilSpell for WordPerfect, but as the old Marine/secrets joke goes, then I'd have to kill you. Not really, but if you deal in military and intelligence matters (Tom Clancy, are you reading this?), then MilSpell is for you.

MilSpell bills itself as a replacement dictionary for WordPerfect, containing military, engineering, and computer-related terms used by the Army, Navy, Air Force, and Marines. Categories include communications, intelligence, logistics, frequencies, medical, transportation, computers, NATO, navigation, missiles, data transfer, test, manufacturing, acquisition, C^3I, electronic warfare, satellites, and programming.

The software sells for $29.95 and is available from Sizzling Software, 2800A Lafayette Rd., #134, Portsmouth, NH 03801; 603-926-8336.

Spellswell 7

At first glance, the 92,000-word dictionary in Spellswell 7, version 1.0.5, might not be of much interest to WordPerfect users. But the good news here is that there are several add-in modules of great use. The dictionary itself, which is fast and facile, sells for $49.95 from publisher Working Software. Add-in Medical or Legal Dictionaries cost $39.95 each; the Geographical or Science Dictionaries $29.95 each; and a Business Dictionary is $19.95.

Just in case you missed the publisher's information in my discussion of Last Resort, here it is again: Working Software, Inc., can be contacted at P.O. Box 1844, Santa Cruz, CA 95061; or by calling 800-229-9675 or 408-423-5696; or by sending a fax message to 408-423-5699.

If you're in desperate need of the top legal word-list, Black's Law Dictionary, you can find it online with Westlaw, the electronic service of West Publishing Company (612-687-7000 or 800-328-9352). This service is extremely comprehensive when it comes to legal research and information — the dictionary is a tiny part of the resources here — but the cost is high.

Along with these resources, the WordPerfect Macintosh forum on America Online and other electronic sources contain lists of words that can be added to your dictionary. There's a Bible-related list of several thousand words, and others are available as well.

Teach WordPerfect to Read with a Scanner and OCR Software

As I write this book in the summer of 1995, one "hot" hardware question among Mac users is whether or not one has a fast (14.4 Kbps) or super-fast (28.8 Kbps) modem. As I discuss in Chapter 15, having such a speedy connection is great for making the most of the Internet capabilities of WordPerfect.

I predict that very soon, the "hot" question will be, "What kind of scanner do you own?" If you don't own at least a small scanner for your Macintosh, and if you work with words and printed matter a lot, frankly, you're cheating yourself.

Yes, I know, a lot of stuff is available online. And yes, you probably have a lot of digital files at hand, and we've already seen that WordPerfect can convert most, if not all, of these.

But there's a wealth of material in print, and perhaps only in print. There are letters you receive to which you must send an answer, and from which you must quote accurately. There are newspaper and magazine articles, contracts, wills, scripts, reports, speeches, news releases, source documents — you name it, it exists in print. If it exists in print, it can be scanned. If it can be scanned, it belongs in your Mac. At least maybe.

There are several kinds of scanners that you can use. Some are handheld, but these have won mixed approval from users and reviewers. At one time a handheld scanner was a reasonable, low-cost alternative to the desktop flatbed variety. This has changed, however.

Part of the reason for this change has been vast improvements in *optical character recognition,* or OCR, software. Many of today's programs are very good, and they produce excellent results, particularly when combined with a compact, inexpensive scanner.

My personal favorite for a desktop scanner is the PaperPort, produced by Visioneer of Palo Alto, California. For around $350 in stores, you get a device that is about a foot long, four inches tall and two inches deep. It can sit between your monitor and keyboard. It plugs into a serial port on your Mac, and the supplied software handles things effortlessly. Just insert a piece of paper and the PaperPort software starts up. It scans a page in under 10 seconds, and you can group and stack pages to form a complete unit. Drag the icons of the scanned items onto one representing WordPerfect (you can set this up in the Preferences dialog of the PaperPort software) and the program automatically invokes an OCR program, reads the scanned image, and starts up WordPerfect with a copy of the resulting text.

In Fall, 1995, Visioneer will release a model with some greater features for handling black-and-white images and other duties at the $370 price level. The original PaperPort will cost about $100 less, and it still does an adequate job. Either model will help you do the job you need to do, and I cannot recommend them highly enough. You can contact Visioneer at 800-787-7007 or 415-493-9599; their address is 2860 West Bayshore Road, Palo Alto, CA 94303. Their e-mail address is Visioneer@aol.com.

A final thought about scanners: Flatbed scanners can be very useful if you are scanning in a lot of photos, or need to scan them in color, or have other demands for scanning that a smaller device cannot meet. Both of the top Macintosh magazines, *Macworld* and *MacUser,* contain numerous ads for worthwhile products. Make sure the one you buy is compatible with your system and is supplied with any software you might need to process scanned images before importing them into WordPerfect.

Really Mass Storage

When I got my first "real" computer (ashamedly, I must admit it was an MS-DOS system), it came with a 10MB hard disk. I wondered how I was ever going to fill a device that could hold the text of the King James version of the Bible — 12 times over.

Today, the Mac "clone" on my desk has a 1 gigabyte hard disk drive, which is 100 times the capacity of that 10MB drive. My other Mac, a PowerMac, has a 160MB drive (yes, I need to upgrade) and my Mac IIsi has an 80MB drive, which I doubled using disk compression software.

As valuable as all of these drives are, here's another predicition. Removable mass storage will become more and more important to Mac users than ever before in the coming years. One reason is that we have too much data on hand. Our hard disks can get over-full. While we might need stuff "some day," you don't need it on your hard disk right now. Having it archived is good enough.

The other force driving the growth in these devices is multimedia. Sound, graphics, and video are major components of today's documents, but they also take up a lot of storage space.

There are several kinds of removable media from which you can choose. Here are some recommendations and comments:

- The original SyQuest drive. These cartridges hold between 44MB and 205MB of data. They are a favorite of graphic designers and printers, many of whom have such devices in-house. You can load up your WordPerfect file, the needed fonts and graphics, and anything else you believe the printer will need, and they can go from your digital media to the film used in offset printing. (Obviously, this costs money and is generally used for high-quality printing projects.) The drives sell for around $500 in stores (at least they did when I last bought one) and cartridges are around $70 for the 88 Mbyte version — less than $1 per megabyte.

- Iomega's ZIP drive, released in 1995, packs 100 megs of data onto a cartridge that is slightly larger than a 3.5-inch floppy disk. The drive costs less than $200, and 100MB cartridges are $19.95 each, or 20-cents per megabyte.

- Not to be outdone, SyQuest has also just released the EZ-135, which is about the size of the Iomega ZIP and similarly priced. The only problem is, of course, that the two drives are not compatible, which means we get another computer-industry replay of the Beta versus VHS debate, but so be it.

- For a really big storage product, check out the DynaMO magneto-optical disc drive from Fujitsu Computer Products. It costs around $1,000, but cartridges hold 230MB apiece, which makes backing up your 1-gig drive easier than with other devices.

Whichever option you choose, know that having some extra storage will make your life easier.

The Most Important Upgrade You Can Make

Make no mistake. There is one thing and one thing only that will make your Mac run better, make WordPerfect more comfortable, and give you the extra oomph you need in so many critical situations.

It is adding random-access memory, or RAM, to your Macintosh. If you have 5 or 8 megs of RAM, the basic for many Macs, then you need to upgrade. If you have 16 megs of RAM, you may still need more.

Adding more RAM is relatively simple; your Mac's manual will give you the basic details, and most RAM suppliers will offer additional instruction. My best advice here is to know exactly what you need and make sure that your supplier gives it to you.

I have a personal bias in favor of TechWorks, a company in Austin, Texas, which has been supplying memory to Mac (and PC) enthusiasts for years. They sell great products, offer incredible customer service, and they know just about everything that can be known about adding memory to a Mac. Call them at 800-695-5928 for more information. I recommend them without reservation.

Chapter 22

Less Than Ten Ways to Enhance Your Output

....

In This Chapter

▶ Printer concerns

▶ Third-party fonts

▶ Paper Direct supplies and templates

▶ Designer issues

▶ Binding and Presentation Options

....

Looking Good!

One of the joys of using WordPerfect is that you can create some of the best looking documents around. One of the challenges might well be finding a printer that does your work justice.

The choice of output devices might well have been made long before you signed up with WordPerfect. It might well have been a laser printer or an inkjet printer. Or it might have been Apple's dot-matrix wonder, the ImageWriter.

If you own an ImageWriter, here's my best suggestion: Find a door in your home or office that won't stay open and use it as a doorstop. Seriously, unless you are using the ImageWriter to fill out multipart forms, or unless you are seriously financially challenged, the dot-matrix printer's days are history. You can get an inkjet for around $200 or so, and for a little more, you can print in very nice color. What are you waiting for?

Choosing a better (or second) printer can be daunting. Indeed, within weeks of this book's arrival in stores, you may well be confronted with other choices than those discussed here. Let's start then with some principles for wise printer shopping.

How to Buy (or Choose) a Printer

Start with the outcome in mind. What kind of work do you do with your computer? Who sees the end product? How important is color? What value do you place on the sharpness of laser output? Do you need a resolution greater than 300 dots per inch? And how much money can you spend?

Answer these questions and you'll come close to the kind of printer you need. If you're just sending letters to grandma and printing up your annual Christmas card mailing list, then an inkjet might be enough for your needs.

Running a business from home? A laser printer might be your answer unless you need to do a lot of work in color. Then it's back to inkjets, such as the Apple Color StyleWriter, the Hewlett-Packard DeskWriter, or the Epson Color Stylus. Are you responsible for the output of an entire department? Then color lasers might be your answer. They're networkable, and the latest ones from Tektronics and Apple Computer are frankly stunning.

But all this begins with knowing where your work will end up. If you know the kind of output you require, you'll know where to go.

If you're unsure of what your needs will be, look at a color inkjet printer. Yes, the cost of consumables (see the next section) is a bit high, but these machines offer the greatest variety of output. In short, a good color inkjet could take you through college and onto your first job.

Know the Cost of Consumables

When you print, you use supplies such as laser toner, printer ribbon, or ink. These are called consumables and therein lies a story.

The story is this: I once bought a typewriter which promised to double as a computer printer. It did great work, but the $3.00 ribbons only produced about ten pages. Bottom line? I got a different machine for printing when I needed one.

The low price — or high price — of a printer should not be the sole determinant of what you buy. Check out the cost of the consumables involved (ink, toner, special paper if needed) and figure out your cost per page. On average, lasers come in at about 2.5 to 3 cents per page; inkjets run between 3 and 5 cents, sometimes higher.

The great Kinko's alternative

Here's a little hint your computer dealer won't necessarily tell you about. You don't *need* a printer. In or near most communities in the United States is a great little place called Kinko's where you can bring in a Mac disk and walk out with printed copy in stunning laser black-and-white or color, since all 800-plus Kinko's have the Apple ColorLaser on hand. Costs range from about 50 cents per page for monochrome to around $1.50 for color, plus the amount of time you rent to use their Mac for printing.

The Kinko's folks are great and usually very savvy about the equipment they have. Most locations are open 24 hours per day, and all have a wide range of specialized paper on which you can print out a document. The stores also feature a full range of copying and binding equipment with which you can quickly and easily produce reports, transparencies, and proposals.

If you have a PowerBook or other Mac portable, here's an extra bonus: you can walk up, plug in, and print, paying only for the copies you turn out. Look in the white pages or call 1-800-254-6567 for an automated guide to the store nearest you.

Whatever printer you select, try to keep at least one set of extra consumables on hand. It's really tough to find a CompUSA or OfficeMax that is open at 3 a.m. when your report is due at 8 o'clock the next morning.

Third-Party Fonts

Another key to looking good in print is to use the proper font. Most books are set in a standard typeface such as Times Roman, with other type used for headings. (This book uses a different set of fonts, but not too many.)

One of the problems new users sometimes have with the wide range of fonts available is the wide range of fonts available. Use too many and your document takes on the appearance of a ransom note cut from a magazine.

WordPerfect itself is supplied with a bunch of Bitstream fonts; more are available from Bitstream and other suppliers. And the great thing about the Mac (using System 6.7 or higher) is that once you install a font in the System folder, it's available to all your Mac applications.

Where can you find good fonts? Look online in the various Mac and desktop publishing forums on America Online, CompuServe, and eWorld. Surf the Mac Web sites on the Internet. You can also find fonts from many commercial sources.

One of the nicer collections of fonts which I've seen comes from Swifte International, of Rockland, Delaware. Called Typecase, you can find it in stores and outfits such as Price Club. The Mac version has nearly 200 fonts in it, including one of my personal favorites, Dateline, which makes your printed output look as if it were produced by an old-fashioned typewriter. (It's great for correspondence, either personal or business.)

Typecase for Macintosh, which sells in stores for under $50, comes on a CD-ROM as well as diskettes, and installation of selected fonts is very easy. Call Swifte at 302-234-1750 for more details.

More advanced collections of fonts are available from companies such as Adobe, which sells a CD-ROM chock full o' fonts of just about every description. I saw this product advertised in one of the Mac magazines for $7,500 — which is beyond the reach of my budget and possibly yours. Adobe also sells an excellent program, Type Manager, which lets you use older PostScript and Type 1 Fonts with ease and clarity. It sells for around $50 (probably less) and is a blessing if you use older fonts.

Finally, be sure to check out Macromedia's Fontographer if you want to do fancy work with your fonts. With this remarkable program, which sells for around $360 in stores and by mail order, you can take a standard font and customize it just about any way you want. It also will convert fonts from a Windows platform for use on the Mac. If you do a lot of cross-platform work or need other specialized font treatments, this is a must-have program!

There's something else to be careful about when it comes to fonts, and it's memory. Too many in your System Folder will eat up your RAM; too many in a document and your laser printing might slow down because WordPerfect is downloading too many fonts to the printer. Oh, and if your printer is RAM-challenged, it'll choke on the document as well. The moral of this tale? Be cautious about the number of fonts you use, make sure you have plenty of RAM in your computer and your printer, and check everything again before you print.

Paper Direct Supplies and Templates

OK, you've figured out which printer you want to use; you've decided on your fonts. Now what about the paper?

Yes, Orestes, I know you've got plenty of white bond paper at hand, but sometimes there's a need for something else, something different, something with pizazz.

At times like this, I recommend Paper Direct, a mail order company that has one of the widest ranges of specialty papers known to mankind. The stuff is classy, it looks and feels substantial, and it makes a great impression.

You can purchase complete sets of a given Paper Direct design, including letterhead, postal cards, business cards, envelopes, and other accessory items. With a matched set of paper products, you can create a coordinated mailing and a professional look on a limited budget.

I've used these products since 1993 and so has my wife, Jean, who does desktop publishing and design. In every instance, the Paper Direct products have made a good impression on the people receiving our materials, and the cost is very reasonable.

Paper Direct also produces a whole range of supplies for creating presentations, certificates, and other items. You can buy binding supplies from them and even supplies for making booklets. Delivery is generally overnight, if ordered by 3 p.m. Eastern, at a cost of $8.95, and I've never had a problem in ordering from them.

The firm is based in New Jersey and offers a toll-free number: 1-800-A-PAPERS (800-272-7377) for catalog requests and orders. Just one question: why are you still reading this and not calling?

There are several other companies out there offering specialty paper by mail order. Some are very good; others strike me as rather garish. But that's my opinion. Look around, see what interests you, and give it a try. Anything you can do to jazz up your work in print will likely be appreciated by those who receive your materials.

When You Need a Designer

The title of this chapter deals with enhancing your printed output. Sometimes, however, you will want an intermediary to come in and assist in creating material for publication. WordPerfect is powerful, yes, and you can do a lot with it, but you may have neither the skills nor the time to do a full design job.

Just as you go to a dentist when you need work done on your teeth, a graphic designer can help you with specialized services that really enhance your appearance. (And no Novocain is required.)

This book is not intended to be a primer on graphic design or desktop publishing. (Instead, let me suggest *Desktop Publishing and Design For Dummies* as the preferred text.) But you should be aware of several things before you sit down with a designer:

- ✔ **Rule 1: Know the language.** Be aware of the terms designers and printers use, and make sure you understand what is being said. Much of the miscommunication that comes about in the design and printing process comes because of inattention on one side or another. By reading a basic text — or by asking questions — you can make sure that what you see in your mind's eye is what you get.

- ✔ **Rule 2: Know the procedures.** Printing is not inexpensive, and it becomes truly expensive when you get something you don't want and have to have a job redone. The solution here is to understand some basics about printing procedures. Know how much multicolor printing costs, be aware of the cost of certain kinds of paper stocks, and know how much a rush job will cost you. Ignorance can hit you in the wallet.

- ✔ **Rule 3: Know what you're signing off on.** When a designer or printer comes to you with a proof and asks for your approval, make sure you know what you're approving and what happens next. Once a job is on the press, turning back gets costly.

- ✔ **Rule 4: Know that WordPerfect can help you.** Not only will WordPerfect's editing, proofing, and spelling tools help you get everything in order so that the copy you turn in is flawless, but you'll be able to export a file in a format that your designer and printer can easily use.

That's not too hard, is it? The bottom line — and I hope you don't mind the digression — is that any word processor can carry you a long way, but when you need more than that, a good designer can take you over the top!

Binding and Presentation Options

Time was that binding a report meant using a stapler. Not any more. You can use spiral binding, heat-sealed binding, and a host of other methods to put your work together.

Selecting a binding format depends in part on your budget and in part on your needs. Loose-leaf formats offer the greatest ease in updating a document; fixed formats can offer greater prestige and a sharper appearance.

Where can you get these materials? I mentioned above that Paper Direct and Kinko's offer various binding options and supplies. You can find others at local office supply stores.

Whichever option you select, keep a thought to the margins of your WordPerfect document and to any duplex (two-sided) printing that you do. Make sure your margins reflect the binding needs, and you're home free.

The 5th Wave — By Rich Tennant

"OK, TECHNICALLY, THIS SHOULD WORK. JUDY, TYPE THE WORD 'GOODYEAR' IN ALL CAPS, BOLDFACE, AT 700-POINT TYPE SIZE."

Chapter 23

Less Than Ten Ways to Get Support

You Don't Have to Go It Alone

Working with a piece of software — particularly something which might be new to you, and particularly when you're away from the office and a company support person — can seem like a lonely experience. You're out there all by yourself, perhaps working against a deadline, perhaps in a hotel room at 3:00 in the morning, trying to get ready for a meeting the next day.

Or perhaps you're just pushing the envelope of using your software, and you've run up against a wall. You want to do something that the program (and perhaps this book) suggests you can do, but you're just not able to complete the task.

Maybe the situation is different: Instead of being all alone, you're a department manager and you have 15 or 20 — or 200 — people you need to get up to speed with WordPerfect, and you need to do it quickly. You want to make sure that everyone is singing from the same page, as it were, and you want them to get the proper training.

Well, friend, you don't have to go it alone. Really. For one thing — pardon the immodesty — you've got this book. No, this isn't a total, comprehensive, microscopic analysis of every nook and cranny of WordPerfect, but if I've succeeded, by now you know the basics of using this program and then some.

This book, however, is *not* your only resource. WordPerfect itself contains an excellent help system. If you're using System 7.5, you can also take advantage of the WordPerfect Guide (see Figure 23-1), a rather nice system that offers more explanations of the program's features along with how-to help. It's based on the Apple Guide program included with System 7.5, which might offer another incentive to upgrade to that version of the system software if you haven't already.

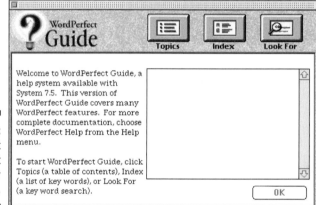

Figure 23-1:
Let
WordPerfect
be your
guide.

While the regular Help menu offers more detailed information, the Guide is an easy, inviting way to find out more about your program's operation.

But even the Guide isn't your only help option. There's support available directly from WordPerfect, both free and paid, as well as support online, in user groups, and from outside trainers. Let's look at some of your options — and how to make the most of them.

WordPerfect Direct Support: *Options and Prices*

From the beginnings of the company in the early 1980s, WordPerfect has been noted for outstanding customer support, at a level that few have matched. Some of that has changed in light of increased demands on companies in general, but you can count on WordPerfect, which is now a division of Novell, Inc., to stand behind its software.

Today, WordPerfect still offers more support than many other firms: For 180 days (or six months, whichever comes first), you can call the company any time between 7:00 a.m. and 6:00 p.m. Mountain Time, Monday through Friday. The call is toll-free from the U.S., Canada, Puerto Rico, and the U.S. Virgin Islands.

On your first call, you'll need to supply the serial number of your software, and you'll be issued a "Personal Identification Number," or PIN. Jot that PIN down somewhere (like the margin next to this paragraph) because you'll need to quote that number every time you call. Using the PIN will not only identify you to WordPerfect's technicians, but it will help the company track problems and keep a record of interactions with you. In turn, using your PIN can keep your call time to a minimum and make sure that you get the answers you need.

After those first six months (or 180 days, whichever comes first), you'll be asked to pay for your support calls, at a rate of $25 per call. That sounds steep, but you do get a couple of benefits. One is more time in which to call — from Monday to Friday, the firm takes Priority Service calls till 10:00 p.m. Mountain Standard time; and they have technicians available from 8:00 a.m. till 4:00 p.m. on Saturdays.

You should be able to find the 800 numbers for these services in the WordPerfect manual, which may be more current than this book. In the absolute worst case, you can reach the WordPerfect switchboard by dialing 801-225-5000. This is a toll call (you pay for it), but you'll get closer to your goal.

If your business needs more than this, you can (a) call and offer *me* a job (I'm partial to very high salaries and beachfront offices) or (b) do the more practical thing and contract for Premium Service from what is now formally known as WordPerfect, the Novell Applications Group. Should you be the one with 200 WordPerfect users to support — particularly across computing platforms — this might be a great answer. (If you are on the beach, however, please call the publisher and track me down. My tan's fading!)

Support Online: WordPerfect's BBS

One observation before we go into details here. This section could not have been written ten years ago. Back then, modems were slow creatures, online services — CompuServe was the main one — measured members in the tens of thousands, not millions, and the CD was just gaining ground as something you *listened* to, not something with data on it.

Anyway, that was then. Now, you probably have a CD-ROM drive hooked up to your Mac (or tucked inside), your modem is so fast it courts meltdown, and you've got more e-mail addresses than Bill Gates. In short, you've come a long way, baby, and so have the means for support in WordPerfect.

For one, WordPerfect has a bulletin board service, or BBS, that you can dial using any Mac communications program. It's available 24 hours a day and has the latest technical notes, upgrades, patches, or anything else WordPerfect chooses to leave there. You can also leave comments and questions for tech support and WordPerfect's developers. The modem number, currently, is 801-226-1605, and you can access at any speed from 1200 bps to 14.4 Kbps.

There's no doubt that WordPerfect's BBS is a neat service, but read on. You can find most, if not all, of the same items through major online services, and usually at a lower cost and with easier access than by making that long-distance modem call.

WordPerfect Goes Digital: CompuServe and America Online

You can get to WordPerfect via the online services, and these offer a great value for Mac users. Log on to CompuServe or America Online (also known as AOL), and you can reach the WordPerfect folks, and fellow users, in a click. Figure 23-2 shows the WordPerfect Center on AOL.

Figure 23-2:
The America Online front door to WordPerfect.

On both services, the WordPerfect forums offer software downloads and patches. They also offer a way to talk with WordPerfect as well as with other users, which can be done via e-mail or through message boards, where various subjects are discussed, sometimes heatedly.

From the main entrance to these forums, it's a short trip to a larger menu and then to the message boards (see Figure 23-3).

Figure 23-3:
Still more
choices,
again on
America
Online.

This larger menu lets you choose from a variety of information about WordPerfect, its products, the message boards, and software libraries. There's a lot of good information available here, and you owe it to yourself to check it out.

One of the best places to get a sense of what users are talking about is from the message boards. On AOL, the free-wheeling discussions cover all sorts of topics of interest to WordPerfect users, and it's a good place to post questions and find answers, as Figure 23-4 reveals.

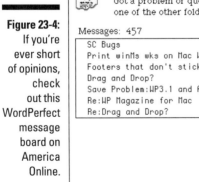
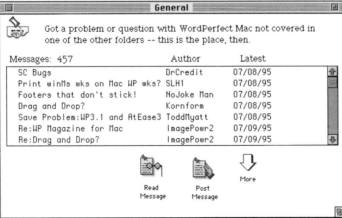

Figure 23-4:
If you're
ever short
of opinions,
check
out this
WordPerfect
message
board on
America
Online.

Understand, however, that while the forum is sponsored and supervised by WordPerfect, not everything posted represents the total viewpoint of WordPerfect or Novell, Inc. When you get into the message board, you'll see some notes that may be less than complimentary about one aspect of WordPerfect or another. These are usually answered by WordPerfect with tact and care, but know that you should weigh carefully all opinions you see on the message boards.

Along with the message boards, the software libraries offer some tremendous things for the WordPerfect user — in other words, Bruce, for you. By delving through the software libraries, you can find sample documents, updates, and enhancements for your program, and, just in case you were wondering, some more macros (see Figure 23-5).

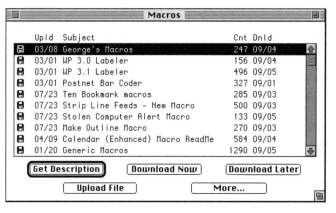

Figure 23-5: Macros from the essential to the inane can be found here.

You can download all sorts of macros for use with your program (ranging from the useful to the inane, such as one that creates a Hangman game for you), and you can also tap into one of the great secrets of the WordPerfect world.

That secret is a monthly online magazine for Mac users called the *WordPerfect Mac News* (see Figure 23-6). This digital *zine* (short for magazine) is produced by WordPerfect, but it's pretty free-wheeling. You'll need the Envoy viewer for this service (available on the CD-ROM version of WordPerfect or downloadable from the AOL file library).

WordPerfect Mac News doesn't take itself too seriously, and users at all levels can find useful articles and features in it. The format fits a standard Mac display comfortably, and the Envoy viewer makes it a breeze to zip through the document. The monthly issues often include files containing the macros-of-the-month, which you can add individually or collectively to bulk up your word processing power.

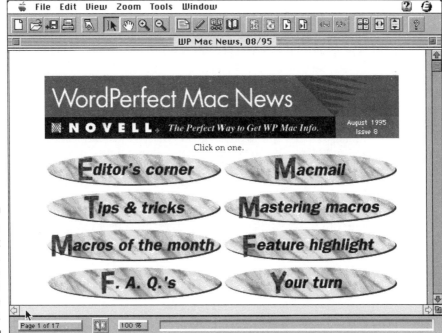

Figure 23-6:
WordPerfect
Mac News,
available
online and
viewable
with Envoy.

Here's a rundown of the places where you can find *WordPerfect Mac News*:

- ✔ Dial the WordPerfect BBS at 801-225-4414.

- ✔ On CompuServe, "Go WordPerfect" and look in the Mac Software Library.

- ✔ On AOL, use the keyword "wordperfect" to get to the forum and check out the Help and Info Files section in the Software Library.

- ✔ Using ftp (File Transfer Protocol), go to ftp.wordperfect.com.

- ✔ With a World Wide Web browser (see Chapter 15), the Universal Resource Locator (URL) is http://netwire.novell.com/servsup/mac/macnews/index.html.

How to Get the Most from User Groups

First of all, show up. If you don't know where your local user group is, check your newspaper, call your local dealer, or call Apple (800-538-9696) to get started on finding one. Follow the prompts, enter your ZIP Code, and you'll be pointed to as many as three such groups in your part of the world.

When you find such a group, become as active a member as you can. Go to meetings, help in the setup and operation of the group (that is, volunteer). Find other WordPerfect users in your group, and, yes, tell people what you think of this program and why you like it. Get some enthusiasm going.

As you attend a few meetings, you'll begin to find answers to the questions you have. Some may be generally Mac-related (the Mac is a great system, but there are a few quirks left); others might tie in to your brand of hardware.

By going to a user group on a regular basis, by keeping your eyes and ears open, and by reading the newsletter the group puts out, you will be able to find computing solutions and increase your knowledge. What's more, by participating, you might be able to help others, and this sharing is one of the key elements in the close-knit nature of the Macintosh community.

Along with the meetings and newsletters, most user groups offer two other key services that can help you with your computer use. One is a software library, which consists of shareware programs, freeware, and items put in the public domain by Apple Computer and others. The other service is a bulletin board system.

Software libraries

Usually for nothing more than the cost of a diskette, or at a very reasonable cost, you can get a disk full of programs, fonts, extensions, and other doo-dads with which you can dress up your system. Be sure you understand the different kinds of software user groups typically distribute:

- Shareware is the term used to describe programs that you can "try before you buy." You get a working copy of the program, but you're expected to send the author whatever contribution or fee is asked for if you continue to use the software beyond a certain trial period. Along with the trial period, the other big difference with shareware is that it's generally distributed by user groups, bulletin boards, and other means — that is, it is shared from one user to another.

- Freeware is distributed in the same manner as shareware, but as the name implies, it's yours free for the asking. There are several nice people out there who do this, and may their tribe increase.

- Public domain software, as I'll define it here, consists of items that may in some circumstances be sold but are given away free in other cases. Most likely to be included in this category are minor patches and updates to System software and some programs. (You should note, however, that System software updates are not technically public domain because Apple retains the copyright.) In these cases, Apple, for example, will charge you for sending you a diskette, but it will give you the item "free" if you get it from a BBS or a user group.

Bulletin board systems

With a bulletin board system, you can contact other (local) users, share information, and get help. Some BBSs are small; others are not. The Berkeley Macintosh User Group, known as BMUG, has a huge BBS system, which, at last count, was planning to offer Internet access as well as local messaging.

Meetings, a newsletter, software, and a BBS seem like enough to ask for from a user group. But wait, there's one more thing! In many cases, these groups offer buying cooperatives that give discounts on popular items. You can't go too far wrong by getting involved with a user group and taking full advantage of its services.

What if you can't join a local user group because there aren't any? Well, you can start a user group, and you can join one that isn't near you but offers useful services nonetheless. The two most popular are BMUG and the Boston Computer Society, which has a Macintosh special interest group with more than 10,000 members. You can reach BMUG at Suite 62, 1442A Walnut Street, Berkeley, CA 94709-1496; 800-776-2684 or 510-549-2684; via both AOL and AppleLink at BMUG; and on CompuServe: 73237,501. The Boston Computer Society, 1972 Massachusetts Ave., Cambridge, MA 02140, can be contacted by phone at 617-864-1700.

What to Look For in a Trainer

Even after reading all of the preceding info in this chapter, you might still want or need more help with WordPerfect. You might want to hire a corporate trainer, preferably someone who has been certified as a Novell/WordPerfect instructor.

What should you look for in a trainer? Obviously, compatibility of attitude and spirit are important: If you frankly don't like the trainer, you're not going to be as successful with him or her as you might be otherwise. Then comes knowledge and adaptability: Does the trainer know his or her stuff, and will the trainer meet your specific needs?

Once those questions are settled, your WordPerfect trainer can be a great help, especially if you are responsible for getting your entire office up and running with WordPerfect.

Where can you find trainers? Ask your local dealer, check out the user group, and ask WordPerfect's support team.

Electronic Newsletters Offer Mac Insights

Like you, I depend on *Macworld, MacUser,* and *MacWeek* to keep me Mac current, but there's more than print as a source of the latest Mac news. *TidBITS,* edited by the talented duo of Adam and Tonya Engst, is a six-year-old weekly chock full of product news, reviews, opinions, and answers. I read it and make use of its information every week. The best way to get your mitts on *TidBITS* is by using e-mail and/or an Internet browser such as Netscape (see Chapter 20).

For information on *TidBITS* (how to subscribe, where to find back issues, and other useful stuff), send e-mail to info@tidbits.com. Send comments and editorial submissions to: editors@tidbits.com. Issues are available at ftp.tidbits.com/pub/tidbits/issues/ and http://www.dartmouth.edu/pages/TidBITS/TidBITS.html. To search back issues with WAIS, use the following URL via a Web browser: http://www.wais.com/wais-dbs/macintosh-tidbits.html.

Also useful is *MacChat,* a "weekly electronic newsletter biased toward Mac users who are production-oriented professionals," according to editor Tony Lindsey, who adds, "Other Mac users may find many, many items of interest as well." Count me in the "other" category, but I get a lot from *MacChat.*

You can subscribe to *MacChat* by sending e-mail to listserv@vm.temple.edu. The subject line of your e-mail message is ignored, so it can say anything. Just make sure that in the body of the message, you include the following line:

SUBSCRIBE MACCHAT your full name

Here's an example: SUBSCRIBE MACCHAT John Smith

You will receive a nice long message explaining acceptance of your subscription, how to end it (if desired), and general listserv info.

Appendix

Installing WordPerfect on Your Macintosh

● ●

*A*s mentioned briefly in Chapter 5, WordPerfect's installation process is relatively easy for most users. Either pop in that first (of eight) diskettes or the CD-ROM on which the program is stored, do a few clicks of the mouse, and the computer does the rest.

Most of the time, that is.

In real life, nothing is totally simple or easy. That's why it's useful to present the basics of installing WordPerfect and to give you something of a heads up on potential problems you might have. Also, I'm going to tell you a couple of things about installing that WordPerfect might not mention in its manual. From the home office in Foster City, California, here we go:

Top Ten Steps to Installing WordPerfect (with Apologies to David Letterman)

10. Make sure all your hard drive is backed up (at least the important data) and defragmented (using Apple Disk Tools or a utility program) before installing.

9. Be sure you have all the installation disks at hand, starting with number one.

8. Restart the computer with all extensions off (by holding down the Shift key during the entire startup process).

7. Make sure you have no other programs running when you install WordPerfect. (By the way, this requirement is standard for most Mac software installs.)

6. If you don't have special needs, click on Easy Install, grab a soda or tea, and relax. At the most, you'll need to flip some disks in and out, or with the CD-ROM, you can truly kick back.

5. If you do have special needs in terms of what you do and don't install, choose the Custom Install option and you'll see a menu of choices from which you can select. WordPerfect will guide you if you need to make a minimal installation (for use on a PowerBook Mac or perhaps for other reasons).

4. As the program installs, it's a good time to either fill in your registration card or call the 800 number to register. (This message brought to you by WordPerfect. Thank you for your support.)

3. Once the program is installed, click on the Quit button to exit the installation process.

2. Surprise! Unlike the old days, you *don't* have to restart your Mac in order to use the program. But if it makes you feel better, do it.

1. Click on the WordPerfect icon, fire up the program, and get busy.

OK, that's the short course. Now to some nitty-gritty, sort of like George Bush's favorite rock band.

Create an Alias

There are all sorts of ways to launch WordPerfect, some easier than others. You can go into your hard disk drive, find the WordPerfect folder, locate the WordPerfect icon, and click on it. Or you can move WordPerfect from its original directory to the Apple Menu Items folder in the System Folder. That will place it in your Apple menu in the upper-left corner of the screen.

If you merely put the WordPerfect program in the Apple Menu Items folder, you lose crucial links to things such as templates and macros. A better way to get WordPerfect's icon in the Apple menu is by creating an *alias* for the program. Figure A-1 shows a WordPerfect alias icon.

Figure A-1:
An alias of
WordPerfect.

WordPerfect alias

To create an alias, follow these steps:

1. **Go to the WordPerfect program icon and click on it once to highlight it.**

2. **Either choose the Make Alias command in the File menu or press the ⌘-M combination.**

3. **After the alias appears, drag it to the Desktop or wherever you want to place the icon, such as the Apple Menu Items folder in the System folder.**

Now, whenever you click on the alias, it will fire up the program as if by remote control.

Isn't that precious? But more than precious, it's a neat way to be able to access your program without hassle.

One Last Thought about Installation

It happens about once every couple of thousand installs, the WordPerfect folks tell me, that when you install the program on a Power Macintosh (or clone), the memory allocation isn't set correctly. You'll find out whether the installation isn't perfect when you get Out of Memory messages when you know you shouldn't get them (that is, when you know you have enough RAM available to run WordPerfect).

The solution? Delete the WordPerfect files, restart your Mac, and reinstall the program, making sure that all extensions are *off*. (You make sure that extensions are off by holding down the Shift key during the startup process until your Mac displays a Welcome screen telling you that extensions are off.) This method cleared things up for me with the Power Computing Power100 Mac clone I'm using; it should work for you.

Index

10/31/9

The Internet For Macs® For Dummies® 2nd Edition	by Charles Seiter	ISBN: 1-56884-371-2	$19.99 USA/$26.99 Canada
The Internet For Macs® For Dummies® Starter Kit	by Charles Seiter	ISBN: 1-56884-244-9	$29.99 USA/$39.99 Canada
The Internet For Macs® For Dummies® Starter Kit Bestseller Edition	by Charles Seiter	ISBN: 1-56884-245-7	$39.99 USA/$54.99 Canada
The Internet For Windows® For Dummies® Starter Kit	by John R. Levine & Margaret Levine Young	ISBN: 1-56884-237-6	$34.99 USA/$44.99 Canada
The Internet For Windows® For Dummies® Starter Kit, Bestseller Edition	by John R. Levine & Margaret Levine Young	ISBN: 1-56884-246-5	$39.99 USA/$54.99 Canada

MACINTOSH

Mac® Programming For Dummies®	by Dan Parks Sydow	ISBN: 1-56884-173-6	$19.95 USA/$26.95 Canada
Macintosh® System 7.5 For Dummies®	by Bob LeVitus	ISBN: 1-56884-197-3	$19.95 USA/$26.95 Canada
MORE Macs® For Dummies®	by David Pogue	ISBN: 1-56884-087-X	$19.95 USA/$26.95 Canada
PageMaker 5 For Macs® For Dummies®	by Galen Gruman & Deke McClelland	ISBN: 1-56884-178-7	$19.95 USA/$26.95 Canada
QuarkXPress 3.3 For Dummies®	by Galen Gruman & Barbara Assadi	ISBN: 1-56884-217-1	$19.99 USA/$26.99 Canada
Upgrading and Fixing Macs® For Dummies®	by Kearney Rietmann & Frank Higgins	ISBN: 1-56884-189-2	$19.95 USA/$26.95 Canada

MULTIMEDIA

Multimedia & CD-ROMs For Dummies® 2nd Edition	by Andy Rathbone	ISBN: 1-56884-907-9	$19.99 USA/$26.99 Canada
Multimedia & CD-ROMs For Dummies® Interactive Multimedia Value Pack, 2nd Edition	by Andy Rathbone	ISBN: 1-56884-909-5	$29.99 USA/$39.99 Canada

OPERATING SYSTEMS:

DOS

MORE DOS For Dummies®	by Dan Gookin	ISBN: 1-56884-046-2	$19.95 USA/$26.95 Canada
OS/2® Warp For Dummies® 2nd Edition	by Andy Rathbone	ISBN: 1-56884-205-8	$19.95 USA/$26.99 Canada

UNIX

MORE UNIX® For Dummies®	by John R. Levine & Margaret Levine Young	ISBN: 1-56884-361-5	$19.99 USA/$26.99 Canada
UNIX® For Dummies®	by John R. Levine & Margaret Levine Young	ISBN: 1-878058-58-4	$19.95 USA/$26.95 Canada

WINDOWS

MORE Windows® For Dummies® 2nd Edition	by Andy Rathbone	ISBN: 1-56884-048-9	$19.95 USA/$26.95 Canada
Windows® 95 For Dummies®	by Andy Rathbone	ISBN: 1-56884-240-6	$19.99 USA/$26.99 Canada

PCS/HARDWARE

Illustrated Computer Dictionary For Dummies® 2nd Edition	by Dan Gookin & Wallace Wang	ISBN: 1-56884-218-X	$12.95 USA/$16.95 Canada
Upgrading and Fixing PCs For Dummies® 2nd Edition	by Andy Rathbone	ISBN: 1-56884-903-6	$19.99 USA/$26.99 Canada

PRESENTATION/AUTOCAD

AutoCAD For Dummies®	by Bud Smith	ISBN: 1-56884-191-4	$19.95 USA/$26.95 Canada
PowerPoint 4 For Windows® For Dummies®	by Doug Lowe	ISBN: 1-56884-161-2	$16.99 USA/$22.99 Canada

PROGRAMMING

Borland C++ For Dummies®	by Michael Hyman	ISBN: 1-56884-162-0	$19.95 USA/$26.95 Canada
C For Dummies® Volume 1	by Dan Gookin	ISBN: 1-878058-78-9	$19.95 USA/$26.95 Canada
C++ For Dummies®	by Stephen R. Davis	ISBN: 1-56884-163-9	$19.95 USA/$26.95 Canada
Delphi Programming For Dummies®	by Neil Rubenking	ISBN: 1-56884-200-7	$19.99 USA/$26.99 Canada
Mac® Programming For Dummies®	by Dan Parks Sydow	ISBN: 1-56884-173-6	$19.95 USA/$26.95 Canada
PowerBuilder 4 Programming For Dummies®	by Ted Coombs & Jason Coombs	ISBN: 1-56884-325-9	$19.99 USA/$26.99 Canada
QBasic Programming For Dummies®	by Douglas Hergert	ISBN: 1-56884-093-4	$19.95 USA/$26.95 Canada
Visual Basic 3 For Dummies®	by Wallace Wang	ISBN: 1-56884-076-4	$19.95 USA/$26.95 Canada
Visual Basic "X" For Dummies®	by Wallace Wang	ISBN: 1-56884-230-9	$19.99 USA/$26.99 Canada
Visual C++ 2 For Dummies®	by Michael Hyman & Bob Arnson	ISBN: 1-56884-328-3	$19.99 USA/$26.99 Canada
Windows® 95 Programming For Dummies®	by S. Randy Davis	ISBN: 1-56884-327-5	$19.99 USA/$26.99 Canada

SPREADSHEET

1-2-3 For Dummies®	by Greg Harvey	ISBN: 1-878058-60-6	$16.95 USA/$22.95 Canada
1-2-3 For Windows® 5 For Dummies® 2nd Edition	by John Walkenbach	ISBN: 1-56884-216-3	$16.95 USA/$22.95 Canada
Excel 5 For Macs® For Dummies®	by Greg Harvey	ISBN: 1-56884-186-8	$19.95 USA/$26.95 Canada
Excel For Dummies® 2nd Edition	by Greg Harvey	ISBN: 1-56884-050-0	$16.95 USA/$22.95 Canada
MORE 1-2-3 For DOS For Dummies®	by John Weingarten	ISBN: 1-56884-224-4	$19.99 USA/$26.99 Canada
MORE Excel 5 For Windows® For Dummies®	by Greg Harvey	ISBN: 1-56884-207-4	$19.95 USA/$26.95 Canada
Quattro Pro 6 For Windows® For Dummies®	by John Walkenbach	ISBN: 1-56884-174-4	$19.95 USA/$26.95 Canada
Quattro Pro For DOS For Dummies®	by John Walkenbach	ISBN: 1-56884-023-3	$16.95 USA/$22.95 Canada

UTILITIES

Norton Utilities 8 For Dummies®	by Beth Slick	ISBN: 1-56884-166-3	$19.95 USA/$26.95 Canada

VCRS/CAMCORDERS

VCRs & Camcorders For Dummies™	by Gordon McComb & Andy Rathbone	ISBN: 1-56884-229-5	$14.99 USA/$20.99 Canada

WORD PROCESSING

Ami Pro For Dummies®	by Jim Meade	ISBN: 1-56884-049-7	$19.95 USA/$26.95 Canada
MORE Word For Windows® 6 For Dummies®	by Doug Lowe	ISBN: 1-56884-165-5	$19.95 USA/$26.95 Canada
MORE WordPerfect® 6 For Windows® For Dummies®	by Margaret Levine Young & David C. Kay	ISBN: 1-56884-206-6	$19.95 USA/$26.95 Canada
MORE WordPerfect® 6 For DOS For Dummies®	by Wallace Wang, edited by Dan Gookin	ISBN: 1-56884-047-0	$19.95 USA/$26.95 Canada
Word 6 For Macs® For Dummies®	by Dan Gookin	ISBN: 1-56884-190-6	$19.95 USA/$26.95 Canada
Word For Windows® 6 For Dummies®	by Dan Gookin	ISBN: 1-56884-075-6	$16.95 USA/$22.95 Canada
Word For Windows® For Dummies®	by Dan Gookin & Ray Werner	ISBN: 1-878058-86-X	$16.95 USA/$22.95 Canada
WordPerfect® 6 For DOS For Dummies®	by Dan Gookin	ISBN: 1-878058-77-0	$16.95 USA/$22.95 Canada
WordPerfect® 6.1 For Windows® For Dummies® 2nd Edition	by Margaret Levine Young & David Kay	ISBN: 1-56884-243-0	$16.95 USA/$22.95 Canada
WordPerfect® For Dummies®	by Dan Gookin	ISBN: 1-878058-52-5	$16.95 USA/$22.95 Canada

Fun, Fast, & Cheap!™

10/31/95

NEW!

NEW!

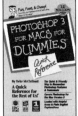

SUPER STAR

SUPER STAR

The Internet For Macs® For Dummies® Quick Reference	Windows® 95 For Dummies® Quick Reference	Photoshop 3 For Macs® For Dummies® Quick Reference	WordPerfect® For DOS For Dummies® Quick Reference
by Charles Seiter	by Greg Harvey	by Deke McClelland	by Greg Harvey
ISBN:1-56884-967-2	ISBN: 1-56884-964-8	ISBN: 1-56884-968-0	ISBN: 1-56884-009-8
$9.99 USA/$12.99 Canada	$9.99 USA/$12.99 Canada	$9.99 USA/$12.99 Canada	$8.95 USA/$12.95 Canada

Title	Author	ISBN	Price
DATABASE			
Access 2 For Dummies® Quick Reference	by Stuart J. Stuple	ISBN: 1-56884-167-1	$8.95 USA/$11.95 Canada
dBASE 5 For DOS For Dummies® Quick Reference	by Barrie Sosinsky	ISBN: 1-56884-954-0	$9.99 USA/$12.99 Canada
dBASE 5 For Windows® For Dummies® Quick Reference	by Stuart J. Stuple	ISBN: 1-56884-953-2	$9.99 USA/$12.99 Canada
Paradox 5 For Windows® For Dummies® Quick Reference	by Scott Palmer	ISBN: 1-56884-960-5	$9.99 USA/$12.99 Canada
DESKTOP PUBLISHING/ILLUSTRATION/GRAPHICS			
CorelDRAW! 5 For Dummies® Quick Reference	by Raymond E. Werner	ISBN: 1-56884-952-4	$9.99 USA/$12.99 Canada
Harvard Graphics For Windows® For Dummies® Quick Reference	by Raymond E. Werner	ISBN: 1-56884-962-1	$9.99 USA/$12.99 Canada
Photoshop 3 For Macs® For Dummies® Quick Reference	by Deke McClelland	ISBN: 1-56884-968-0	$9.99 USA/$12.99 Canada
FINANCE/PERSONAL FINANCE			
Quicken 4 For Windows® For Dummies® Quick Reference	by Stephen L. Nelson	ISBN: 1-56884-950-8	$9.95 USA/$12.95 Canada
GROUPWARE/INTEGRATED			
Microsoft® Office 4 For Windows® For Dummies® Quick Reference	by Doug Lowe	ISBN: 1-56884-958-3	$9.99 USA/$12.99 Canada
Microsoft® Works 3 For Windows® For Dummies® Quick Reference	by Michael Partington	ISBN: 1-56884-959-1	$9.99 USA/$12.99 Canada
INTERNET/COMMUNICATIONS/NETWORKING			
The Internet For Dummies® Quick Reference	by John R. Levine & Margaret Levine Young	ISBN: 1-56884-168-X	$8.95 USA/$11.95 Canada
MACINTOSH			
Macintosh® System 7.5 For Dummies® Quick Reference	by Stuart J. Stuple	ISBN: 1-56884-956-7	$9.99 USA/$12.99 Canada
OPERATING SYSTEMS:			
DOS			
DOS For Dummies® Quick Reference	by Greg Harvey	ISBN: 1-56884-007-1	$8.95 USA/$11.95 Canada
UNIX			
UNIX® For Dummies® Quick Reference	by John R. Levine & Margaret Levine Young	ISBN: 1-56884-094-2	$8.95 USA/$11.95 Canada
WINDOWS			
Windows® 3.1 For Dummies® Quick Reference, 2nd Edition	by Greg Harvey	ISBN: 1-56884-951-6	$8.95 USA/$11.95 Canada
PCs/HARDWARE			
Memory Management For Dummies® Quick Reference	by Doug Lowe	ISBN: 1-56884-362-3	$9.99 USA/$12.99 Canada
PRESENTATION/AUTOCAD			
AutoCAD For Dummies® Quick Reference	by Ellen Finkelstein	ISBN: 1-56884-198-1	$9.95 USA/$12.95 Canada
SPREADSHEET			
1-2-3 For Dummies® Quick Reference	by John Walkenbach	ISBN: 1-56884-027-6	$8.95 USA/$11.95 Canada
1-2-3 For Windows® 5 For Dummies® Quick Reference	by John Walkenbach	ISBN: 1-56884-957-5	$9.95 USA/$12.95 Canada
Excel For Windows® For Dummies® Quick Reference, 2nd Edition	by John Walkenbach	ISBN: 1-56884-096-9	$8.95 USA/$11.95 Canada
Quattro Pro 6 For Windows® For Dummies® Quick Reference	by Stuart J. Stuple	ISBN: 1-56884-172-8	$9.95 USA/$12.95 Canada
WORD PROCESSING			
Word For Windows® 6 For Dummies® Quick Reference	by George Lynch	ISBN: 1-56884-095-0	$8.95 USA/$11.95 Canada
Word For Windows® For Dummies® Quick Reference	by George Lynch	ISBN: 1-56884-029-2	$8.95 USA/$11.95 Canada
WordPerfect® 6.1 For Windows® For Dummies® Quick Reference, 2nd Edition	by Greg Harvey	ISBN: 1-56884-966-4	$9.99 USA/$12.99/Canada

For scholastic requests & educational orders please call Educational Sales at 1. 800. 434. 2086

FOR MORE INFO OR TO ORDER, PLEASE CALL ► 800. 762. 2974

For volume discounts & special orders please call Tony Real, Special Sales, at 415. 655. 3048

Macworld® QuarkXPress 3.2/3.3 Bible
by Barbara Assadi & Galen Gruman

ISBN: 1-878058-85-1
$39.95 USA/$52.95 Canada

Includes disk with QuarkXPress XTensions and scripts.

Macworld® PageMaker 5 Bible
by Craig Danuloff

ISBN: 1-878058-84-3
$39.95 USA/$52.95 Canada

Includes 2 disks with PageMaker utilities, clip art, and more.

Macworld® FileMaker Pro 2.0/2.1 Bible
by Steven A. Schwartz

ISBN: 1-56884-201-5
$34.95 USA/$46.95 Canada

Includes disk with ready-to-run data buses.

Macworld® Word 6 Companion, 2nd Edition
by Jim Heid

ISBN: 1-56884-082-9
$24.95 USA/$34.95 Canada

NEWBRIDGE BOOK CLUB SELECTION

Macworld® Guide To Microsoft® Word 5/5.1
by Jim Heid

ISBN: 1-878058-39-8
$22.95 USA/$29.95 Canada

Macworld® ClarisWorks 2.0/2.1 Companion, 2nd Edition
by Steven A. Schwartz

ISBN: 1-56884-180-9
$24.95 USA/$34.95 Canada

Macworld® Guide To Microsoft® Works 3
by Barrie Sosinsky

ISBN: 1-878058-42-8
$22.95 USA/$29.95 Canada

Macworld® Excel 5 Companion, 2nd Edition
by Chris Van Buren & David Maguiness

ISBN: 1-56884-081-0
$24.95 USA/$34.95 Canada

NEWBRIDGE BOOK CLUB SELECTION

Macworld® Guide To Microsoft® Excel 4
by David Maguiness

ISBN: 1-878058-40-1
$22.95 USA/$29.95 Canada

ORDER FORM

IDG BOOKS WORLDWIDE

Order Center: **(800) 762-2974** *(8 a.m.–6 p.m., EST, weekdays)*

Quantity	ISBN	Title	Price	Total

Shipping & Handling Charges

	Description	First book	Each additional book	Total
Domestic	Normal	$4.50	$1.50	$
	Two Day Air	$8.50	$2.50	$
	Overnight	$18.00	$3.00	$
International	Surface	$8.00	$8.00	$
	Airmail	$16.00	$16.00	$
	DHL Air	$17.00	$17.00	$

*For large quantities call for shipping & handling charges.
**Prices are subject to change without notice.

Ship to:

Name _____

Company _____

Address _____

City/State/Zip _____

Daytime Phone _____

Payment: ☐ Check to IDG Books Worldwide (US Funds Only)

☐ VISA   ☐ MasterCard   ☐ American Express

Card # _____ Expires _____

Signature _____

Subtotal _____

CA residents add applicable sales tax _____

IN, MA, and MD residents add 5% sales tax _____

IL residents add 6.25% sales tax _____

RI residents add 7% sales tax _____

TX residents add 8.25% sales tax _____

Shipping _____

Total _____

Please send this order form to:
**IDG Books Worldwide, Inc.
7260 Shadeland Station, Suite 100
Indianapolis, IN 46256**

*Allow up to 3 weeks for delivery.
Thank you!*

❏ YES!

Please keep me informed about IDG's World of Computer Knowledge.
Send me the latest IDG Books catalog.